## DATE DUE

PRINTED IN U.S.A.

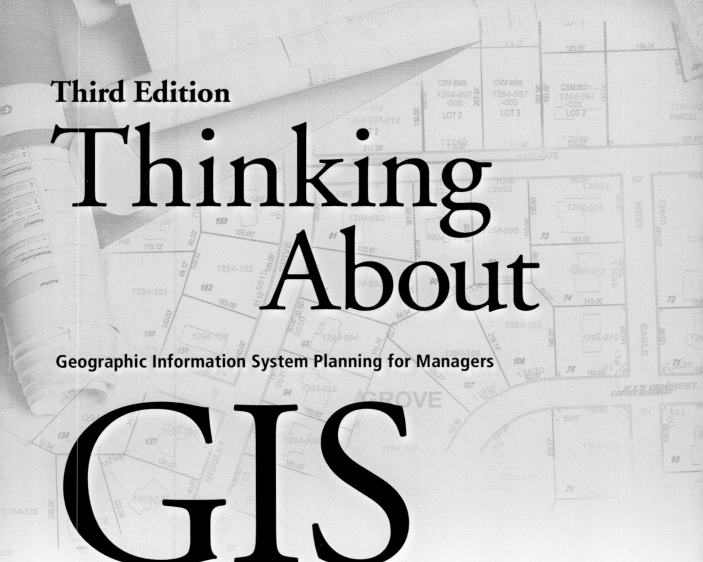

**Third Edition**

# Thinking About

**Geographic Information System Planning for Managers**

# GIS

## Roger Tomlinson

ESRI PRESS

REDLANDS, CALIFORNIA

Ask for ESRI Press titles at your local bookstore or order by calling 1-800-447-9778. You can also shop online at www.esri.com/esripress. Outside the United States, contact your local ESRI distributor.

ESRI Press titles are distributed to the trade by the following:

In North America:
Ingram Publisher Services
Toll-free telephone: (800) 648-3104
Toll-free fax: (800) 838-1149
E-mail: customerservice@ingrampublisherservices.com

In the United Kingdom, Europe, and the Middle East:
Transatlantic Publishers Group Ltd.
Telephone: 44 20 7373 2515
Fax: 44 20 7244 1018
E-mail: richard@tpgltd.co.uk

Cover design by Takeshi Kanemura
Interior design by Savitri Brant

Dedicated to Mr. Leonard Hassall, geography teacher at Newmarket Grammar School, Suffolk, England, who turned my heart and life toward geography.

R. F. T.

# Contents

# Foreword

For a number of years, Roger Tomlinson has been advocating that one of the key ingredients to successful geographic information systems (GIS) is the use of a consistent planning methodology. He developed a methodology that has evolved over the years, and he continues to adapt it through his personal consultation practicum and in association with the evolution of technology. At the ESRI International User Conference and other venues, Tomlinson teaches his method as part of a very popular "Planning and Managing a GIS" seminar. In observing the attendance of these seminars, I notice that they tend to attract two primary groups of people. The first group is composed of senior managers who oversee GIS and other information technologies in their organizations. The second group is composed of more technical managers responsible for the actual implementation of GIS and other information technologies. That these two markedly differing groups come together year after year to glean Tomlinson's wisdom always strikes me as significant and as an excellent starting point for a book on GIS planning.

Roger Tomlinson wrote this book for those two kinds of managers, intending to bridge the communication gap between them. Senior executives in public- and private-sector organizations often have the general idea that GIS would be good for their organization, and they know how to get the resources allocated to make it happen. What they lack is enough understanding about the capabilities and unique constraints of geospatial data technologies to direct their technical managers (the second audience) and ask the right questions. Conversely, these line GIS managers tend to have a solid grasp of the technology and the unique characteristics of GIS but know much less about how the GIS must operate within the broader context of the organization itself. What they need is information that will allow them to anticipate the questions their bosses are going to ask. This book effectively and successfully serves the needs of both groups.

While these are the primary audiences, the book also has value for the student of GIS who wishes to learn how to do the middle manager's job. It is an invaluable source of tuition for students to understand what being a GIS manager in a large organization is all about and what they have to be able to do.

While Roger has rightly become known as the "father of GIS" as a result of his early work in using computers to model land inventories for the Canadian government in the early 1960s, I believe that his greatest contribution to the field is the rigorous method of GIS planning that is described in this book. I hope that you find his work as informative and beneficial as have my colleagues and I at ESRI.

Jack Dangermond
President, ESRI

# Acknowledgments

The errors are mine. The methods described in this book have evolved over the years with help from many people. These include the associates of Tomlinson Associates Ltd. in Canada, the United States, and Australia. Many contributions were made by my colleague Larry Sugarbaker as we developed the "Planning and Managing a GIS" seminar together. Deep thanks to Dave Peters for help and careful review of chapter 10 and particularly of the City of Rome case study. Generous input has been received from the staff of our clients worldwide and the staff of the corporations that eventually served our clients. They have been the real-world laboratory in which the ideas were tested. This book exists because Jack Dangermond thought it was a good idea to show the world what we put him through and because Brian Parr and Christian Harder turned the methodology into readable words. Candace Lyle Hogan is responsible for the new face on the third edition. Their support has been patient and constant. None of this would have come about without the continuing work and friendship of my wife Lila. Not only has she read every word and corrected most of my mistakes, but she still smiles. To these I owe my heartfelt thanks.

Roger Tomlinson

# Introduction

If you're holding this book, perhaps it's because you've been charged with launching or implementing a geographic information system, a GIS, for your organization. Yours could be the type of organization that has historically used GIS—a local government, a transportation authority, a forest management agency. Or it could be the type of organization—such as a corporation, a political action group, or a farm—that has only recently begun to discover the positive implications of geographically enabled decision making.

The GIS you've been tasked with implementing could be intended to serve a single, specific purpose or to perform an ongoing function. It could even be what's called an *enterprise GIS,* one designed to serve a wide range of purposes across many departments within your organization. (You'll learn as your GIS evolves that a well-planned implementation can start out as a project and grow, or scale up, into a full-blown enterprise system.)

Whatever the mission of your organization or the intended scope of the initial GIS implementation, the good news is that the fundamental principles behind planning for a successful GIS are essentially the same. These principles are based on the simple concept that you must think about your real purposes and decide what output, what information, you want from your GIS. All the rest depends on that.

This book details a practical method for planning a GIS that has been proven successful time and again during many years of use in real public- and private-sector organizations. It is a scalable approach—the methodology can be adapted to any size GIS, from a modest project to an enterprise-wide system.

## Why plan?

So why should you plan? What's wrong with just buying some computers and GIS software, loading some data, and sort of "letting things happen"? Can't you simply adapt as things move along, tweak the system, learn as you go? In fact, doesn't all this advance thinking slow things down and create even more work? On the contrary, evidence shows that good GIS planning leads to GIS success and absence of planning leads to failure. Whether you are working with an existing system or creating a GIS from scratch, you must integrate sufficient planning into the development of your GIS; if you don't, chances are you'll end up with a system that doesn't meet your expectations.

Knowing what you want to get out of your GIS is absolutely crucial to your ultimate success. Too often, organizations decide they want a GIS because they've heard great things from their peers in other organizations, or they just don't want to get left behind technologically. So they invest considerable sums of money into technology, data, and personnel without knowing exactly what they need from the system. That's like packing for a vacation without knowing where you're going. You pack everything from your closet just in case, but it turns out that sweater isn't needed in Fiji and you forgot the sunscreen. You've wasted time and energy, and worse yet, you're still not ready. When you try to develop a GIS without first seriously considering the real purpose, you could find yourself with the wrong (expensive) technology and unmet needs.

You must determine your organization's GIS needs from the outset of the planning process. GIS has many potential applications, so it's important to establish your specific requirements and objectives from the beginning. That way you will avoid the chaos that results from trying to create a system with no priorities or ends in mind. The methodology described in these pages will show you how to describe and prioritize what your organization needs from a GIS, so that you can plan a system that meets these requirements.

The key undertaking of managers—and those who plan on their behalf—is to understand their business and identify what would benefit that business. From GIS, the fundamental benefit comes in the form of what we call *information products.* An information product is data transformed into information particularly useful to you—for example, economic data analyzed in relation to a specific location—and delivered to you, via computer, often in the visual form of a map. If it's something that helps you do your work better, faster, more efficiently, then it's an information product.

Your GIS can quickly become a money pit if it's not creating useful products for the organization, ultimately jeopardizing the very existence of the GIS initiative and perhaps your own job. Conversely, a GIS can prove its worth and justify its existence if it manages to help streamline existing workflows and create useful information products. These are the ultimate benefits reaped by any successful information system.

Once you've identified the information products you seek, you can determine what data you need to make them. Then you can deal with the issues of tolerance to error and the concepts of database design on which efficiency will depend. From the type and amount of handling the data requires to make it usable (data requirements), you can specify the system scope, the capabilities you need from software (software functionality), and what your system requires in the way of support from the hardware and the network (hardware and network requirements). From these itemized necessities, you can develop accurate cost models to allow for clear and meaningful benefit–cost analysis. Having laid this groundwork, you can identify issues affecting implementation—institutional, legal, budgetary, staffing, risk, or timing issues—and look at how to mitigate them. The end result is an effective, efficient, and demonstrably beneficial GIS within the organization.

Implementation and maintenance can be expensive, but good planning will make your ongoing GIS efforts cost-effective in the long run. This book will teach you to evaluate the benefits of the system relative to its cost and how to make the case to management in a way that makes them advocates for your own success.

The entire planning process can take some time, and you may find that some of the steps can be minimized or eliminated in certain situations. But it is nonetheless important to think carefully about each step, to really get your head around the subject. You'll be glad you took the time.

## GIS means change

Technology changes under us like the swell of a tide. To harvest the immense long-term benefits of GIS, you have to plan ahead in fast-paced times.

Rapid advancements in technology—both in software and hardware—continue to exert their strong effect on the GIS planning process. Your GIS can develop faster and much more iteratively now because of improvements in software usability and advanced off-the-shelf GIS functionality. The hardware that supports this grows ever more affordable—CPU seconds are approaching zero cost. The days when we designed system architecture around the limitations of software and hardware are over.

Now the driving determinants in system design are the location of human and data resources in the organization and the communication between them. Distributed systems and communications are becoming increasingly important. Quite complex applications can be done on the server level now. That's where the technology is going. Follow it, and you won't be left unsupported.

Geospatial data also has become more accessible and plentiful, due in part to the increase in geographic measurement being driven by new technologies (GPS, lidar, etc.) and by real-time sensors capturing data to make it available as Web services. Many standard and commonly used datasets are now readily available in digital form and at a much lower cost than even just a few years ago.

This relative abundance of affordable and reliable spatial data significantly widens the scope of potential GIS applications. Rapid prototyping and development tools such as ESRI ArcGIS Desktop with ModelBuilder, Microsoft Visual Basic, and CASE technology allow for quick exploration and testing of such applications. In other words, you can now explore a greater range of options; you can do targeted planning on selected business areas and build databases incrementally, scaling them up as needed.

These days, most GIS users handle spatial data within one of three paradigms: In the first GIS framework, the traditional stand-alone desktop information system, the user can conduct an integrated set of GIS functions on a wide variety of data types. In the second, the developer environment, software developers can combine a set of application-neutral, individual function components to create new applications. The third is the server environment. Here, a set of standardized GIS Web services (e.g., mapping, data access, geocoding) support enterprise-wide applications. (We see many examples of enterprise GIS now in organizations such as federal agencies, state and local governments, utility companies, national mapping organizations, and transportation agencies.)

These three environments currently interoperate but are moving rapidly toward more unified models and interfaces. The more enterprise systems are in place, the more interoperability standards will be required. Integration is becoming the theme of the future.

Geographic information systems integrate seemingly disparate information quickly and visually, which facilitates communication, collaboration, and decision making. Through GIS, geography is actually becoming an organizing tool. In much the same manner as enterprise-wide financial systems converted the way organizations were managed in the 1960s through the 1980s, now geographic information systems are transforming the way organizations and government agencies manage their assets and serve their customers or citizens.

The focus is shifting from application-oriented architecture to a server-oriented one, making real-time geographic information available to anyone who surfs the Internet. The results of GIS capabilities—quick complex analysis, maps showing statistical connections—used to be limited to the few. Now GIS technology, fully emerging on the Web, offers affordable and direct access to such information products. The combination of new GIS server technology and intuitive, easy-to-use Web clients is opening up the GIS domain to everyone.

We've learned that individual geographic information systems themselves tend to evolve over time, but now we're discovering the value of GIS as a facilitator for a kind of organizational evolution. GIS means change—a new GIS implementation (into an organization that hasn't had GIS before) is a change agent. But once in place, GIS capabilities can be used to help an organization adjust to change, forecast changes ahead, and take advantage of the opportunities incumbent with change.

The ever-widening availability and continual advancements of technology have made it impossible to ignore that we live and work in a perpetual atmosphere of change. Planning is no longer a one-time event, but rather an ongoing process. More and more, organizations and public policy makers have come to identify GIS as important to their objectives. But to harvest GIS's potential requires coordination, collaboration, and an enterprise view of GIS management. GIS planning itself is increasingly important if all these objectives are to be achieved.

# GIS: The whole picture

*No GIS can be a success without the right people involved. A real-world GIS is actually a complex system of interrelated parts, and at the center of this system is a smart person who understands the whole.*

GIS is a particularly horizontal technology in the sense that it has wide-ranging applications across the industrial and intellectual landscape. For this reason, it tends to resist simplistic definition. Yet the first thing we need is a common understanding of what we're talking about when we refer to GIS. A simple definition is not sufficient. In order to discuss GIS outside the context of any specific industry or application, we need a more flexible tool for elaborating: a model.

Figure 1.1 on the next page presents a holistic model of a functional geographic information system, which turns data, through analysis, into useful information. At the center, you can see that GIS stores spatial data, replete with its logically linked attribute information (from the left), in a GIS storage database, where analytical functions are controlled interactively by a human operator to generate the needed information products (shown on the right).

Let's understand the GIS model better by examining its individual components. Spatial data is a term with special meaning in GIS. *Spatial data* is raw data distinguished by the presence of a geographic link. In other words, something about that piece of data is connected to a known place on the earth, a true geographic reference. The features you see on a map—roads, lakes, buildings—are ones commonly found in a GIS database as individual thematic layers. Most can be represented using a combination of points, lines, or polygons. Linked to these geographic features, and usually stored in a table format, is nonspatial information about them, data such as the name of the road, seasonal temperatures of the lake, owner of the building. These various characteristics applied to place are called *attributes* in GIS parlance, and, in fact, it is

# Parts of a geographic information system

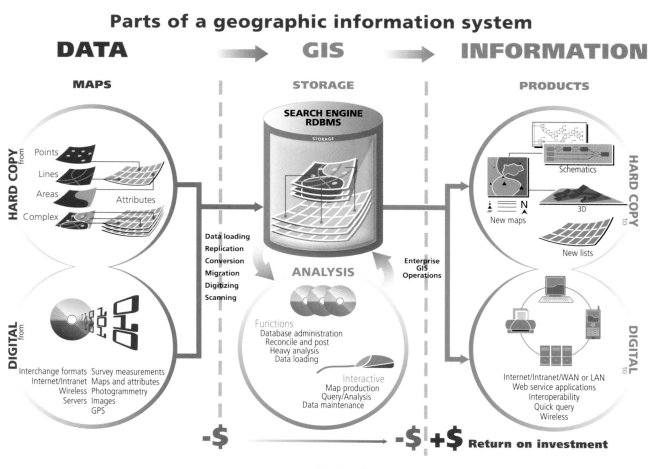

Figure 1.1 **Parts of a GIS**

the range and depth of these attributes that make spatial data such a powerful tool in the hands of a dynamic, working GIS.

So where does this data come from? Not surprisingly, good old-fashioned paper maps and other hard-copy records still supply much of the physical and human data needed for GIS. After all, printed paper maps have been the standard vehicle for conveying geographic information since the earliest recorded history. By scanning or digitizing the features drawn on our organization's paper maps, we mine this rich data source. And by establishing logical links to other digitized hard-copy records in

our organization—tables, lists, documents—we further convert data for use in the GIS, doing this until we've digitized and linked all the relevant paper documents at our disposal. More and more, spatial data is available in digital form; you can buy it or acquire it via data-sharing arrangements or over the Web.

Measuring and survey devices, including GPS receivers, photogrammetry images, and survey instruments generate troves of GIS-usable data, which can be shared quickly by means of the Internet and common interchange formats. All these sets of data with logical links—after being systematically integrated under the primary organizing key of geographic location—can be stored and managed as a unit, called a *database.*

Along with all its features and attributes, this linked unit of spatial data—the GIS database—resides in the GIS storage system, where it is available for software functions such as analysis and mapmaking. The power of the computer is used to ask questions of the spatial data, to search through it, compare it, analyze it, and measure it. You use the GIS to do things that would be very laborious or even impossible to do in any other way. These GIS software functions are under the interactive control of the GIS operator, whose job is to create the needed information products.

Identifying the information products your organization needs is central to the GIS planning process, so we do it at the beginning. Information products come in many forms—new maps, new lists and tables, schematics, 3D visualizations, the results of interactive queries presented on-screen, as hard-copy maps and reports, or as transmittable digital information—but they are all intended to improve job performance. And when these end-product reports, which inform your choices, actually lead to better decision making, you know you've planned your GIS well. This is the harvest, the accomplishment that represents the ultimate success of GIS.

## Scope of GIS projects

Understanding the scope or range of operation of your project will help you develop an effective plan for GIS implementation. Is it a single-purpose project, a department-level application, or a multi-department—perhaps even multiagency—enterprise system? The same guiding principles of GIS planning apply to all three scopes, regardless of subtle differences between project types, but some of the planning steps may not be needed on small projects or department-level applications.

Most organizations end up testing the GIS waters with a single-purpose project carried out within a single department. The expected result is a project-specific output, such as information needed to make a decision. A site analysis to locate a new landfill is an example of this modest scope: a one-time effort that has an end date, with the project paying the acquisition cost and no long-term support expected.

The second level of GIS implementation is also within a contained scope, but without the limited time frame. With a department-level application, the objective is just as straightforward, but this time the need is ongoing: a department expects output from GIS to support at least one established business objective or function. For example, anytime a change in land-use zoning is proposed, the city planning department must notify all property owners within three hundred feet of the property in question. The business objective is notification of all those owners; GIS supports this by generating the appropriate mailing lists. The GIS is located right there in the department responsible for the targeted workflow, and this department manages the system. For this reason, support from the departmental head is crucial; developing the GIS application depends on it. Funding to cover GIS staff, hardware, software, applications, and maintenance requires corporate approval.

Finally, enterprise-wide systems are the broadest in scope of the three, allowing employees to access and integrate GIS data across all departments of the organization. Here, fully in alignment with the organization's mission, GIS takes its most versatile, active role. The objective is for GIS to boost an already established strategic direction, supporting the entire organization over the long haul. Advocacy from upper management is essential, as is long-term support from multiple departments. Enterprise GIS addresses the business needs of many or all departments, becoming a powerful tool inside the organization as a whole. For example, in a transportation company using multiple GIS applications and huge databases of geospatial data across all departments, GIS is a mission-critical element of the company's operating strategy. Corporate involvement is integral to ensuring data sharing among the many divisions. An enterprise-wide GIS allows the integration of this data with the business functions and processes.

The power of GIS can be leveraged the most at the enterprise level, where there is much to be gained from GIS's adeptness at bringing people and knowledge together: with consistent information available across the organization, decision makers get a clearer picture of reality; data is regularly updated; and more data is shared, reducing duplication of effort.

As GIS software continues to expand more and more into enterprise implementations, other trends lead industry observers to predict that the next step will be society-wide—GIS will become as much a part of our lives as computers are today. GIS servers are already providing the software architecture to enable multiuser access, extending the capability for serving maps and data on the Web in a ready-to-use fashion (through Web clients).

GIS's potential as integrator is only beginning to be tapped, but already GIS-based applications have brought modest changes into the daily life of people, just as GIS has brought major change into the daily business of many organizations. As GIS-based applications become more widespread and available, who knows what societal changes will develop?

Interest in Web services and in service-oriented architecture (SOA) is growing, and with it the public's access to knowledge previously available only to GIS specialists. Thanks to the Internet and technologic advances, GIS is currently evolving from the enterprise to society.

## The who, what, when, where, why

Let's borrow a page from the reporter's notebook and set this story up via those famous "W"s of the newsroom: *who*, *what*, *when*, *where*, and *why*?

*Who should plan a GIS?* You, the GIS manager, must take the lead role in the planning process, but you should never go it alone. You need the senior-level decision makers on board with you, advised and informed throughout the process. Failure to keep these budget keepers apprised can lead to reduced or eliminated funding. To ensure their support, keep them actively engaged in the planning process and educated about the work. You rely on them also to tell you what information products are going to be needed at their level. Include in the planning process those who will be directly using the system as well. If they aren't involved, you'll probably fail to meet their real needs.

A note on consultants: if you decide to hire GIS consultants, have them lead you through the planning steps—never hire a consultant to do the planning for you. You and your colleagues need to do the planning—it's your GIS system, your job, and your reputation at stake. You'll be making decisions as a team throughout the planning process. If you do use a consultant to help you, a GIS team within the organization should still carry out the work, under the consultant's guidance.

In Canada there is a saying: "Consultants disappear like the snow in springtime." The point is, at the end of the process you will be left with the system to implement. If you haven't been totally involved in planning and writing the implementation strategy, you might be in for a very difficult and painful time.

*What to plan?* GIS is a complex system of interconnected parts. So it will come as no surprise that you must consider six different major components in any GIS plan: information products, data, software, hardware, procedures, and people.

**Information products:** Information products are what you want (need) from the GIS. This desired output may take the form of maps, reports, graphs, lists, or any combination thereof. Mission critical: identify these products with sufficient clarity early in the planning process.

**Data:** By knowing what information products you want, you can plan for the acquisition of the needed data. What can you get that already exists? What can you create from existing sources? What levels of map accuracy and scale will you require? And don't forget data format, a factor related to the next component, software. Sometimes data format alone drives the software decision, as in the case of the city municipal government planning a data-sharing arrangement with a county GIS department that already uses a particular software.

**Software:** Software programs provide the functions needed to perform analysis and create the information products you want. Sometimes customized software sits on top of the main GIS software package. Updates need to be planned to keep the versions current. There are also support and operating system issues related to software.

**Hardware:** GIS is demanding of hardware. You must take an unflinching look at your organization's computational resources and upgrade accordingly to support GIS. Typically, a few powerful workstations support the heavy lifting and geoprocessing, though in larger systems this is increasingly handled by GIS servers on a network. Simple computers ("thin clients") on the network provide the user access for database query and display purposes. A robust internal network and wide bandwidth ("fat pipe") to the Internet are also required to facilitate file sharing, data acquisition, and reporting.

**Procedures:** As an important component of GIS planning, *procedures* refers to the way people do their jobs and the changes they will have to make to do their jobs using your new GIS system. You need a migration plan to facilitate this transition from the old way into the new, plus you need to address how the existing ("legacy") systems will coexist (or not) with the GIS.

**People:** GIS is a thinking process that requires the right people. Will you need to hire or are the right ones already on staff? How will you hire, train, and keep the staff with the specialized skills it takes to build or use your system? Over time, staffing will be your single biggest cost.

*When to plan?* You plan from the beginning, and the planning process continues after the GIS is installed. Successful GIS projects attract positive attention, which means that before long people will identify other things that they'd like to see from the GIS. This will move you to revisit one or the other of the planning stages. Armed now with the empirical experience of a functioning GIS, each new iteration of the planning process becomes better calibrated to the real world.

Also, you plan in a particular order, each step illuminating where to go with the next. This only stands to reason. How could you plan to acquire the data for a map, for example, unless you'd already identified that map as part of an information product you need?

*Where to plan?* GIS planning, to be most effective, must be carried out in the business world, not from the vacuum of your office. Because GIS has the potential to create common connections between disparate things, it is inherently a horizontal technology that can touch literally every person in an organization if the company's leaders want it to (and many do). The thorough and diligent GIS planner must meet people in the organization to learn what information they need and how they need to get it. Only by taking the time to witness people doing their work can the GIS planner ever aspire to true understanding of the business processes. And how can a planner create anything of use to anyone without this knowledge?

*Why plan GIS?* Good planning leads to success and poor planning leads to failure. This is true whether you are starting from scratch or building from an existing GIS. It seems obvious on the surface, but time after time GIS projects fail because of poor planning. Like any complex information system, GIS implementation and maintenance are costly. Every component of the system—the data, the software, the hardware, the staff—cost an organization dearly. But everything exacts a lesser toll if it is considered beforehand and selected carefully.

Would you rather spend a dollar at the beginning on planning or ten thousand later to make up for not planning? The point is, even spending a lot of money is no assurance of getting the right thing. Besides, planning can be interesting: you meet a lot of people, learn a lot about your organization, and you may end up knowing more than the CEO about how the place really runs. Planning is especially rewarding toward the end when you do the benefit–cost analysis and see how much money your organization will be saving over time—and all because you led the implementation of a well-planned GIS.

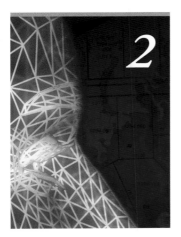

# Overview of the method

*2*

*Like a good roadmap, an overview of the method lets you know where you are going.*

The planning methodology introduced in this book shows you the steps of GIS planning—how to assess what your requirements are and which system will meet those needs—and how to implement the GIS in your organization once your plan is approved.

This ten-stage GIS planning methodology evolved from years of experience in planning large and small implementations in public- and private-sector companies. The size and nature of your organization will determine which of the component stages are most relevant to your situation. A full enterprise-wide implementation almost certainly requires you to undertake all the stages in full, while for a smaller project, you'll be completing some steps quickly or even skipping a few. Regardless of the size of the undertaking, all situations are unique; you will need to understand all of the steps in the process before adapting the methodology to suit your circumstances.

## The ten-stage GIS planning methodology

Stage 1: Consider the strategic purpose

Stage 2: Plan for the planning

Stage 3: Conduct a technology seminar

Stage 4: Describe the information products

Stage 5: Define the system scope

Stage 6: Create a data design

Stage 7: Choose a logical data model

Stage 8: Determine system requirements

Stage 9: Consider benefit–cost, migration, and risk analysis

Stage 10: Plan the implementation

The following ten chapters of this book detail each of the ten stages. Let's take a quick tour of the method.

## Stage 1: Consider the strategic purpose (chapter 3)

Start by considering the strategic purpose of the organization within which the system will be developed. What are its goals, objectives, and mandates?

This stage of planning ensures that the GIS planning process and final system fit within the organizational context and truly support the strategic objectives of the organization. This stage also allows you to assess how information created by the GIS will affect the business strategy of the organization.

## Stage 2: Plan for the planning (chapter 4)

GIS planning should not be taken lightly. Forget about actually implementing a GIS for the moment. Just planning a GIS takes a commitment of resources and people. Before you begin, you need to know that your organization understands the distinction between planning and implementing and that it is prepared to provide enough resources for the planning project.

Making the case means understanding what needs to be done and what it will take to get it done. The result of this stage is a project proposal that makes that case and explicitly seeks approval and funding to launch the formal planning process.

Commitment to the planning process is essential to a successful GIS implementation, especially in municipal government agencies and other bureaucratic public-sector organizations. The project proposal helps secure this political commitment. This is the moment to introduce the GIS planning process to the highest level executives of your organization and to arrange to keep them fully informed of your progress. If you receive approval for your planning project and a commitment of resources at this point, your chances of having a successful GIS are high.

## Stage 3: Conduct a technology seminar (chapter 5)

Once your project plan is approved, you can activate the in-house GIS planning team to begin its most important endeavor: identifying exactly what the organization needs from a GIS.

Defining the specific GIS requirements is the primary task of the planning process. You must meet with the customers or clients of the GIS (those who will use the system or its output) to begin gathering specifics about the organization's needs from the user's perspective. A highly effective method of soliciting input is to hold one or more in-house technology seminars.

In addition to its information gathering purpose, the technology seminar is an ideal opportunity for you to explain to key personnel the nature of GIS, its potential benefits, and the scope of the planning process itself. By involving stakeholders at this early stage, you help to ensure subsequent participation in the planning work ahead.

The technology seminar is also the place where initial identification of information products begins.

## Stage 4: Describe the information products (chapter 6)

Knowing what you want to get out of your GIS is the key to a successful implementation. And what you want comes in the form of information products: maps, lists, charts, reports, whatever you need to inform your decision making and streamline workflows.

This stage must be carefully undertaken. You will talk to the users about what their job involves and what information they need to perform their tasks. Ultimately you need to determine things like how each information product should be made and how frequently, what data is required to make it, how much error can be tolerated, and the benefits of the new information produced. You will help each person declaring a specific need for such information from the GIS to write an *information product description (IPD)*.

This stage should result in a document that includes a description of all the information products that can be reasonably foreseen, together with details of the data and functions required to produce these products.

## Stage 5: Define the system scope (chapter 7)

Once the information products have been described, you can begin to define the scope of the entire system. This involves determining what data to acquire, when it will be needed, and how much data volume must be handled, then charting all this on a *master input data list (MIDL)*.

You will also assess the probable timing of the production of the information products. Here, you may discover it's possible to use one input data source to generate more than one information product, and you can build this into your development program. Each refinement helps clarify your needs and increase your chance of success.

## Stage 6: Create a data design (chapter 8)

In GIS, data is a major factor because spatial data is relatively complicated. In the conceptual system design phase of the planning process, you review the requirements identified in the earlier stages and use them to begin developing a database design.

## Stage 7: Choose a logical data model (chapter 9)

A logical data model describes those parts of the real world that concern your organization. The database may be simple or complex but must fit together in a logical manner so that you can easily retrieve the data you need and efficiently carry out the analysis tasks required.

Several options are available for your system's database design. You will review the advantages and disadvantages of each approach at this stage, while considering various issues affecting the design: data accuracy, update requirements, error tolerance, and data standards.

## Stage 8: Determine system requirements (chapter 10)

Here, you envisage the system design in its entirety by examining as a whole what you will require of a system: the GIS functions, user interface, communications bandwidth, and core capacity. This is the first time in the planning process that you examine software and hardware products.

You review the information product descriptions (IPDs from chapter 6) and the master input data list (MIDL from chapter 7) in order to summarize and classify the functions needed to make these products. This will enable you to inform vendors of what you require in the way of software functionality. You will consider issues of interface design, effective communications (particularly in distributed systems), and platform sizing in order to determine the appropriate hardware, software, and network configurations to meet your needs.

## Stage 9: Consider benefit–cost, migration, and risk analysis (chapter 11)

Following conceptual system design, you need to work out the best way to actually implement the system you have designed. This is where you begin preparing for how the system will be taken from the planning stage to actual implementation.

As part of that preparation, you may need to conduct a benefit–cost analysis to make your business case for the system. To convince management to fund the GIS implementation, you will probably be called upon to show how various risk factors weigh in, such as migration from the old system to the new.

## Stage 10: Plan the implementation (chapter 12)

Until now, the focus of the planning methodology has been on what you need to put in place to meet your requirements. The focus at this stage switches to how to

## Let each step inform the next

- If you know what information products you need, you can determine what data should go into your GIS.
- If you can determine what data should go into your system, you can also determine what needs to be done to the data to produce your information products.
- If you know what you want to do to your data, you can determine what functions your system needs to be able to perform and begin to design an appropriate technological solution.

put the system in place—acquisition and implementation planning. Now you will address such issues as staffing and training, institutional interactions, legal matters, security, existing legacy hardware and software, and how to manage change. The plan that results from this last stage of the methodology will contain your implementation strategy and benefit–cost analysis. This plan becomes your final report, which can be used both to secure funding for your system and as a guide for the actual implementation of the system.

The final report equips you with all the information you need to implement a successful GIS. It will become your GIS planning book to help you through the implementation process.

Developing the final report should be the result of a process of communication between the GIS team and management so that no part of the report comes as a surprise to anyone. The report should contain a review of the organization's strategic business objectives, the information requirements study, details of the conceptual system design, recommendations for implementation, time-planning issues, and funding alternatives.

The purpose of this GIS planning methodology—and my intention with this book—is to guide you through these stages in your thinking. Use it to give senior executives the context for the questions they must ask about GIS in their organization; let it inform you as a planner or new GIS manager how to answer those questions.

# Consider the strategic purpose

*Strategic purpose is the guiding light. The system that gets implemented must be aligned with the purpose of the organization as a whole.*

It all starts with the organization. To develop an effective GIS, the GIS planner must have a clear understanding of what the agency or company does, its working plan to do it, and how GIS can help accomplish the mission. Organizations adopt GIS on the assumption that it will make their work easier and cheaper to do or better for the customer or constituency. Fostering any or all of those GIS benefits begins with understanding how the organization works. A successful GIS is one that is aligned with the purpose of the organization as a whole, thereby helping provide what it needs to stay true to that purpose.

How do you find out what your organization needs? As the GIS planner, first you examine the strategic business plan—most organizations have one. It states the goals as they are envisioned plus the actions required to meet them. A strategic business plan consists of some or all of the following components:

**Mission statement:** Describes the purpose of the organization.

**Guiding principles:** Outlines the behavior of the organization as it carries out its mission. For example, descriptors of the guiding principles in a customer-driven organization might be *user friendly, collaborative, responsive,* and *providing better service.*

**Goal statement:** What the organization hopes to accomplish, in general, over a given amount of time. For instance, your organization could determine that over the next five years it wants to automate all the business processes in three of its departments.

**Program direction:** The current direction or strategy of the efforts. In other words, if you were to add up everything the different programs are doing, the sum of these efforts should achieve the overall organizational goals.

**Employee development and support:** The plan for providing employee training and staff development.

**Public interaction:** How the public or your constituency participates in developing and updating the strategic plan. Such involvement can be direct or through indirect methods such as surveys or focus groups.

Every bit of this information, in any form you can find it, will contribute to your overall understanding of the organization's strategic direction and purpose, which will inform your GIS planning. Be creative and thorough in discovering what the organization is all about. If it does not have a strategic plan, examine its mandates and responsibilities to get a sense of organizational purposes and objectives. The planner's job is easier, however, if the organization has an established strategic plan; if senior management's objectives match those of the strategic plan; and if there is commitment throughout the organization to achieve its goals.

Equally important in setting the direction for GIS planning is your understanding of the specific business model intended to achieve the goals in the strategic plan. In effect, this model sets out for each program area what is defined as successful. (In this envisioning of business success, note whether technology is prominent in the picture; for sustained support of GIS development, technology must be recognized as an important tool in achieving success.) The business model also provides insights into business sustainability—how revenue will be available for business costs over time.

Both the strategic plan and the business model establish the framework within which you will do a GIS benefit–cost analysis (chapter 11) as well as your assessment of what additional information would help the organization accomplish its goals and objectives. Understanding what the organization does and its vision for the future allows the GIS manager to design valuable information products, ones that further those objectives. Without considering the organization's strategic purpose, you risk wasting time on planning that is peripheral to its needs.

If the organization does not have a strategic business plan, it may take some work to find out what the real business is and thereby what the real needs are. But even a relatively detailed business plan tells only part of the story. You need to uncover the organization's secrets, its objectives, how its workflows really operate, what makes it tick. You need to know all of this to plan for an effective GIS.

To really understand the business, you must also analyze the mandates and responsibilities of each functional division that will be involved with GIS. Undertaking this analysis requires active engagement of the stakeholders. Go into individual departments and seek answers to these questions:

- How do the individuals who make decisions currently do it?
- What do they need to know to perform their tasks?
- What information products are appropriate for these tasks?

Imagine the following scenario: You go into a government department of forestry to talk to the staff and begin by asking a forester, "What do you do here?"

"My job is to manage the harvesting of timber in the best interests of the people of the state," she replies.

OK, that's how she sees her job. Next you ask, "What do you need to know to do that?"

She talks around the subject at length, listing many of the datasets she uses, before she finally gets to something tangible: She really needs to know which trees to cut down, when to cut them down, and how to cut them down. This simple statement contains the crux of the information you need to know, but you had to ask probing questions and be a good listener to filter out all the rest. Now that you know what she really does, you can start to identify some information products she will need on her desk, information products that will actually tell her which trees to cut down, when, and how, based on the methodology she already uses.

It will take several conversations like this to get a handle on the information that individuals need to carry out their jobs, fulfill their mandates and responsibilities, or accomplish the objectives of the strategic business plan. Asking these questions should help those you interview focus on the specifics you're after:

- What are your job responsibilities?
- What do you have to achieve?
- What do you have to produce?
- What do you need to know to carry out your responsibilities?
- What information can GIS produce and put on your desk that will provide what you need to know and help you monitor or keep track of your responsibilities?

In this way, the strategic direction of the organization will reveal itself and, with the answers to these questions from a range of individuals, you will be able to envisage the scope of the information they need to succeed. Answers given by management may differ significantly from those of the rank-and-file, so you will "blend" the responses in order to get a clear picture of the information required from GIS.

Asking the same questions in different departments will help delineate workflows within departments and their interaction with workflows in other departments. Ultimately, a comprehensive overview of the organization's processes will emerge. With this insight, the GIS planner can begin to examine the following:

- What data is available now that can be used to create the information products needed?
- Where is this data?
- What new data is required?
- What data handling functions are necessary to turn the available data into the required information products?

When you know what functions are needed and what data these functions must operate on, you have enough information to define the technological requirements (e.g., hardware and software).

The link you establish between strategic objectives, information, and data gives you an audit trail. You identify how information fits into the organization and the benefits of creating new information. This is the start of a benefit–cost analysis for GIS: What is the benefit of creating an information product for the organization, and what is the cost of producing that product?

Once the information products are available, they will help the organization to fulfill its mandates and responsibilities, meet its objectives, and progress in the direction intended. Even better, the new information products allow the organization to change its strategic direction in response to new opportunities or to identify new markets. This moment, when an organization's leaders finally grasp the full strategic implications of their GIS, is a sweet moment indeed for the GIS planner.

# Plan for the planning

*Since the GIS planning process will take time and resources, you need to get an approval and commitment at the front end.*

Planning for a GIS usually requires a serious commitment of time and money. It can take from six months to a year to look at the overall needs of a large organization, during which time you'll be depending on its personnel and funding. That's why you need specific permission to plan, along with management's commitment to provide the resources. You ask for both within a planning proposal document, which you will write and submit as soon as possible.

A planning proposal is a useful tool for making the case to management for the resources to complete your GIS planning project. This project proposal should explain exactly what's involved: the stages and costs of planning, in time and money, including the use of in-house staff resources.

Develop this proposal early to get the organization behind you. Make sure that management signs off on your proposal before going further. With management support beginning at this stage, your chances of a successful GIS implementation are high. Approval and commitment of resources are essential, and they need to come from the top—from senior management. You might have to start discussions with middle management and work through the chain of command, but eventually you will have to sell the idea to the higher-ups.

Your proposal can make a convincing case to top management by pointing out that both the success rate and the benefits of GIS increase significantly with better planning. In fact, it's the planning study you are proposing that will give the GIS planning team the opportunity to identify what the organization needs most from a GIS: the specific information products that could bring such improved efficiency into its day-to-day work.

It is also worth mentioning in the proposal that planning is more important than ever, despite positive changes in the economics of computing that foster the illusion you could just dive in. In the early days of GIS, when the massive hardware installations required to run the systems could cost more than a million dollars, organizations looking at GIS could easily justify spending significant time and resources on planning. With that kind of money at stake, they had to make sure they were going about things wisely. Ten percent of the total system cost was an entirely reasonable amount to allocate for planning. But in today's computing environment, with adequate hardware available for thousands rather than millions of dollars, 10 percent of the hardware budget would amount to only a few thousand dollars, not an adequate amount for in-depth planning. The proportion of funds needed in the planning stage relative to the overall budget has shifted.

These days, the ultimate cost of GIS implementation will depend heavily on data rather than hardware or software. Therefore, while your planning project proposal will include cost estimates for hardware and software as well as information on anticipated staffing needs, it will have to show that the most significant investments will be in data acquisition and development, not in hardware and software. The data costs for your GIS may surpass the hardware and software investments, once you factor in things like measuring equipment, labor, conversion costs, maintenance, and the licensing of commercial data.

As your investments in data grow, so too will the time and resource requirements of ongoing maintenance. So despite the perennial lowering of costs for equipment, the need for thorough and thoughtful GIS planning is as important today as it ever was.

## Planning project proposals

Let's look at a couple of successful project proposals. The first one was developed by an in-house GIS advocate working at a national park; the second by a GIS consultant, laying out a planning proposal for an Australian state government effort. At Jasper National Park in Canada, the in-house planning team submitted a document called a *terms of reference* to the park service senior management with the purpose of seeking funding for the GIS planning process. The organization of the proposal is shown in figure 4.1.

Figure 4.2 illustrates the sections of a successful proposal submitted by Tomlinson Associates Ltd. to the state government of Victoria, Australia, for involvement in a large-scale GIS planning project. Bear in mind that this is a document produced by consultants aiming to get work assisting the GIS planning process.

A note about hiring consultants: they can help, but you must be the one who drives the process, works with it, writes reports, and makes trade-off decisions. A consultant should not entirely do your GIS planning—you must assume that responsibility. When the consultant leaves, you will be left with the system to implement.

These examples give you the general idea about what constitutes a project proposal. You can adapt them to the specific needs of your own organization in the document you present with your plan for planning to meet those needs. Your proposal should be detailed and deal with all aspects of the GIS planning process. Although there are no set guidelines for creating GIS planning project

**Jasper National Park**
**Terms of reference**

**Work outline**

1.0 Project description

       1.1 Background

       1.2 Objectives of the project

       1.3 Project deliverables

2.0 User needs analysis

       2.1 Situational assessment

       2.2 Client base

       2.3 Business requirements and information products

       2.4 Data requirements

       2.5 Technology requirements

3.0 Software/hardware assessment

4.0 Database requirements

5.0 Implementation plan

6.0 Schedule of payment

**Contract conditions**

       Parks Canada responsibility

       Timing and duration

       Proposal guidelines

**Appendix 1**   Documents for review

**Appendix 2**   Ecosystem database inventory

**Appendix 3**   Client list

       1. Jasper National Park clients

       2. Corporate clients

       3. Tri-council research

       4. Agency clients

       5. Private industry clients and general public

       6. Information management

**List of bidders for GIS user needs**

Figure 4.1   **Outline of an in-house planning proposal**

**Strategic framework for GIS development**

Introduction
Project team
Outline of the proposed methodology
    Staff seminar
    Information product definition
    Benefits
    Data requirements
    Error tolerance analysis
    Information priority
    Functional requirement
    Benefit–cost analysis
    Implementation planning
    Request for tender design (technical contents)
    Strategy report
Project deliverables
Work organization
Procurement process (optional)
Project timing
Involvement of government staff
Administrative and cost notes
Cost assumptions
Cost summary
    GIS planning project
    Cost break down—by fiscal year
    Cost break down—by primary year
    Optional cost—electoral office procurement process
Appendix 1:   Background and experience of Tomlinson Associates Ltd.
Appendix 2:   Curriculum vitae of key personnel

Figure 4.2   **Contents of a GIS consultant's planning proposal**

proposals, it is a good idea to deal with each phase of the planning methodology in a distinctive section (as in figure 4.3). Within each section, include potential staffing needs and staff time commitment. Figure 4.3 illustrates the basic sections of a proposal using parts of the GIS planning methodology.

Once you present your proposal, it is imperative that it be reviewed and approved and the resources committed. You have not asked for money just for hiring a consultant; you have requested a commitment of in-house time and staff resources. Since the GIS planning process will use these resources, you need to get approval and commitment before you take the next step. This will ensure that the planning process will be carried out. Make sure that management signs off on your proposal to plan for a GIS, and ask for a memo that describes its importance to the organization, which can be used to apprise everyone in the organization.

```
Project description
        Background
        Objectives
        Deliverables

Requirements study
        Preparation
        Needs assessment
        System scope

Conceptual design
        Database design
        Technology design
        Hardware
        Software

Implementation planning
```

Figure 4.3   **Stages of the GIS planning methodology as proposal sections**

## Assemble the GIS team

After you receive the go-ahead, you can prepare to evaluate your organization's requirements in more detail, and for that you need teamwork. Now that you have commitment to the planning process, you'll need to confirm who should be involved in it and brief all the participants on their roles and responsibilities.

Your planning project needs to be conducted by an in-house GIS team. The "guiding" team should be made up of the team leader and two other people, one of whom should be from the permanent staff of the organization or agency concerned. The second person on the team should have participated in at least one previous GIS planning study and be fully conversant with the methods and techniques employed. The third person should be from the permanent staff of the organization or, if it's an agency, from the region, city, or municipality concerned; this is the one appointed to be the on-site or local organizer.

In a small organization, the project team could be just one person, but it is more effective to have a group consisting of a team leader—part of the three-person guiding team—and one person from each department requesting information from the GIS. The individuals from these departments will assist by clarifying the needs of those departments.

After the in-house team has been established, you can meet with department heads. The memo you obtained earlier from the CEO or director of your organization stressing the importance of the GIS planning process should request the support of all department heads. As you meet with the department heads, you will probably find that they want to know the following: What is the role of the department in the planning process? What time commitments will be necessary? Who will be needed? In response, you can answer their questions, making it clear that some of their personnel will be involved in the planning and may need to spend several days in the process. This must be stated upfront so that staff are

**Plan ahead for the time commitment**

These guidelines regarding resource requirements are based on the experiences of the author in planning a number of GIS implementations at a variety of regional and municipal organizations:

- From start to finish, the GIS planning process in a typical region, government, department, or small municipality takes four to eight months, longer for complex or large organizations.
- The aggregate total of work hours amounts to six or seven person-months, more time for complex or large organizations.
- The leader of the in-house GIS team is committed for 70 percent of his or her working time (and would probably opt for more if other duties didn't intrude).
- Departmental staff involved will spend two to six days in the development of each information product description (more about this in the next two chapters).
- All levels of staff will be affected in some way and are thus indirectly involved with the study.

given time away from their normal duties to help with the planning with full support of their manager.

If all you're undertaking is a single-purpose project within your own department, you may only need to visit one department manager, your own, to get the green light. Even so, it is important to get support, and to stress that the planning will take some time and that you will not be able to do as many other things during this period.

For a project of any cross-departmental scope, you should definitely visit all the department heads separately

to secure their support. Find out what is needed for them to reach a level of comfort with your GIS endeavors.

Of course it would be ideal if your small team of people came with GIS planning experience, but regardless, a GIS team guiding the planning process with consistency in approach and method inspires confidence and cooperation. You'll need both for the all-important task ahead. Now that departmental commitment has been secured and the GIS team assembled, you are ready to assess further the needs and requirements of your organization.

# Conduct a technology seminar

## 5

*Think of the technology seminar as a "town-hall" meeting between the GIS planning team and the potential users of GIS in the organization.*

Having studied the organization's strategic plan, you have the official word on the goals of the work it does; now you're going to find out how the organization actually works toward those goals and how GIS can help those workflows move more smoothly to their objectives. You're going to hold a big meeting—a kind of group study—with all the potential users to find out what people need from GIS to do their jobs better.

You have already assembled your in-house GIS team and secured the support of department heads for their staff to be involved, so now you can bring everyone together for a technology seminar. Think of this as a kind of town-hall meeting, wherein the in-house team shares the vision of GIS and reviews the planning process, while everyone affected has a chance to voice what they want from GIS. The deliverable for this meeting will be the initial list of information products, divided by department.

This is a training event to raise awareness of GIS and explain the roles of those involved. Depending on the size of the organization, you can host one or more technology seminars—whatever it takes for your colleagues to understand the planning process and the fundamental concepts behind GIS. One approach is to run an event over two or more days, in order to accommodate all the people who expect information from the GIS. In a large organization, you may have thirty or more participating; in a smaller one, maybe a dozen or less.

# Overview of a seminar

Before going into more detail, let's take a look at what it is about a technology seminar that moves the planning forward. You will see from the description of one, below, that a seminar supports the planning process by eliciting an itemized first listing of the output desired from a GIS and by bringing everyone on board and up to speed on GIS. Of course, such events vary according to the nature of the organization, but basically the agenda for any GIS technology seminar should include the following:

- Describing a GIS
- Defining GIS terminology
- Explaining GIS functions
- The planning process—steps and responsibilities
- Preliminary/first identification of information products
- Business workflow improvement opportunities

Successful planning requires effective communication among those involved. Spend some time during the seminar explaining the nature of GIS, defining the basic terminology and describing the functions that systems can perform. This will help everyone in the organization establish a shared vision of GIS and a common language in which to clearly articulate their requirements.

Participants want to know when and how they will be involved in planning and what is expected of them, so start right off by saying that this seminar begins their participation in the planning process. This is their first forum, and in it they will define the deliverables; by identifying the information products they need from GIS, they will be laying the foundation of the planning process. Tell them you will open the discussion to audience participation shortly, but first you want to spend some time defining GIS and outlining the stages of the planning process. Explain how each planning step logically follows one upon the other, building on the information gathered in the one before. Emphasize that the first step—identifying the output participants require from GIS—is the most important because it sets the course for

planning. And this is why their involvement is so crucial: it's up to them to declare what they want out of the system (or at least what they think they want).

Then open it up for discussion and begin to capture what the participants say. Use a whiteboard and assign someone to take good notes. Ask people directly: what's the job you do and what information do you need on your desk? They will probably think about it and say they don't know what they need. Keep prompting them and eventually they will give you some ideas.

A forester with a timber inventory to manage might say she could use a better harvesting map. An urban engineer tracking sewer repairs might say he needs an accurate inventory of sewer hookups, one that's updated automatically whenever completed work orders are submitted back to engineering.

Even after you explain that in GIS we call this kind of output—anything that meets your specific workflow needs—an *information product,* some people will get hung up in limiting their thinking to maps, under the assumption that GIS is a mapping system only. So be sure to mention early on that sometimes the best GIS output comes in the form of lists derived from spatial analysis, such as a record of all the customers in a trade area. One result of GIS spatial analysis of all the properties in a flood zone could be the series of addresses of people to be contacted in an emergency, another example of new information coming in the form of a list. While such lists can be subsequently mapped, the real value of these information products comes from the GIS process of spatial analysis, not from its mapmaking function.

Because you're involved in a session of collaborative brainstorming, the first ideas will trigger others and before you know it, most people in the group will have described the workflow story in their own context. Write what you're hearing on the board, making a list of the information products indentified. (Try to get consensus in the naming of each information product.) You can expect to collect ten, twenty, even fifty information

**Purpose of the technology seminar**

The purpose of the seminar is to do the following:

- Introduce GIS to the participants (if necessary)
- Introduce the planning process to the participants
- Explain to participants the reason why the work is being done
- Make clear the nature of the contribution required of participants and how their efforts will improve the chance for success overall
- Introduce GIS terminology and methods that will be used throughout the planning and final implementation
- Afford participants the opportunity to assess their work needs and identify the information that would help them do their job better and more efficiently
- Compose the list of information products needed, by name and by department, including the name of the person requesting the product

The technology seminar is the first face-to-face contact between the GIS planning team and the staff involved in the planning study, so an underlying objective of the seminar is to establish a good working relationship between the two groups. Toward this end, members of the planning team should demonstrate that they possess the following:

- Competence in GIS and, preferably, in the business of the company
- Experience in related GIS planning efforts elsewhere
- Ability to elicit the participants' views on information needs and management practices without pushing their own views
- Ability to aid the organization in clarifying and describing its own requirement

product ideas by the end of the technology seminar. At this point, it doesn't matter which information products take precedence over others—some may never even get built—you simply want to start from the largest universe of possibilities you can muster. You can count on the process itself to lead to an emerging sense of priorities, as well as a great deal of cooperation and cross-fertilization of ideas.

For now, all you need is the title of the proposed information product, a few words describing its intended use, the scale of any output maps required, and the name of the person who wants it. The person's name is very important, so it is required; you may need them for more details later on. It also serves as an indication that someone wants the information product so much that they're willing to support it themselves, and there is no point in taking note of any other kind. The person set

to actually use the product is the one who really knows why it's needed, and he should be willing to associate his name with it. Make it a rule: no name, no information product.

One more thing: It is not a good idea to let the head of the department design all of the information products. An authority figure's viewpoint acts as a filter, and at this early stage we want the ideas coming in unfiltered.

## Set the stage

GIS means change, and whenever you introduce change into organizations there will be internal debate and usually some resistance. Building trust and alliances with colleagues who will be affected by your efforts is an important dimension of achieving success. Enabling everyone to get prepared and stay informed is considerate and fosters trust, so you should distribute a set of well-written (and carefully proofread) documents to all participants prior to the seminar. Include in the package any relevant memoranda authorizing the study, the agenda of the first meeting, and the timetable for the study. Also provide some introductory GIS information that people can study before coming to the meeting. You could photocopy articles or sections of textbooks (with the publisher's permission) or even purchase copies in bulk of a certain book if you find one you like. (See "Further reading" on page 227 for a list of books appropriate for this purpose.)

You'll discover at the meeting that some people will have read your documents from front to back, others not at all, and most will have skimmed them with varying degrees of interest. Look for the people who really have taken to the GIS introductory materials; these are people who, like you, have recognized something inherently interesting about GIS and can be recruited as allies in your GIS campaign.

Limit the number of staff invited to a single seminar to twenty-five or thirty people organization-wide, with each manager making the selection for his or her department. Smaller GIS efforts in smaller agencies obviously require smaller teams. Among the required attendees are the senior administrative officer of the organization and the heads of all departments involved. Their attendance alone, even if they are figureheads, sends a signal of senior management's commitment to the effort, which should stimulate interest in all invitees to attend. Especially encourage experienced staff members to attend; they bring intimate knowledge of their own department's processes. It may be useful to invite representatives of other organizations with GIS experience, such as those in neighboring states, regions, or provinces. But these should be carefully selected. The focus of the meeting is on your own organization. Particularly, include the people involved with any GIS efforts already established in your organization.

Arrange to hold your technology seminar away from the office—better for brainstorming. Local hotels, universities, and conference centers typically make for safe, easy-to-find locations with appropriate meeting facilities. The "no cell phone" rule is good practice. The ideal location should offer a large room with comfortable chairs and ancillary rooms nearby to allow the group to break up into smaller working units. The main room should have several flip charts or whiteboards, ample marking pens, an overhead projector and screen, computer projection facilities if desired, and one or two large tables. The smaller rooms will require flip charts or whiteboards as well.

## Plan the program

The typical seminar takes place over two days. The first part of the meeting—or the first day—should include the following agenda items, which may vary in sequence somewhat:

- Welcome and statement of commitment to the project by the senior administrative officer of the organization.
- Overview of current GIS status in the organization, including current GIS procurement or GIS activities, if any.
- Introduction to GIS by the team leader to establish basic GIS concepts and common terminology. This might include a definition of GIS, the parts of a GIS, and the functions of a GIS. This alone could take up a full day.
- Explanation of the needs assessment process, with the team leader emphasizing that the contribution of participants is central to the work. A key goal of the meeting is for participants to describe the information products they need.
- Brief overview and examples of information product descriptions (IPDs).

Expect many questions and issues surrounding the descriptions of information products. Be prepared to explain the generic GIS functions in detail (see the "Lexicon" section on page 209) and stress the difference between data (the raw elements of information) and information products (those raw elements transformed into information useful in doing work). Show how interim information products will evolve, and how those used in one area might find application in other areas. Encourage people to look for these cross-department applications.

## Assess information needs

On the second day (or after the earlier discussions if you have only one day), begin the initial assessment of information needs. This amounts to brainstorming, so encourage open-mindedness because, though the result you want is short and concise, the way to get it may be long and roundabout. At this stage in planning, all you're after is a brief identification of the information products needed: descriptive title, map scale, name of individual who needs it, and scope (someone else who might use it). The key to success in this step is to get participants to think about their overall information needs, freely and creatively as well as realistically, so that ultimately they come up with something that really works for them. This may be something they may not have thought of before, or even something that changes their workflow altogether. New ideas can be fruitful, so allow participants to spend some time on assessing their information needs.

Finally, you want to end up with a piece of paper listing a logical name for each information product, attached to the name of the person who needs the product on his or her desk to perform his or her work. One team member should act as reporter and fill in an "information products needed" form as each new idea is brought into the discussion.

Start the assessment of information needs by asking one department head to state broadly the responsibilities of the department. Write a concise version of this on the flip chart or whiteboard. Then ask other members of the department about their responsibilities. Ask them to identify the kinds of tasks they are responsible for, the types of decisions they have to make, the need for information at their workplace, and the conditions they regularly monitor in order to do their jobs. Capture the essence of this information on the whiteboard.

Now go back and start over, this time asking these same staff members to identify a single information product they could see as useful. Discuss the product only until you have a good idea of what it contains, making sure that it is an information product and not a dataset. (A dataset is simply a grouping of related data, while an information product is the result of one or more datasets turned into information in a form particularly useful in doing your work.) Decide on a brief descriptive title and write this on the board. Add the scope of the proposed product, that is, who else in the organization will require it. If it's a map-based information product, make sure you note the scale. Identify the name of the individual who needs the product—the person who needs it on their desk to do their job. That person must be prepared to define it more clearly in the next stage of planning. If nobody is willing to "own" the proposed idea, drop it from consideration. This will prevent your list from swelling with mere idle thoughts and half-baked ideas. Identify a second information product from the same department and continue in this fashion until that department is out of ideas.

Now move on to another department. Repeat the process until there is at least one information product identified for each department. A great deal of cross-fertilization of ideas, corporate-wide understanding, and potential for cooperating are frequent outcomes of the seminar. Better ways of doing business can be recognized; opportunities for revised workflows based on GIS can be identified. This can be noted on the whiteboard for future examination. These benefits come when the group is kept together listening to the requests of other departments. If time becomes a constraint, and at the risk of losing some cross-fertilization, you may decide to split into separate rooms to allow each department to work further on its initial list. At the end of the day, bring the whole group together to clarify any problems and to collate a list of the information products needed. This allows you to check for duplication.

Figure 5.1 is an actual list of information products, organized by department, that was developed at an internal technology seminar for a city government. You can see

| Information products for a city | |
|---|---|
| **Engineering and public works** | **Housing and property** |
| Public works program map and list | Legal surveys index query |
| Sanitary sewer analysis | Select area plan production |
| Road needs map and list | Legal surveys drafting (CAD) |
| Pedestrian system needs | Dwelling unit analysis |
| Annual sewer needs map and list | Social housing acquisition analysis |
| Basement flooding situation | Housing protection analysis |
| Sidewalk ramping needs | Housing potential map |
| Minor hard services needs | Residential loans and complaints map and list |
| Detailed engineering design (CAD*) | Existing housing and demographics map and list |
| Storm sewer analysis | City property map list |
| Maintenance analysis map and lists | Development activity map and list |
| Route optimization map and lists | Social housing map and list |
| Sidewalk snow removal analysis | Amenity map for selected area |
| Sidewalk route analysis | Waiting list analysis |
| Snow removal scheduling | Architect/landscape design drawing (CAD) |
| Lane map and public notification lists | Architect/landscape technical drawing (CAD) |
| Fleet tracking | Interior design drawings (CAD) |
| Waste receptacles/litter analysis | Streetscape design drawings (CAD) |
| Complaints analysis | |
| Park site maintenance analysis | **Economic development** |
| Stop signal location analysis | Development projects map and list |
| Traffic/parking changes | |
| Parking needs analysis | **Fire department** |
| Traffic counts | Fire suppression water supply map |
| *Acronym for computer-aided design | Emergency response building floor plans |
| | Planning department site plans |
| **City clerk's office** | Fire emergency demographic analysis |
| Ward profile analysis | Emergency route selection |
| Citywide election data map and list | |
| Ward/poll/voter election data map and list | |

Figure 5.1   **List of descriptive names, organized by department, developed at a seminar**

| Planning and development |
| --- |
| Site planning existing conditions |
| Permit parking program map and list |
| Development agreement analysis |
| Zoning analysis |
| Cash-in-lieu-of parking map and list |
| Street and lane closure analysis |
| Development information map and list |
| Circulation address labels and lists |
| Reservation of special-needs housing locations |
| Registered special-needs housing location map |
| Property location map and application cross-reference |
| Area monitoring map and list |
| Citywide monitoring map and list |
| Official plan designations map |
| Area monitoring map and list |
| Vacant land assessment |
| Census tract monitoring map and list |
| Spatial market analysis |
| Neighborhood monitoring map and list |
| Transportation flow density map |
| 3D simulation of urban section |
| Perspective views of urban section |
| Ward monitoring map and list |
| User-defined area monitoring map and list |
| Overlay mapping system |
| Employment analysis map and list |
| Accident rate analysis maps and lists |
| Spot speed survey map and list |

| Planning and development (continued) |
| --- |
| Development site impact analysis map and list |
| Pedestrian flow map and list |
| Intersection operation analysis map and list |
| Employment/FSI capacity map and list |
| Office and retail vacancy rates map and list |
| Summary of development projects map and list |
| Commercial activity map and list |
| Capital works project status list |
| Public land facilities list |
| Inspection status by district map |
| Cumulative development activity |
| Inspector performance activity map and list |

| Recreation and culture |
| --- |
| Recreation site analysis and design |
| Recreational/cultural site location analysis |
| Recreational/cultural opportunity analysis |

| Legal department |
| --- |
| Lane and street index map and list |

| Police department |
| --- |
| Special-event planning |
| Emergency route response map and list |
| Recent occurrence analysis map and lists |
| Police response property map and lists |
| Crime occurrence—best suspect system |

Figure 5.1 (continued)

that the product titles alone, in most cases, explain what they're about without more detailed information.

## Rank the benefits

With this initial list of information products in hand, you can now perform what is known as a benefit scan. A benefit scan is a somewhat bureaucratic term for an overall look. You should ask how the information products identified in the technology seminar would benefit the organization as a whole. Think back to the strategic business plan. How do the information products fit into it? Most importantly, which budgets will each product benefit?

Review the list of information products with the GIS team and management representatives and check off the ones most important in terms of the value of the benefits they could bring. Try to rank them from most to least important.

This preliminary, ranked list of the most beneficial information products will help in the next stage of planning. You'll be selecting the most important or

mission-critical ones from the list, and for those that are technically achievable, you will draft fully detailed descriptions. (You will find a more detailed account of these information product descriptions in the next chapter.) This is how your initial list spawns your next to-do list: the first round of information products to be developed.

## Go with the workflow

During both the technology seminar and while you're ranking the information products according to how beneficial each could be, you are delving into how the organization actually does its work, getting a sense of how various tasks flow from one to the other. This can be a very productive endeavor, with people thinking about their organization's workflows and the information products that could facilitate them. GIS planners need to understand these workflows because the GIS tools are often required to operate within a larger workflow.

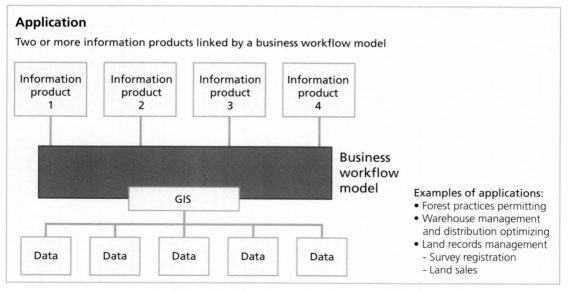

Figure 5.2  **A GIS application turns data into useful information**

In this business context, workflows are models of complex business processes used to gain more efficient operations within the organization. Typical complex business processes include things like land-use development approvals, building loan approvals, permitting, conservation land planning, power outage response, service delivery, and distributed facilities management.

When facilitating such a business workflow process requires more than one information product, you create these related and interdependent information products from one GIS application. An application is two or more information products produced from the same software and linked by a business workflow model, as in figure 5.2.

For example, imagine you work within a city's planning department. On a regular basis, people come into your office requesting building permits. This request triggers a well-established business workflow model that involves locating the property, determining if there are any building restrictions on the lot, and notifying all persons who own parcels within 200 feet of the permit location. But what if you had GIS and its output in a form particularly useful to you: information products. Using GIS capabilities, you could develop an application program that locates the subdivision within which the lot falls (we could call this information product #1); displays a map of the subdivision, which shows any building restrictions like utility easements and building setbacks (information product #2); and finally, selects all properties within 200 feet of the permit location and exports their ownership records to a mailing list (information product #3). In this case, the application creates three information products

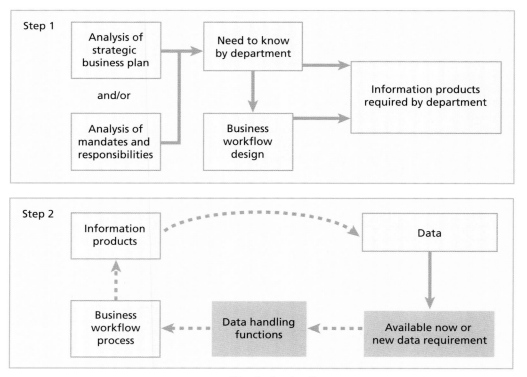

Figure 5.3   **Study logic diagram**

that reproduce an existing workflow associated with approving a building permit.

Applications compose the centerpiece of GIS and the culmination of the planning process. If you ever get the chance, ask a GIS manager what applications his or her system is running. If they are savvy planners, their eyes will gleam as they tell you about these complex applications, the information they produce, and how they are streamlining existing workflows. You might get the same glimmer during the technology seminar when people start thinking about their workflows with an eye toward improving them. A typical scenario evolves when you begin to press them for what information products they want: people realize they need to take a hard look at their business processes at the same time. If they are having trouble determining information products, suggest that they define the actual workflow process and see what information products come out of that.

GIS is an enabling technology that allows people to think about changing their workflow. So this is where you ask "do you want to redesign a workflow in any part of your organization?" And if the answer to that question is yes, you need to think about who's going to do it. If it's necessary to contract out the work, you must take into account how long it will take because it has to be completed before the GIS can be integrated.

What's the business workflow design and is there an opportunity to rework how the organization does business to gain efficiency or to capitalize on a new opportunity? Be sure to ask these questions and discuss the issue because this may be where a very high percentage of the benefit from GIS comes into an organization. Big gains result from the reduction of time or the number of steps in a process and from having a centralized database instead of replicated databases all over the place.

You must consider business workflows in your planning. In step 2 of figure 5.3, note that data and data handling move through the business workflow process. As you enter the next phase of planning, describing the information products and the data that comprise them (chapters 6 through 9), you will see why it's so important to keep this in mind.

# Describe the information products

*Know what you want to get out of it.*

The technology seminar provided you with an initial list of information products and names of the people who requested them. This is your starting point. The whole unfiltered list frames the scope of expectations that exist in the organization. The next step is to take the most urgent and important of these information products, as defined by your ranking, and start looking at them in detail. At this point, with your help, the people requesting them will begin to develop thorough descriptions of information products—specifications that will allow the actual product to become a working reality.

For the GIS to create an information product for you, you must first envisage it and write down descriptions of everything about it. These information product descriptions (IPDs) are the building blocks of the planning process.

In creating these IPDs, you are specifying for the first time the output your GIS must be able to generate. Once you know that, you can detail the prerequisite input on the master input data list (MIDL) in the next chapter. After that, in chapter 10, you will use specifications derived from the IPDs and MIDL to configure the best system design to support your GIS, which you will recommend to upper management. These IPDs are the tools you'll leverage to gain approval for spending money on GIS

## IPDs: The building blocks of GIS planning

In pinpointing its characteristics, an IPD defines what is required to make the information product and what is expected of it. In particular, what you need from your information product in the way of maps, lists, and scanned documents especially helps in clarifying the output required from the system. Determining these output requirements in turn clarifies what must go into the system, the data input. To be useful, each information product description should include all of the following components that pertain to it:

- **Title** or name of the information product.
- **Name** of the department and name of the person who needs it.
- **Synopsis:** a narrative summary providing an overview of the information product in layperson's terms. One paragraph is usually sufficient.
- **Map requirements:** either a map sketch or an actual example from another source, including a legend. Can be 3D output.
- **List requirements:** details of any information to be presented in the form of a report, list, or table, including headings and typical data entries.
- **Scanned documents:** details of textual information to be included, such as Adobe PDF, Microsoft Word, and .txt files, as well as images and videos; scanned document retrieval.
- **Image requirements:** details of images to be displayed as part of the information product. Include on scanned documents form.
- **Schematic requirements:** examples of type of schematic output required; goes on map requirements form; if not applicable, note "NA."
- **Steps required to make the product:** details of the data elements and software functions needed to generate this single information product. Remember to include any steps that involve functions using mobile handheld devices.
- **Frequency of use:** an accounting of how often the product will be created and by how many people each year.
- **Logical linkages:** details of any linkages that need to be established between data elements in the database.
- **Error tolerance:** an estimation of acceptable levels of error in the information product.
- **Wait and response tolerances:** network timing issues and user demands; time requirements.
- **Current cost:** the costs of producing the product using current methods.
- **Benefit analysis:** the benefits to your organization of having this GIS-created information product.
- **Sign-offs:** signature of the person requesting the product on the last page (after initialing all the pages) to signify approval of the IPD, and the signature and initials on the benefits pages of the head of the department to which benefits from the information product will accrue. (Although not really a descriptive component, these signatures are so important to the IPD's usefulness that they are included here.)

hardware, software, and data. IPDs are very important, and it's at this stage in the planning process that you will create them by doing the following:

- Clarify the information products that need to be produced by the system
- Establish what data is needed to create the information products
- Identify the system functions that will be used to create the information products
- Assess the benefit to the organization of having each information product

If this seems like hard work, you are being astute and realistic. This is the mental heavy lifting necessary to create well-defined specifications for the information products that you're ultimately going to build. "Pay me now or pay me later" warns the craftsman's adage. In some ways, because it is such a creative endeavor, this is also the most interesting part of the process. After this crucial step, what remains of planning your GIS will fall into place systematically.

## The individual components of an IPD

Each information product description is composed of one or more forms, like the ones in the case study starting on page 42, but each descriptive component in the IPD does not necessarily require a separate form. For example, anything to be scanned—text documents, images, videos—can go on the product's scanned documents form. Or, one of the maps required for an information product could be a schematic, so your schematic requirements would be specified on the map requirements form. When thinking about GIS, keep in mind that there is a fundamental difference between images (pictures) and plans or diagrams (lines) and design your forms accordingly.

Not every IPD will contain all of these components, but they are listed here individually because considering whether each is needed or not is part of a sound planning methodology. Later on, IPDs will help you to specify what is required to make each information product and to verify that each contains all the needed elements once it's created. So you want to be sure your descriptions are thorough.

### Title

The title should be a precise, pithy two- or three-word name for the information product, developed from the list of possible names collected at the technology seminar. The title must identify what the information is used for in a way that a layman can understand: in other words, name it "Sewer Backup Map" rather than "Engineering Situation Analysis."

### Name of the department and person who needs it

Associating the department and requesting person's name with the information product fosters their taking responsibility for developing it into what they really need. Placing his or her name, along with the title, on every page of the IPD reinforces ownership of each information product.

### Synopsis

This is an easy-to-understand explanation of the information product and its purpose. This succinct narrative summary is usually the first page of the IPD.

### Map requirements

This section describes each map required in the output (if a map is indeed required), both visually and by listing its features (legend). It is important to include some sort of hand-drawn sketch or perhaps an actual example of the desired map previously prepared. The sketch can be simple but should show at least one of every feature type the final product is expected to display. If users need the map at two different scales, indicate this as well (draw both versions).

The sketched map or example should include the following information:

- Map title
- Legend showing how data is presented thematically on the map
- Any special symbology required
- Colors required
- Scale bar
- North arrow

  (You can include any 3D representations or schematics you need on the same form with the maps.)

## List requirements

An information product is not always a map. It could be simply a list of figures, a table, or a report; any of these could be stand-alone or part of an information product that also includes a map. All these, along with spreadsheets, databases, and other text files, fall within the broad category called *tabular data*. Identify each of these lists, tables, or reports with a title, appropriate column headings, typical entries, and an indication of the source file for the data.

If predefined report formats exist, identify them as well. Reports can usually be automatically converted into appropriate formats. (Keep in mind that report creation capabilities should be flexible enough to accommodate change in the future.)

## Scanned documents

Text-based documents of a more narrative nature than lists often compose an important part of an information product, too; things like Adobe PDF files, Microsoft Word documents, and plain old reliable .txt files. In this descriptive category, include the likely number of pages per document to be retrieved from the GIS, as well as the database keys used to select them. Where appropriate, indicate the need for document display. Specify whether users need to view the document, copy the whole (or portions of) the document to hard copy, or copy the

### Three-dimensional representation

Three-dimensional (3D) scene generation capabilities in geographic information systems are not yet true virtual reality, but significant steps are being made toward creating 3D representation and three-dimensional symbology. Already, databases can be extended to include geometry models for textured 3D solid objects representing buildings and other objects in the landscape. The ability to show a 3D symbology of points, lines, polygons (spheres, cubes, strips, dotted lines, etc.), and realistic out-of-the-box texture patterns exists. Extensive libraries of 3D objects—to simulate 3D space—will be available, along with translators from common 3D object formats, such as OpenFlight, 3-D Studio (realistic 3D models with a CAD orientation), and VRML. Symbology attached to these models can be geospecific in the shape of a 3D marker symbol or geotypical in the shape of a feature in a feature class. Continuous multiresolution global viewing of geographic information is becoming possible, which enables the dynamic 3D viewing of the information working directly from a geodatabase. In short, three-dimensional representation is becoming easier, quicker, and more flexible, and the foundation is being built for future development.

whole (or portions of) the document digitally. Also, note whether changes can be made to any of the documents or images.

## Image requirements

An information product may also include an image file or 3D representations. In fact, the entire product could be that image. These days, most agencies hold a wealth of information in the form of image files: digital photographs, satellite imagery, scanned floor plans, and diagrams. You should complete this portion of the IPD for every kind of image that users want to retrieve from the GIS, including scanned documents and video clips. Include in their description the key identifiers that will be used to search for and find the required images. The document and image requirements can be specified on a single sheet. IPDs for documents and images should include the number of pages that will be retrieved (typical and maximum), the key identifier to be used to search for data (an address, for example), and what you expect to see on the document.

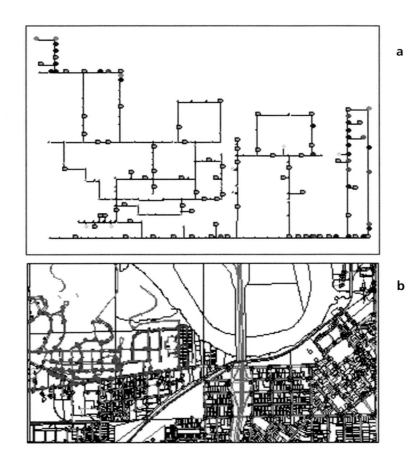

Figure 6.1    **Schematics: (a) Orthogonal schematic of the
selected set; (b) the same overlaid with street network**

## Schematic requirements

An information product may present data in the form of schematics for ease of understanding. These diagrammatic presentations can approximate the real world in many ways: by using geographic coordinates, with a geoschematic emphasizing the topology of a network or other system, or as a pure schematic showing only the flow paths as linkages. A water system geoschematic connecting the fire hydrants, for example, could speed the response to a large fire by quickly showing firefighters where to draw water. Figure 6.1 shows two schematics representing an electrical network.

## Steps required to make the product

The components of the IPD described above (map, list, document, image, and schematic requirements) clarify details of the information product required. Once you know this much about the information product, you can begin to evaluate the steps needed to make it. These steps should account for both the data elements and functions required to make the product.

As you start to examine datasets, you'll notice that sometimes conflicting names are used in different departments to refer to the same dataset. Carefully study the files and naming conventions and establish one standard name for each dataset. You may even have to create a directory of synonyms just to sort things out (more on data dictionaries later). It is good practice to settle on a single, simple, descriptive title that is unique to the dataset. You will use these titles later to create a master input data list (chapter 7), which will make use of much of the information you are gathering at this IPD stage of planning.

You should now write a step-by-step description of how to make the information product, in the order of the manual steps (many of which will be automated later) required for the GIS to provide the thing you want. This procedural description covers all stages, from the initial request to completion of the product. Of course, with GIS there are often several ways to do something, but for now all you need do is specify one logical and direct method. This will suffice to clarify the thinking about the user's real objectives and identify all the data required. Later on, the system will be fine-tuned to create an application that makes elegant use of the system functions.

Often, the most effective way to identify the sequence of steps needed to make an information product is to think of how you would create the product by hand using hard-copy data sources. Setting down the steps for this method is not difficult, but it requires logic and a linear thought process. The key is to stay focused on the end product you envision and not to get distracted by other possibilities inherent in the data or by functions that you don't need. Rigorous care at this stage will often resolve questions about data availability and suitability and identify sources of potential error.

For an example of how you might chart the steps required to make an information product, take a look at figure 6.10 on page 48. Here are some additional tips that will help make your step-by-step description easier to write and more useful thereafter:

1.  Use one dataset at a time and use its standard name. Write down the source scales of any maps that will be used as a reminder of the source data's resolution.

2.  Use the generic function descriptions provided in the lexicon at the back of this book. They are easy to understand and will translate into any system-specific piece of software.

3.  For every time a function is used, explain the work it's doing on the dataset and clearly identify the specific data elements accessed in the process. This is very important, as the dataset could contain many more data elements than the ones you need, and you must be sure to work with the right one(s). You will also cross-check the product output requirements against the right-hand column of steps on your chart to make sure that all the data elements needed in

## A rapid prototyping tool

When datasets are already entered into the GIS, recent advancements can make the development of prototype GIS applications far quicker and easier than ever before. Wizard-based and graphic-based construction of GIS applications is possible using a wide variety of data types and geoprocessing functions. A rapid prototyping tool (RPT) gives you the advantage of combining datasets already entered into the system with a series of geoprocessing function steps to produce information products. These products can be simple or complex; in fact, they can be extremely complex. They can be combined models. The output can be examined as the model goes through several stages of development.

RPT will continue to play an important role in iterative design, as a model can be shared between people who can add to it, revise it, and implement it. An accepted model can be published, rather in the way an application is currently published, but with the steps in the model graphically illustrated and amenable to revision.

Future directions of development may lead to building interfaces between RPT and business workflow applications (such as Visio Enterprise, ABC Flowcharter, or Workflow Analyzer), wherein RPT can both construct the information products required by the business workflow and interface with CASE tools in physically designing the databases the models need.

the product have been produced by the functions working on the datasets.

4.  Always operate on the assumption that the results of using any function are available for use in later steps. For more complicated processes, you can represent the steps visually in the form of a flowchart to aid in communication. The steps to make the product should be clear and should help identify the data needed, functions invoked at each step, details of any interim products, and the final product.

5.  If data is not readily available, now is a good time to think about how you will obtain it—from the government, a data vendor, or in-house creation.

6.  If the organization's staff is not aware of the range of GIS functions available or the terminology to describe them, they may need to seek further training in basic GIS functionality.

Don't overlook the capabilities of mobile devices in the array of functions at your fingertips. A range of handheld devices and tablet PCs with differing capacities and operating systems are now available to interact with GIS. You need to consider these mobile devices both in terms of communications limitations as well as capabilities. And this stage of the process is the time to do it so that you'll know, for example, if an application needs to be available on desktop PCs as well as handheld computers. These devices offer important new capabilities for GIS developers, including the ability to operate through loosely coupled architecture for disconnected editing of the central database in the field.

### Frequency of use

You also need to estimate the overall demand for the information product—how many times per year will it be generated? The frequency may range from once per year (a map to hang on a wall) to ten thousand times per year (some emergency routing products). Write down the numbers of maps you anticipate producing, lists you think you will generate, and documents you will retrieve each year. Then, for the IPD, try to project these numbers out to five years. Include a simple table in the IPD summarizing these frequency-of-use estimates.

After determining all of the functions and when they are used in the process, you can count the number of times each function will be used in the creation of the information product. You may have some products that require multiple functions, and those functions may have to be invoked many times. After you determine the number of times per year the product is generated, you can multiply that by the number of times a specific function is used to make the product. The result is the number of times the function is used in a year to make that product (figure 6.2).

You are now getting a first view of how often you will use the functions in your system. On completion of your first round of IPDs, you can create a list of the functions that will be required from the GIS overall. Such a list will be useful in evaluating your choices among potential GIS software packages and in scoping your system requirements for hardware, as you'll see in chapter 10. Both this list and the summary of totals become important tools for ensuring that you plan for a system that will effectively and efficiently meet your needs. (The process of determining frequency of function use is discussed further in the case study at the end of this chapter.)

## Logical linkages

The next step in describing an information product is to determine the relationships required between the data elements and also between datasets. These relationships are called *logical linkages,* and they must be in place when you build your database later on. In the IPD, you need to establish how data from different datasets will be joined to create the end product.

There are three types of logical linkages:

1. Relationships between lists and graphic entities: these are relationships between features (points, lines, polygons) and their characteristics (attributes, i.e., names attached to items).

2. Relationships between maps or map layers: these are relationships between the different kinds of maps (or data layers) that you require (i.e., can they be overlaid, are they the same scale and map projection).

3. Relationships between attributes: these are relationships between characteristics and between data elements (i.e., does this data item have to know about that data item).

Don't look for every linkage you can establish, but do look for linkages you need that might not be there. When you perceive necessary logical linkages not currently in the source data, you're identifying a problem that must be solved before this information product can be made. If, for example, you know that you need a linkage between a house and a sewer, it needs to be in the database. If you find out after you've built your database that you need such a linkage between a house and sewer, you might have to revisit every house and sewer to input the data. This may not be significant with a town of only 500 dwellings, but if you have 120,000 dwellings to revisit,

| Number of times a product is created in one year | X | Number of times a function is used during creation of the product | = | Number of times a function is used to create the product in one year |

Figure 6.2 **Frequency of function use equation**

the problem becomes onerous indeed. Information about linkages becomes more significant as the size of your database increases.

## Error tolerance

Error tolerance is the amount of error that you can accept in the information product. The question you must answer is "how wrong can it be?" When someone requests an information product, it's because they expect it to provide a benefit, such as saving staff time or increasing operational efficiency. If the information product contains errors that require time to correct or another method for determining the right answer, you receive neither the savings in staff time nor improvements in efficiency.

The IPD should address possible errors, the result of errors, the impact on benefits, and the amount of error that is acceptable. That is, you must establish how much error can be tolerated in the information product without losing its usefulness.

It is important for users to think about error and consider what level of accuracy is important in terms of cost versus reliability. The user's view of their own needs is their bargaining position in the discussions on data quality during implementation. Once costs and benefits are weighed, users may not get their desired accuracy, but at least they'll be prepared for this and cognizant of the degree of reliability they can count on in the information products.

The levels of quality control established to ensure that data meets user needs can significantly increase costs. Achieving the elusive final 10 percent of accuracy may cost 90 percent of the total costs of building the database. With users, you should determine the maximum amount of error that can be tolerated while still sustaining the intended benefits from the information product. You need to find out where the balance is between accuracy requirements and data-entry and quality-assurance costs.

There are four types of error:

- Referential: an error in a reference to something, such as a wrong address, label, number, or name
- Topological: a linkage error in spatial data, such as unclosed polygons or breaks in networks
- Relative: an error in the positioning of two objects relative to each other
- Absolute: an error in something's true position in the world

Error tolerance is expressed numerically but differently depending on the type of error, as you can see in figure 6.3. Usually, referential and topological errors are expressed as a percentage of the total error, while relative and absolute errors are expressed in linear distance.

Figure 6.4 shows examples of each type of error from various information products.

In thinking about data, remember there is no such thing as inherently "good" data. In working terms, there is useful data and useless data. Data carries no intrinsic value or accuracy. There is no accuracy that data should contain in theory—only the accuracy that affects people doing real work; in other words, the accuracy demanded from the data to create a useful information product. Data remains useless if its accuracy is not related to the reality of what the data is being used for.

## Wait and response tolerances

Wait and response tolerances are related but distinct concepts that must be included in the IPD. Wait tolerance is a measure of how robust the computer and network system must be, that is, the maximum allowable time (with the computer up and running) between the last keystroke and the full display or output of the information product. For some emergency dispatch uses, the wait tolerance can be as low as 0 to 1 second; for other applications it can be up to an hour, or so high it's almost irrelevant.

Wait tolerances can influence how you design your computer network, while response tolerances have more

| Error type | Specific error | Tolerance |
|---|---|---|
| Referential | Incorrect street address | 2% |
| Topological | Incorrect street network | 0% |
| Relative | Sewer line shown on the wrong side of the street | ± 2m |
| Absolute | Floodplain not aligned with property boundaries | ± 10m |

Figure 6.3 **Expressing error tolerance**

to do with the human process. Response tolerance is the maximum allowable time between the arrival of the request or critical data at the GIS office (or wherever processing takes place) and the delivery of the information product to the user. Gauging how much time can be spent in responding to the request for an information product will help you understand how many GIS office hours, staff members, etc., will be needed to meet the demand. You know the response tolerance is set too high, for example, when the forest is burning on Sunday but the maps aren't available until Monday.

## Current cost

The next step in building an IPD is to document what it currently costs you to create the information product without GIS. Your estimate should include both labor and materials and account for how many times a year your organization incurs this total expense.

The cost figures you calculate can be used in cost-cost comparisons to help justify the implementation of the GIS. For example, if an information product costs a few hundred dollars and is used only once or twice a year, the automation costs will not be recovered in a reasonable amount of time. On the other hand, if you have an information product that takes a lot of staff time to create and is needed frequently, the current cost will probably justify automation. This step helps you identify the level of effort required for each information product being requested. It also helps explain to management the magnitude of the work being attempted by the GIS, and

sometimes explains why the information product is not made using current methods.

## Benefit analysis

For the final step in preparing the IPD, the person who needs the information product on his or her desk should perform a benefit analysis. Also, the GIS manager should have a grasp on what benefit will result from the information created through GIS. You should be able to weigh the costs of system and data acquisition (the input) against the benefits your organization expects from the output. Consider the following three categories of benefits:

- Financial savings: actual cash saved from current budgets if GIS made the required information products (i.e., reductions in current staff time, increases in revenue).
- Direct benefits to organization: beneficial results of implementing the GIS, which were not available before. These could include improvements in operational efficiency and workflow, or the reduction of a liability, for example.
- External benefits: benefits that accrue to others who are not directly using the GIS. For instance, the general public benefits from lower fire insurance rates, indirectly, when better fire response times result from the fire department's immediate access to reliable maps.

Once you've added up the benefits of each information product, you can compare the benefit total with the cost of

| Referential error | |
|---|---|
| Possible occurrence | Incorrect street address. |
| Results of error | Delivery to wrong property. |
| Impact on benefits | Time wasted during delivery reduces benefits of having product. Pizza may get cold. |
| Concerns for error tolerance | Must balance data entry and checking costs with amount of acceptable error. 2% of addresses wrong. |

| Topological error | |
|---|---|
| Possible occurrence | Incorrect street network. |
| Results of error | Route may take longer than necessary. |
| Impact on benefits | Loss of life or property because an emergency services vehicle is delayed. |
| Concerns for error tolerance | If loss of life may occur, zero tolerance may be required. |

| Relative error | |
|---|---|
| Possible occurrence | Sewer line shown on the wrong side of the street. |
| Results of error | Excavation for sewer repairs in the wrong place. |
| Impact on benefits | Increase in on-site costs. |
| Concerns for error tolerance | How much error can the sewer line have before it's ineffective? It might still be effective if it is only a little off-center, but if it is on the wrong side of the road, it's ineffective. ±6' (2m). |

| Absolute error | |
|---|---|
| Possible occurrence | Floodplain boundary not aligned with property boundaries. |
| Results of error | Uncertainty of location. Are you in the floodplain? |
| Impact on benefits | Owners paying for flood insurance when it is not needed. Owners not being protected when they are in a floodplain. |
| Concerns for error tolerance | Need to balance costs of data, costs of checking, and the amount of acceptable error. ±30' (10m). |

Figure 6.4 **Examples of the four types of error in information products**

implementing the GIS, including acquiring data needed for the information products.

## Sign-offs

To finalize the information product description after each IPD is complete, ask the person writing the description to review and initial every page—and to sign the last page—of the IPD. This sign-off on each page confirms that it accurately describes the information product requested. If there is no signature, there should be no information product. It is best to make this clear from the beginning, so the person responsible can make an effort to ensure that the final description meets the need. People sometimes don't realize the amount of work that goes into building a GIS, so it's important to make clear to them early on that their organization is going to be spending treasure on their behalf and it is imperative to spend it on information they truly need.

Another person's initials and signature are essential as well: the department head overseeing the budget to which the benefits will accrue must initial and sign the benefits pages. If he or she will not sign the benefits pages, find out why and make the needed revisions. If you can't reasonably accommodate the changes, then there is a fundamental problem with the information product.

Again, no department head signature, no information product. This harkens back to the first recommendations I made to you—be sure to gain upper management's full support from the beginning of the project, and regularly inform management of progress. A consistent and rigorous approach to approvals is what makes GIS successful in established organizations. And the time-honored way to win approval is to demonstrate how benefits will outweigh costs soon enough and time after time.

One further note about benefits: calculating benefits is always a difficult task, but a critical one in the GIS planning process. At one time, most economists professed the theory that the only legitimate value that could be attached to data was the value someone was prepared to pay for it. In practice, this is ludicrous because no one buys data just for the sake of buying it. People buy data because they want to do something with it that is going to create information that will benefit them. We need new models—methods to calculate the benefits that accrue from having the information—so I developed one.

You will find my methodology for measuring the benefits of information—benefit–cost analysis—described in chapter 11. The methodology has been tested and proven successful in Canada, Australia, and in state and federal governments in the United States. The organizations that used the methodology accepted the outcome and the results from it, which is the real measure of success.

The case study that follows is a walk through the creation of an information product description. Much of the information gathering and writing of an IPD is best done by the person requesting the information product, with the help of the GIS planner or planning team. Creating the IPDs is probably the single most important task in the entire GIS plan-

ning process—and the most fruitful. Not an ounce of effort is ever wasted in thinking about the nature and details of desired information products. At some stage in running a GIS, all of the information in the IPDs will be needed by the GIS manager to plan his or her day-to-day work. Sooner or later, the thinking is going to have to be done to explain the work to users and senior management and to run the system itself. Doing this thinking when faced with daily production demands in a production GIS shop is a recipe for GIS manager madness (or at least frustration and overwork). It is better to do it during planning, before production begins and not after.

## Case study: Tracking the IPD

The rest of this chapter tracks the creation of an actual information product description, step by step. The context is a real one, within an actual case study of a major North American city. Gary works in the city's engineering department. Charged with the maintenance and repair of the sewer system, he envisions an information product that will help his staff deal with frequent sewer backups. During his city's recent technology seminar, Gary spoke up to request a sewer incident situation map as part of the information product he needs the GIS to produce.

The background is as follows: In this city the sewers are generally known to be in a terrible state. The original lines date from the middle of the nineteenth century. At one time they were combined sanitary and storm sewers, but were separated later on. Fast-forward to the present and the city's engineering department is dealing with frequent complaints of trouble. The aging and modified sewers tend to flood, causing people's houses to get filled with backup sewage—a very unpleasant situation to say the least. Every year there are fifty sewer backup incidents, on average, all over the city. This is not a trivial situation. When a backup occurs, homeowners telephone city hall for action and the engineering department must react quickly.

Gary needs to be able to call up the sewer backup information product that displays the information he needs about a particular area. But before the GIS can create it and keep it at hand for him, Gary will have to describe it thoroughly in terms of the components required for it to be built into the database. He will have to write an IPD, engaging your help as a planner.

The first components of this information product description will appear on every IPD form, as shown in figure 6.5: title or name of the information product, the department requiring it, and the person who needs it. As the person identified on the IPD, Gary is responsible for making sure the IPD accurately describes the

information product he needs. Once the IPD is complete, he will need to sign each page, verifying that the description is correct. The head of the engineering department will have to initial the benefits pages of the IPD as further verification that the information product as described is exactly what they need.

Now we'll examine in detail the other components of Gary's IPD, beginning with the first page, which summarizes the information product in a brief synopsis.

## Synopsis

In a nutshell, Gary needs to be able to input the address of the sewer complaint and have the GIS return an information product that includes a map, a report, and

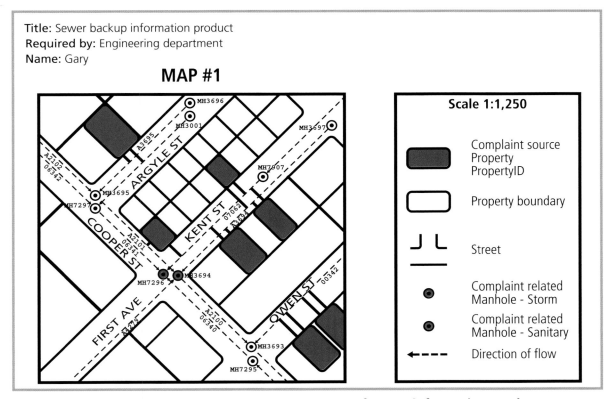

Figure 6.5   **Sewer backup situation map: Part of Gary's information product**

photos. The map should provide a view of the property or properties involved, the sewer segments under suspicion, the segments connected to them (both upstream and downstream), manhole locations, and any other potentially relevant landmarks in the immediately surrounding area. Also, Gary needs a report documenting both the complaint history in the same segment area and the known condition of the segment, according to the most recent inspection reports. (This documentation for the report will be created from tabular data—lists of information transformed into the entry format for the IPD, as illustrated on this page and the next two pages.) Any available photos of the suspect sewer segments might also help him do his work, so he'd like to see the GIS retrieve them, too.

## Map requirements

To fulfill the descriptive elements of this IPD component, Gary makes a sketch of the type of map he needs. Gary thinks that a map in support of the sewer incident report should illustrate the following:

- Property numbers (addresses)
- Locations of the houses whose sewers are backed up
- Property ID numbers of the affected houses
- Sewer segments the houses are connected to
- Street names
- Manhole numbers

## List requirements

Gary needs three lists. He makes note of all the information needed to build them. First, he needs to see a list providing pertinent details about the complaint (figure 6.6):

- Address of the affected property
- Property ID number
- Name of the occupant/owner
- Housing type: e.g., single-family residential
- Zoning

**Title:** Sewer backup information product
**Required by:** Engineering department
**Name:** Gary

|  |  |  |  |  |  |  |  | List #2 |
|---|---|---|---|---|---|---|---|---|
| List title: Suspect sewer report | | | | | | | | |
| Headings | Storm or sanitary | Segment # | Manhole To | Manhole From | Capacity | Size | Grade | Material |
| Typical entries | Sanitary | A2101 Cooper St. | 3694 | 3695 | 350 gps | 10" | 2° | Metal |
|  | Sanitary | A3694 Kent St. | 3694 | 3697 | 220 gps | 8" | 5° | Concrete |
| Source | SIMS | SIMS | SIMS | SIMS | SIMS | SIMS | SIMS | SIMS |

Figure 6.7   **IPD format for List #2**

Title: Sewer backup information product
Required by: Engineering department
Name: Gary

| | | | | | | | | Connection | |
|---|---|---|---|---|---|---|---|---|---|
| **List #1** | | | | | | | | | |
| List title: Complaint source | | | | | | | | | |
| Headings | Address | Prop ID | Owner occupant | Housing type | Zoning | Previous complaint | Type | Sanitary | Storm |
| Typical entries | 26 Cooper St. | 32968 | M. Dewe | SFR | 5ac | Oct. 1985<br>Nov. 1986 | Basement flood<br>Basement flood | To 07062 | To 07062 |
| | 17 Kent St. | 37210 | A. Brown | SFR | 5ac | ---- | ---- | To A3694 | To 07062 |
| Source | Complaint file | PDIS | PDIS | PDIS | PDIS | Complaint file | Complaint file | SIMS | SIMS |

Figure 6.6   **IPD format for List #1**

| Date installed | Class (phys. cond.) | Date last inspected | Date last cleared | No. of floodings | Previous incidents | TV report | Estimated flow |
|---|---|---|---|---|---|---|---|
| 1936 | 3 | Sept. 1986 | Sept. 1986 | 5 | Oct. 1975<br>Nov. 1982<br>Mar. 1987<br>Jul. 1987<br>May 1988 | File #123 | 250 L/hr |
| 1944 | 4 | Oct. 1975 | Oct. 1975 | 1 | None | | |
| SIMS | SIMS | SIMS | SIMS | SIMS | SIMS | SIMS | Inspector |

Figure 6.7 (continued)

**Title:** Sewer backup information product
**Required by:** Engineering department
**Name:** Gary

| | | List #3 | | | | | | | |
|---|---|---|---|---|---|---|---|---|---|
| List title: Management report | | | | | | | | | |
| Headings | Sewer section | Flooding dates | | | | | | | Total # of floodings |
| | | 1 | 2 | 3 | 4 | 5 | 6 | 7 | |
| Typical entries | A2101 | Oct. 1975 | Nov. 1982 | Mar. 1987 | Jul. 1987 | May 1988 | | | 5 |
| | 03624 | | | | | | | | |
| Source | SIMS—Management report | | | | | | | | 1 |

Figure 6.8 **IPD format for List #3**

- Date of previous complaints
- Type of complaint
- Details about the relationship between previous complaints and the sanitary sewer or the storm sewer (some previous backups can be traced to this source)

The IPD entry format for this list is the same for the other two lists, all containing categories for headings, typical entries, and source information. The data for this first list, named Complaint source, comes from one of three sources: the complaint file itself (a 5-by-7-inch card file); a city mainframe database of property development information stored by the assessor's office, called the *PDIS*; or the *SIMS* (sewer information management system), the sewer characteristics file maintained in Gary's department on a PC.

Gary needs a second list pertaining to the suspect sewer segment itself, which should contain the following information and more (see figure 6.7 on page 44):

- Segment number
- Manhole details
- Sewer capacity

- Sewer size
- Sewer grade
- Construction materials
- Date of installation
- Physical class
- Last inspection date
- Date last cleared
- Number of floodings
- Previous incidents
- TV report file number
- Estimated flow

The third thing Gary needs in list format is information from the previous management reports on sewer backup incidents, including where and when incidents occurred, so Gary prepares the list shown in figure 6.8.

## Documents

After describing the maps and lists, Gary specifies any text files he may need to access. For example, the transcript of the inspector's last taped voice report, which he wants, qualifies as a document.

**Title:** Sewer backup information product
**Required by:** Engineering department
**Name:** Gary

| Scanned document display | | |
|---|---|---|
| **#** | **Dataset name:** Sewer characteristics (SIMS) file | |
| **Document title:** Sewer TV reports file | | |
| **Number of pages per retrieved document** | Typical 2 | Maximum 5 |
| **Search keys (all)** | | |
| **Spatial:** Sewer segment number | | |
| **Attribute:** --- | | |
| **Data elements** (required to be seen) Sewer interior TV scan (manhole to manhole) of suspect sewer segments | | |
| **Action:** (Check as appropriate) | ✓ Visually observe | Read only |
| | Copy whole | Hard copy |
| | Copy whole | Digital |
| **Change:** (Check as appropriate) | ✓ Copy part | Hard copy |
| | Copy part | Digital |
| | Add data | Which elements |
| | Delete data | Which elements |
| | Edit data | Change errors |
| **No change permitted** | ✓ | |

Figure 6.9   **IPD specifications for the images**

## Image requirements

The engineering department employs a robotic video system capable of delivering images showing pipe condition in the segment. These images are all date-stamped and referenced to the segment number. (The form shown in figure 6.9 specifies, next to "Spatial," that Gary will retrieve these documents based on sewer segment number.) Gary tells you he needs to be able to observe the images and transfer some to hard copy without changing the documents on which they appear.

Now that you know what Gary wants—maps, lists, text files, and images—start thinking about how this information product, with its disparate data sources, can be produced:

- What data do you need to make the information product?
- Where will the data come from?
- Which functions are needed to create the products?
- How do the component parts relate to one another?
- What common data elements in the different datasets are needed to link them together?

This is where Gary needs your help and expertise as a GIS planner. He can tell you that, currently, only the

**Title:** Sewer backup information product
**Required by:** Engineering department
**Name:** Gary

| | Gary's description | |
|---|---|---|
| **Step 1** | A staff member receives a complaint phone call and uses the complaint system file to get details of previous complaints of that type at that address. | |
| **Step 2** | The staff member matches the complaint address with the owner/occupant name, housing type, and zoning information using the property development information system on the city's mainframe. A property, residential, or occupant file may need to be accessed. | |
| **Step 3** | Now the staff member needs to obtain data about the sewer segment at fault. First, the correct sewer segment based on the street address of the complaint must be found. Then, the characteristics for each suspect sewer segment must be found. | |
| **Step 4** | Next, the staff member needs a map of the complaint property that includes the boundaries of the property. | |
| **Step 5** | Next, the staff member needs to identify sewer segments within one kilometer that are adjacent to the suspect sewer segment. A map showing upstream and downstream sewers within the one-kilometer region is needed, overplotted with information about the city. | |
| **Step 6** | Finally, the staff member needs to add street boundaries to the area of interest. The street boundaries are at a different scale than the rest of the information, so a scale change is necessary. With all of this data, final maps and lists can be created. | |

Figure 6.10 **Steps to make Gary's information product**

| Data needed | Function needed |
|---|---|
| **Complaints system file** <br> *Note: There is tight security on this file.* | **Keyboard data input** of address and nature of complaint. <br> **Attribute query** to determine previous complaints (date and type). |
| **Property development information system (PDIS)** <br> (City mainframe database) <br> Property file <br> Residential file <br> Occupants file | **Attribute query** on PDIS to match complaint address with owner/occupant name, housing type, zoning. |
| **Sewer characteristics file (SIMS)** <br> From land-use maps (1:1,250) <br> Sewer plan and profile sheets <br> Sewer log file <br> Sewer TV reports file <br> Drain card file <br> *Note 1: Sewer data must be linked to a sewer segment number, which is linked to a street address.* <br> *Note 2: This file does not currently exist in digital format.* | **Attribute query** on sewer database to match street address with sewer segment number. For each suspect sewer segment, identify manhole (to and from), capacity, size, grade, material, date installed, physical condition, date last inspected, date last cleared, and dates of incidents. |
| **Legal survey map** <br> (1:1,250) | **Attribute query** by street address (matched to property identification number, if necessary) to identify complaint property boundary. |
| **Sewer network map** <br> To be created at 1:1,250 scale in topological network form, with manholes as nodes, sewer segments between manholes. | **Attribute query** to identify suspect sewer segments. <br> **Network analysis** to identify adjacent sewer segments within one kilometer of suspect segments. <br> **Graphic overplot** sewer segments and city to identify the area of interest within the city. |
| **Topographic map** <br> (1:2,000) | **Spatial query** (by region) defined by sewer segments. <br> **Scale change.** <br> **Graphic overplot** selected street boundaries, selected sewer network, and selected property boundaries. <br> **Display, edit, label, symbolize, plot, create list.** |

Figure 6.10 (continued)

property information and a sewer map exist in the city engineering department; he will have to contact the water company to get the sewer condition data. You can tell him that the sewer condition data should be linked to the property file to allow sewer segment numbers to be linked to street addresses. Discovering that digital sewer data is lacking within the organization, you suggest that creating it would be beneficial.

## Steps to make the product (data and functions required)

Together, you've figured out what you need to know about the information product envisioned in order to list the steps required to make it. Figure 6.10 gives details of the step-by-step process of building Gary's information product. From his description of the workflow (left column), you identify the datasets (middle column) and system functions (right column) required to make the

product intended to facilitate the workflow. This organized document—the "steps to make the information product" table—is a vital component of the IPD.

The table's far-right column contains very important information. It specifies not only the system functions needed to create the information product but also every data element that must be taken from the dataset and included in the product. You'll use this later to confirm that all the required data elements will actually be in the product.

Also later on, you will make good use of this right-hand column's listing of the required system functions. In fact, now as part of the IPD, you should use the information from this column to make a simple table, like Gary's (figure 6.11), listing these necessary functions and specifically how many times each will be used to make the product. This table helps you and Gary calculate your descriptive entry for the next IPD component.

## Frequency of use

Now that you know the number of times each function is used to make one product, you can multiply that by the number of times per year that the product will be created. This annual figure will give you an idea of functional use, a primary indicator of the type of software system capable of supporting it (see pages 110–111 in chapter 10).

Gary estimates that each year his department will require fifty of the information products needed to respond to sewer backup complaints. Now you can rank the functions, listing the most frequent first, according to the number of times each will be used in a year to produce this information product fifty times.

1. Attribute query: 250
2. Create list: 150
3. Graphic overplot: 100
4. Data input: 50
5. Spatial query: 50
6. Network analysis: 50

**Title:** Sewer backup information product
**Required by:** Engineering department
**Name:** Gary

| Function | Number |
| --- | --- |
| Attribute query | 5 |
| Create list | 3 |
| Graphic overplot | 2 |
| Data input | 1 |
| Spatial query | 1 |
| Network analysis | 1 |
| Scale change | 1 |
| Display | 1 |
| Edit | 1 |
| Label | 1 |
| Symbolize | 1 |
| Plot | 1 |

Figure 6.11 **Function utilization table (per information product)**

7.  Scale change: 50
8.  Display: 50
9.  Edit: 50
10. Label: 50
11. Symbolize: 50
12. Plot: 50

The function that will be used the most is attribute query. So now you know that the software Gary's organization implements must be able to perform attribute queries efficiently, at least for the benefit of this information product.

## Logical linkages

Gary needs a link in the GIS database between street address and property boundaries in order to select the lot lines for the map. He also needs a link between a sewer segment number and the sewer network segment, the actual line in the digital database. These are key linkages between items in a list and a graphic entity in the database.

---

**Title:** Sewer backup information product
**Required by:** Engineering department
**Name:** Gary

| List to graphic entity |
| --- |
| Street address to property boundaries (polygon) Sewer segment number to sewer network segment (line) |

| Map to map |
| --- |
| Ability to graphically overplot property boundaries on sewer network map and topographic map |

| Attribute to attribute |
| --- |
| Street address to property attribute (PDIS) Street address to sewer segment number Sewer segment number to sewer characteristics file (SIMS) attributes |

Figure 6.12   **Logical linkages**

---

Some map-to-map linkages are also required. Gary must be able to overlay the property boundaries on the sewer network map and the topographic map—meaning they'll need to be available at a common scale and projection. Note that the degree of scale change of any dataset required to make the overlay should not be too large. Although scale changes of more than 2.5 times in either direction should be avoided generally, you may have to live with more, if the more closely projected or scaled data is not available. Heed the information systems creed: be guided by the error tolerance.

Finally, three attribute-to-attribute linkages must be made: the street address needs to be linked to the property attributes in the property development information system (PDIS); the street address must be linked to the sewer segment numbers (to determine which segment in which sewer is backing up into each house); and the sewer segment number needs to be related to the sewer characteristics file. It is useful for the IPD to list all the linkages in one place, as in figure 6.12.

Unfortunately, no sewer segment map exists, so it is not possible to link sewer segment numbers and sewer characteristics. Without these segment numbers, it is also not possible to link street addresses to sewer segments. To the uninitiated, this may sound like a simple thing to correct: just manually determine and append the data. But in fact, the cost of creating such things can be enormous—in the millions of dollars for even a medium-sized town or city. This is because creating a sewer network map involves scanning old sewer plans, digitizing the real position of the manhole covers from aerial photography, and sliding the images in behind those digital points.

Fortunately, Gary's city government recognized long ago how beneficial this new database could be and decided that its development should be an infrastructure cost in the engineering department's budget, not a cost for the GIS budget. In your own organization, you may need to figure out smart ways to get these

**Title:** Sewer backup information product
**Required by:** Engineering department
**Name:** Gary

| Type of error | Possible occurrences | Result of error | Impact on benefits | Error tolerance |
|---|---|---|---|---|
| Referential | Street address error | Wrong identification of property | Erroneous situation analysis | 0% error |
| | Sewer segment number error | Wrong identification of suspect sewer segment | Wasted time while errors are resolved | |
| Topological | Link between property and sewer not established | Property not included in analysis | Incomplete situation analysis | 0% (complete topology required) Links between property and sewer are particulary important |
| | Break in topology of sewer network | Adjacent sewer segment would not be included in analysis | Potential source of problem may be missed | |
| Relative | Location of sewer line within street | Wrong site for excavation | Increase in on-site cost | ± 1m |
| Absolute | NA | NA | NA | NA |

Figure 6.13 **Error tolerance table**

databases built or else be prepared to include them in your GIS budget.

## Error tolerance

It is up to Gary to think carefully about how much error the product could tolerate and still remain useful. Is it really necessary to check every address three times to get zero errors? Even a simple operation such as rechecking an address could severely increase the cost of creating the information product. Yet error and accuracy matter because they affect the reliability of the system as a whole. To assess how much error is tolerable, Gary must ask the question "how wrong can we be?"

Gary identifies three types of error of the possible four (see figure 6.13). He specifies 0 percent error tolerance

on referential and topological errors. This is the ideal, but if costs seem too high, he is prepared to revisit his error tolerance. Even if Gary ends up changing it, he'll derive a lot of value from examining the issue of error tolerance and discussing it with you, as the GIS planner, in specific terms. By examining acceptable error, he begins to understand the effect of errors on the information product's reliability and cost.

## Wait tolerance and response tolerance

Because the sewer backup represents a time-sensitive issue, but not life threatening, the network wait tolerance does not apply. Gary designates one day as the response tolerance, measured as the time between the first telephone complaint and availability of the complete information product at the backup site.

| Title: Sewer backup information product<br>Required by: Engineering department<br>Name: Gary | | |
|---|---|---|
| To create product | Hours | Cost ($) |
| Labor<br>    Professional<br>    Technical | 100 | $2,237.00 |
| Materials | | $100.00 |
| Total cost | | $2,337.00 |

**Figure 6.14   Current cost without GIS**

## Current costs

Gary estimates that using current non-GIS methods takes one hundred hours to create this information product, or $2,237 in labor costs each time the product is created. In addition to labor costs, he accounts for another $100 in material costs, for a total cost per information product of $2,337 right now. Creating this information product fifty times per year—without the GIS—costs $116,850 annually. That is the current cost of creating the product within an operational budget for sewer maintenance of $12 million per year.

## Benefits analysis

The GIS could create the same product in four to eight hours, compared to one hundred hours of manual effort, reducing the time involved by more than 90 percent. Some staff members would remain involved, but still, staff time savings of more than 80 percent would be realistic. This represents a real cash savings.

In addition, with GIS creating it faster, the product could be available within a day, as opposed to three weeks later. This is a direct benefit to the organization, helping them react more quickly to a flooding situation. With this faster reaction time, perhaps they could solve the flooding problems quickly enough to keep homeowners from becoming angry, and minimize liability. Improved timing may also make it possible to coordinate repairs with maintenance operations already under way, another agency benefit. Gary can see that it's entirely reasonable to expect benefits of at least $100,000 per year.

One more direct benefit to the agency will be a reduction in liability. Long delays in solving backup problems have already led to a backlog of ten court cases involving unresolved sewer backup problems, including a class action suit for $600,000 by a group of homeowners. The cost of legal preparation by engineering department staff alone could be reduced by an estimated $50,000 per year.

Future and external benefits include improvements to the environment as a result of resolving the flooding and sewage backup problems more quickly. Currently, when the sewers back up, their flow is diverted to the storm sewers, which normally run into the lakes and streams. Some of the polluted storm sewers are diverted to the local waste processing plant, increasing its volume substantially. The costs of extra processing could be lowered by $10,000 per year.

As you can see on the last page of Gary's IPD (figure 6.15), these benefits could result in savings of $160,000 per year. Expanded over ten years, the benefits would amount to $1.6 million, without even taking inflation into account. These figures strengthen the case for building the new databases. You can now compare the benefits that will result from the new information against the costs of data acquisition and system implementation.

Gary's department head recognizes the benefits of GIS from this comparison, too, and indicates his approval of Gary's completed IPD by signing off on the benefits pages. With Gary initialing every page, then putting his signature on the last page, his IPD is ready to be handed off officially to the GIS team.

**Title:** Sewer backup information product
**Required by:** Engineering department
**Name:** Gary

Savings
Current data compilation is time-consuming—100+ person hours for each flooding (fifty per year). This time could be reduced by 90 percent. Staff time savings of 80 percent per year on current workload.

**Benefit—$100,000/year**

Benefit to agency
Timing of product output will be improved significantly. Information provided on basement floodings just after the storm occurs.
Solutions may be applied in time to verify the correction during the rainy season.

The improved timing will make it possible to coordinate repairs with maintenance contracts currently under way, which would save considerable sums.

Reduced liability. There is currently a backlog of ten court cases awaiting trial. The number of court cases increases as time goes on. Staff spends considerable time collecting data for court cases. Legal costs would be reduced.

**Benefit—$50,000/year**

Future and external benefits
By resolving basement-flooding problems, the environment is improved. To relieve basement floodings, sanitary sewers are pumped into the storm sewers, and there is an increase in pollution levels in freshwater streams and lakes. Sewage treatment costs would be reduced.

**Benefit—$10,000/year**

Gary Zzyyxyx _____*Gary Zzyyxyx*_____

Department head _____*Zzlly*_____

Figure 6.15    **Signed benefits page: end of IPD**

The sample forms used in this case study have facilitated the successful collection of IPDs in state, regional, and municipal organizations over many years by Tomlinson Associates Ltd. They can be found in the ESRI Virtual Campus course by the author called "Planning for a GIS." Visit http://campus.esri.com/ to see the course catalog. Examining these forms will help you complete the information needed to ensure that your requirements are fully evaluated.

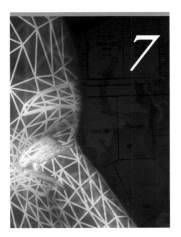

# Define the system scope

*Scoping the system means defining the actual data, hardware, software, and timing.*

Defining the system scope is the stage where you further organize your information in order to answer the following questions:

- How much data is needed?
- What hardware and software is required to input and store the data?
- When must the system be put into place if the organization's expectations are to be met?

In the previous chapter, you learned how to create information product descriptions. IPDs are important planning tools that collate and summarize the essential information about what users want out of the system. In this chapter, using another summary document (called a *master input data list*), we take a more detailed look at how data should go into the system to generate those information products. We'll enumerate the basic software functions required to input your data, along with the other system capabilities you'll need for your GIS. Finally, with a Gantt chart, you will illustrate the activity planning that reflects project timing according to your information product priorities.

## Master input data list (MIDL)

In creating the IPDs, you identified the data needed. Now you're going to use this knowledge to create a new document: the master input data list (MIDL). The MIDL is a detailed list of all the datasets that need to be entered into the GIS system to generate all the information products. The MIDL should identify each dataset (with its name, ID number, and source agency name) and include assessments of the data volume (amount), format, availability, and cost.

The MIDL

- is the master list of data that needs to go into your system; and
- identifies the work that will be involved in putting the data into your system.

The MIDL will guide the effort of setting up your database when the time comes, so estimate as closely as you can how much work will be required, such as the amount of digitizing and alphanumeric data input, along with how much data must be available each year (see figure 6.2).

To be included in the MIDL, each dataset must be needed and specified for at least one information product. No other data should be described in the MIDL. If someone comes to you offering "good" data to include in the GIS, ask that person "which information product needs this data?" Even so-called good data should not make it into the MIDL unless it is necessary for the creation of at least one information product. Having this business rule in place forces people to think in terms of the end products from the GIS; without this rule, your GIS data directories would quickly grow into an array of layers and features that nobody understands because they don't ever get used.

A member of the GIS planning team should be responsible for creating the MIDL; it's perfectly appropriate for the team leader to undertake this task. Whoever is responsible should bring a working knowledge of the characteristics of data, both the data at hand in the organization and that coming from elsewhere. If GIS planning becomes your career, with experience you'll learn to create the MIDL at the same time as you create IPDs. This way, as you identify the datasets necessary to make information products, you can record the dataset names and characteristics directly onto the MIDL as you go (see "Data shoe box," page 59).

## Components of an MIDL

A master input data list includes the following four components:

1. Data identification details
2. Data volume considerations
3. Data characteristics
4. Source data availability and cost

## Data identification details

This is the information that uniquely identifies each dataset. Because different people or departments may have different names for the same data, it is important to create a common identification name or number that can become the standard throughout the organization.

## Data volume considerations

The volume or amount of data you need will affect your system design. Spatial data tends to demand a lot of disk space; having adequate, scalable storage will save you grief down the road. If you're lucky, some of the data will come spatially referenced in the format and scale and projection you need it. But realistically, much data will require conversion from another format. Some will not even be digital data; these nondigital datasets will require conversion to a GIS-readable format. The amount you'll need to store, as well as the amount you'll have to preprocess, affects your working strategy for data storage and handling. You should evaluate the number of datasets you need overall, their size, and the quantity and size of their attribute files. Will you need two datasets or two hundred? Are the attribute files associated with these datasets large or small?

## Data characteristics

Understanding the format and pedigree of the data you intend to incorporate into the GIS will guide your database design and, ultimately, the selection of software and hardware. You need to know whether the data is available as digital files already in an appropriate GIS format: is the format one you can use directly in your system or do you need to convert the data from another format before using it? What are the data characteristics that will determine your input method (scanning, digitizing, or text input)? Note the detailed breakdown in figure 7.1 even calls for counting the number of keystrokes, for example; the more specifics the better.

## Source data availability and cost

Later on as you develop your implementation strategy, facts about the availability of data and its cost become imperative. Sometimes, it is cheaper and easier to re-create data than to edit and update existing commercial or government data. Some of the questions you need to answer are the following:

- Does the data exist in a digital format or will you need to convert it?
- What is the cost of acquisition? Do royalties need to be paid?
- Is it possible to partner with another agency to share the cost of data?
- What is the cost of converting data from one format to another?
- Who is going to be responsible for updating and maintaining data?
- Are there any restrictions on the use of data?

## Assembling the MIDL

The components of the MIDL (figure 7.1) summarize the information to be collected for each dataset. You will fashion your own according to what is appropriate for your project.

The master input data list details the basics—data name, source, volume, the outright cash cost, and any significant variables, like conversion and availability schedules; the specific items of information will vary somewhat depending on the project. As a general rule, it's a good idea for every project to gather as much metadata as possible.

Capture everything that will affect your acquisition and use of the data you need. Data about the data (metadata) doesn't use much storage, and taking the time to set it up correctly will pay dividends down the road when stakeholders start questioning the basis of your analyses. (Today's modern GIS systems have built-in metadata handling capabilities.)

Any book on IT planning would be remiss not to drag out the shopworn phrase "garbage in, garbage out" to drive home the importance of stocking your GIS with only the most reliable and accurate data. This is not to say that lower resolution or more generalized spatial data cannot be loaded into a GIS; just be sure that the associated metadata reflects its limitations.

| Component | Details needed | Notes |
|---|---|---|
| **1. Data identification** | Dataset name | |
| | Dataset number | |
| | Source agency name | |
| | Internet location (URL) | |
| | Metadata available | Yes or no |
| **2. Data volume considerations** | Source data medium | |
| | Digital data format | |
| | Percentage available now in digital format | |
| | Primary record type | Line, sheet, etc. |
| | Primary record volume | Number of primary records |
| | Total data volume | |
| **3. Data characteristics** | | |
| Scanning considerations | Sheet size | In inches or centimeters, typical and maximum |
| | Minimum scan resolution | In dpi, without compression |
| | Legibility | Percentage of total data volume in high, medium, low, and difficult categories |
| Graphic portion | Size | In inches or centimeters, typical and maximum |
| | Schematic | Yes or no |
| | Photo image | Yes or no |
| | Map projection/datum | |
| | Measurement (COGO) data volume | Typical and maximum volume or coordinates Typical and maximum number and size of observations |
| Digitizing effort | Polygons per sheet | Typical and maximum |
| | Lines per sheet | In inches or centimeters, typical and maximum |
| | Points per sheet | Typical and maximum |
| Text portion | Lines per sheet | Typical and maximum |
| | Data elements per record | Number of fields per record, typical and maximum |
| | Total alphanumerics per sheet on input | Number of keystrokes, typical and maximum |
| **4. Data availability and cost** | Percent coverage available now | Or date when it will be available |
| | Currency | Date of data capture and date of most recent update |
| | Restrictions on use | |
| | Cost of dataset acquisition | |
| | Royalties | On acquisition and use |

Figure 7.1 **Components of the MIDL**

## Data shoe box

Because some of the information required for the master input data list (MIDL) is detailed and requires time to assemble, it is a good idea to begin collecting information for this document while preparing the IPDs. You can use the data inventory form shown in figure 7.2 to enter information about datasets identified during the IPD building process. Don't get hung up trying to answer all the questions right away. The idea is to give each dataset a name and a number and describe the data well enough to recognize it when you return to it. You can fill in the other portions of the form later. As you can see, this form covers most everything you can think of to describe data, including dataset name, source, scale, projection, format, description, and volume.

It's good practice to attach sample data to the form. This might include representative maps, with a copy of the legend, or all the columns for two to three records of tabular data (lists). Such samples serve to clarify the functions that the user must perform to create or use the data. These data samples, with inventory forms attached, should be collected together in a physical place, what we call a *data shoe box*. If data is not represented with a sample in the shoe box, it is considered nonexistent in terms of the GIS. Many people new to GIS are unclear about what data exists in their organization. The shoe box is the test! Use a separate data inventory form for each dataset, staple a sample of the data to it, and put it all in the shoe box.

| Data inventory | |
|---|---|
| Interviewer: | Date: |
| Name: | Department: |
| Phone#: | Division/Office: |
| Dataset name: | Dataset number: |
| Source agency: | Metadata? (circle)      Yes    No |
| Data format: (circle)    Map      Manual data file      Air photo      Automated data file      Imagery | |
| Other: | Source data medium: |
| Digital data format: | |
| Percentage available now in a digital format: | |
| Total data volume (# of pages, CDs, maps, etc.): | |
| Scale of source data: | Map projection/datum: |
| Photo image?      Yes    No | |
| Digitizing effort (per sheet): | # of polygons: |
| | # of lines: |
| | # of points: |
| Date of data capture: | Date of last update: |
| Percent of coverage available now: | |
| Date entire coverage is available: | |
| Restrictions on use: | |
| Cost of dataset acquisition: $ | |
| Royalties on acquisition and use: $ | |

Figure 7.2    **Data inventory form**

59

# Functions to input data

Once you've collected the information for the MIDL, you can evaluate the basic system capability functions necessary to put each dataset into the GIS. For every dataset in the MIDL, list the functions required to put the data into the database. These data handling functions will differ depending on the type and characteristics of the data to be input. For example, it's a different set of operations altogether for the computer to input a hard-copy map than to input a digital image, as you can see with the differences between these two datasets in figure 7.3 below. (You need only list the individual functions once for each dataset.)

For now, set aside this list of functions required to input the data. Later on, you will combine it with the list of functions required to make each information product, identified in the IPDs in chapter 6 (see figures 6.10 and 6.11). Eventually, in combining your two lists—the type of function and number of times the function will be used (from the MIDL and IPDs)—you will have the complete list of software functionality your system requires. That will be the piece of paper software vendors will need to see in order to compete for your business.

# Case study: Basic system capability input functions to create the map

Continuing the case study example from chapter 6, Gary is thinking about what it will take to create the sewer backup information product that will help him do his work in the city engineering department. He needs the information product to help him create his incident report, and for that he needs a sewer segment map illustrating the location of each sewer segment together with the segment numbers. Having identified the two datasets required for this, Gary has listed both on the MIDL.

Now he must evaluate the basic system capability functions needed to merge the two datasets. First, Gary outlines the steps needed to input the data.

## Dataset 1: Sewer plans on paper maps (1:11,000)

1. **Scan**—to create digital raster files
2. **Raster to vector**—converts cells to lines
3. **Edit and display**—corrects errors introduced during conversion

|  | Data needed | Data handling functions required |
|---|---|---|
| Dataset A | Digital image data (remote-sensing image supplied on CD–ROM) | File transfer<br>Reformat<br>Create and manage database |
| Dataset B | Hard-copy map data (property parcel boundaries available only on map sheets) | Digitize<br>Reformat<br>Create topology<br>Add attributes<br>Create and manage database |

Figure 7.3 **Different input functions for different datasets**

4. **Create topology**—produces sewer network
5. **Add attributes**—adds sewer segment numbers
6. **Edgematch**—creates single seamless digital file
7. **Create and manage database**—implements a tiling storage structure for easy access
8. **Update**—maintains sewer segment data

### Dataset 2: Aerial photographs in digital format

1. **File transfer**—copies aerial photographs to the GIS database server
2. **Use handheld GPS**—to create a vector file of manhole locations (points)
3. **Add attributes**—adds manhole characteristics
4. **Symbolize**—adds appropriate manhole symbols for display
5. **Rubber sheet**—stretches to fit sewer to known position of manhole
6. **Create topology**—incorporates sewer segments into sewer network
7. **Update**—includes new sewers or manhole locations as added

Having thought this through, with the detailed outline above, Gary can now make his succinct list of the basic system capability functions needed for each of the datasets. This is enough to work with from now on, so he needs only to make note of them as shown in figure 7.4.

Later, in figuring out the basic system capabilities the GIS requires, the GIS planner will add these functions (and those required to generate all the other information products Gary and his colleagues have specified) to the list of necessary functions identified in the "Steps to Make the Product" section of the IPD.

## Setting priorities

At the technology seminar, you began to get a sense of which information products were more important than others to your organization's workflows. Now you must clarify those priorities because, of course, all the information products required from a GIS cannot be created at once. You need to prioritize your list according to the relative importance of the contribution of each product to your organization's objectives. These priorities will be ranked using a scoring method, a group-consensus method, or some combination of the two. Remember, this ranking is the thing that will guide which information products get delivered first, so make sure the process you use incorporates the input of upper management.

When assigning priorities, you must rank information products in strict numerical order—no two can have the same rank. For your process of prioritizing, choose either (or some combination of) the scoring method or the group-consensus method.

| Dataset 1: Sewer plans | Dataset 2: Aerial photographs |
|---|---|
| Scan | File transfer |
| Raster to vector | Input GPS points |
| Edit and display (on input) | Add attributes |
| Create topology | Symbolize |
| Add attributes | Rubber sheet |
| Edgematch | Create topology |
| Create and manage database | Update |
| Update | |

**Figure 7.4   Two datasets: Basic functions needed for each**

## 1. The scoring method

The GIS team leader creates a simple model by which each information product is scored based on the benefit it will provide: ease of production, relevance to the organization's strategic plan, whatever. The planning team members decide the appropriate criteria for scoring. The GIS team leader can allocate scores alone initially or in consultation with the rest of the team throughout the process. Once the team is satisfied, the list of information products and their priority scores—ranked in order of the highest first—is submitted to executive decision makers for comment and approval. Senior management should and will make the final decision on priorities.

## 2. The group-consensus method

This method is a less structured approach to assigning priorities: you get all the managers and decision makers into a room together and work until consensus is reached on the priorities assigned to all the information products.

Consultants are not welcome in that room; they should never participate in this stage of the GIS planning process. External consultants should not be allowed to do the prioritizing of the information products; they don't have enough of a vested interest in the organization's missions and objectives. It's management's concern where to place priorities. As conditions change in the future, rankings may need to be adjusted, but this initial assignment of priorities gives your GIS implementation essential direction and validity.

# Determining system scope

With both the IPDs and the MIDL in hand, having described the information products and the data to build them with, you can begin to evaluate the scope of your system. Determining the range of the system involves considering the following:

- Data priorities
- Data handling load, workstation requirements, and location
- Data storage and security requirements
- Data readiness for use

## Data priorities

In the same way that you ranked the information products by priority, you should rank the datasets based on what data the MIDL says you need first. Reorder the MIDL based on the order in which data is required to make the information products. On the new version of the list, datasets to be used first will have the highest priority. The end product of this simple step should be the assignment of data priorities to each dataset in the MIDL. In the list itself, the highest priority (most immediately needed) data will be on top.

## Data handling load

Once you know what the priorities are, you can use the IPD and MIDL to calculate a quantifiable data handling load that a software and hardware system will be called on to support. Data handling load is simply an estimate of how many products the system will create per year and the amount of work that the system has to do to create each product. You can use the data handling load as a guideline for determining the computational power and storage dimensions of the system that you'll need to implement.

The amount of computational work required to produce an information product depends on processing complexity and data volume. At this point in predicting data handling load, rough estimates of processing complexity and data volume will do to approximate the number of "boxes on desks" required, that is, the number of workstations or terminals necessary for individual users to interact with the GIS. (The sizing of server platforms is addressed in another step.)

Workstation processing complexity is either high or low. You can assess complexity according to the number of steps it takes to make the information product, weighted (mentally) by the number of advanced functions used (e.g., topological overlay, network analysis, 3D analysis). (In the lexicon at the back of the book, functions considered to be complex are signified by an asterisk.)

Data volume, either high or low, is the amount of data the system uses in producing one information product. Make your estimate from the number of different datasets needed to create the product, weighted (mentally) by the volume of data (number of items and size of area) that must be extracted from each dataset to make the information product. All you have to do is assign a high or low evaluation. For some information products, this will be an obvious selection; for others you'll have to use your judgment. Again, estimates are adequate for this stage in the planning process.

Go through your list of information products and assign to each one a high or low value for processing complexity and then for data volume. Next, try to match these characteristics with the type of workstation that will be required for each information product. Consider two workstation types:

1.  High-end: Dual Core Intel Xeon Processor 5160; 3.0 GHz, 4MB L2, 1333; 2GB memory; RAID 2 x 500 GB hard drive; 20-inch flat-screen display; approximate cost in 2007 = $5,500.

2.  Standard: Dual Core Intel Xeon Processor 5130; 2.0 GHz, 4MB L2, 1333; 16MB memory; 80GB hard drive; 17-inch flat-panel display; approximate cost in 2007 = $3,600.

Figure 7.5 indicates the suitable workstation type (high-end or standard) for different combinations of processing complexity and data volume.

Based on data processing complexity and data volume assessments and your own experience (or with the advice of a consultant), you can now estimate how much workstation time each information product will need. Multiply the total number of workstation hours necessary to create the product, by the number of times the product is needed per year. You can use this calculation to make a preliminary appraisal of how many workstations of each type you'll need in each department.

Occasionally one information product will use all the available hours on one workstation. More frequently, several information products may be produced from a single workstation or be made at different workstations in different parts of the department in different locations.

Terminal servers (also known as client-server systems) are usually employed where the data handling load is high and multiple users need access to the same data. They are particularly appropriate for very large datasets.

| Processing complexity | Data volume to be handled | Type of workstation required |
|---|---|---|
| High | High | High-end |
| High | Low | High-end or standard |
| Low | High | Standard |
| Low | Low | Standard |
| High-end: Dual Core Intel Xeon Processor 5160 | | |
| Standard: Dual Core Intel Xeon Processor 5130 | | |

Figure 7.5 **Assessing workstations for information products**

## Data hosting and user locations

The locations of machines on which data will be hosted, as well as where users will operate from, affect network communication requirements and should be considered in advance. For the purposes of estimating, let's assume that an information product will be generated in the user's department (although in the era of Web services, this is often not the case).

If you are a single user in a single department with a single computer using either high- or low-complexity processing and not hosting a Web site, this part of the analysis is extremely simple. On the other hand, if you need to consider the location of numerous databases, along with users with different types of workstations and in different departments, the situation is more complex. We examine this more in the "Distributed GIS and Web services" section in chapter 10. For each department, whether in the headquarters building or at a remote site, you need to calculate the following:

- The total number of workstations using GIS, first for high-complexity processing, then for low-complexity processing (if both, use high)
- The number of users who will be using their workstations concurrently at the time of peak usage

If any of the departments are hosting a Web page based on GIS data, you also need to factor in the anticipated number of visits or hits per hour; either measure is helpful. Hits are best but more difficult to estimate. You should use one or both in your analysis.

You can put together your own estimates in a table, as in figure 7.6, which will aid you in assessing your network communication requirements. The example here, estimating usage for three departments in headquarters and two remote offices, shows that forty people will be considered high-use clients, with fourteen of them needing simultaneous high-use access. Also, counting users from all locations, eighty-two will require low-use access, twenty-nine of them needing it concurrently during peak hours.

It is also useful at this stage to make some notes on the computer system with which the GIS leader or manager will access the system. The GIS leader usually has special superuser privileges and specialized mission-critical, rapid-response applications and should be equipped with a high-performance machine.

| Location | | Processing complexity | | | | Intranet/Internet |
|---|---|---|---|---|---|---|
| | | High | | Low | | |
| | | Total users | Peak concurrent users | Total users | Peak concurrent users | Visits or hits per hour |
| Headquarters | Planning | 8 | 2 | 16 | 5 | 250 |
| | Engineering | 12 | 5 | 5 | 3 | |
| | Operations | 2 | 2 | 30 | 10 | |
| | Totals | 22 | 9 | 51 | 18 | 250 |
| Remote sites | Exning | 10 | 3 | 21 | 6 | 500 |
| | Gazeley | 8 | 2 | 10 | 5 | 400 |
| | Totals | 18 | 5 | 31 | 11 | 900 |
| | Grand totals | 40 | 14 | 82 | 29 | 1,150 |

Figure 7.6 **Estimating peak network usage**

## Scoping hardware requirements

At this stage of the process, you need to take a quick look at the basic hardware requirements so you can make intelligent progress on this topic later (in chapter 10). The basic configuration for computer systems can be thought of as a three-tier option:

- Servers: multiuser UNIX or Microsoft Windows server/workstations
- High-end workstations: Dual Core Intel Xeon Processor 5160; workstation with lots of RAM for running core GIS software
- Standard workstations: Dual Core Intel Xeon Processor 5130; for Web access to GIS resources and thin desktop-client applications

System performance expectations have changed significantly over the past few years. In particular, better platform performance and lower hardware costs continue to enhance productivity.

## Data storage and security

The type and cost of the disk space you'll require depends on the volume of data your system must handle and on how much you need to protect your data. You should be keeping track of data volume amounts within the MIDL. Use the total data volume recorded in the MIDL to estimate the actual amount of disk space required by the information products. Then add 50 percent more to allow for indexing.

Data volume can be calculated as the number of gigabytes or terabytes of storage space required and can be classified as shown in figure 7.7.

Your organization may require some level of data security measures to protect against accidental or deliberate loss and corruption of data. Most organizations also restrict access to sensitive data to prevent misuse. A network-based mass storage system can be secured against loss, for example, by including mirror sites as backups as well as tiered username and password protection. Stand-alone personal computers offer much more limited security features. You would classify computer security levels from high to low:

1. High security: Full mirror, RAID level 1 (highest) protection (100 percent redundancy of data on mirror; no need to rebuild data in the case of disk failure).
2. Medium security: RAID level 5 protection (a much lower level of protection than RAID level 1). A disk failure will have an effect, and it is difficult to rebuild a database in the event of a failure.
3. Low security: Tape or compressed disk backup (you're only as good as your last regular backup).

The appropriate amount of storage and security and what it costs are shown in figure 7.8.

## Data readiness

There is an important difference between data availability and data readiness. Data availability is the date on which you can receive data from its source. This date follows the acquisition or gathering of data (including negotiation of any agreements about data use).

Data readiness is the date on which the data is in your system, processed, and ready for use in the creation of an information product. *Readiness* means that all the data entry, editing, reformatting, and conversion processes are complete.

| Data volume | Storage space required |
|---|---|
| High | Over 100 terabytes |
| Medium | 1–100 terabytes |
| Low | Less than 1 terabyte |

Figure 7.7   **Disk space for information products**

| Data storage options | Disk space | Security | Approximate cost (2007 prices) |
|---|---|---|---|
| Enterprise network mass storage | 1–10 terabytes | High security | $1.50–$10.00 per gigabyte |
| Work group server | 80 gigabytes to 1 terabyte | Medium security | $1.50–$4.00 per gigabyte |
| Personal computer | <80 gigabytes | Low security | $1.25–$3.50 per gigabyte (SATA) $2.50–$4.50 per gigabyte for Serial Attached SCSI (SAS), 15,000 rpm |

Figure 7.8  **The price of protection**

# What affects timing?

To effectively manage the complex process of creating information products from scratch in a logical sequence, careful planning of time and resources is essential. To plan for a successful GIS, you need to understand the factors that can affect the readiness of data and when it is needed, and how these factors guide your production schedule for information products.

These are the factors that affect project timing:

- Data input timing
- Timing for programming information product applications
- Product demand timing
- System acquisition timing
- Training and staff issues

## Data input

How you get your data into the system will have a major effect on your timetable. As in most new GIS efforts of any size, you will probably be creating your database yourself, a very labor-intensive process. Each method of inputting takes a different amount of time, and each is suited for a certain type of data. The four most common methods of data entry are digitizing, scanning, keyboard input, and file transfer.

In the case study of the engineering department, the mandate was to link the sewer segment numbers, characteristics, and street addresses in the database. The high cost of producing this new database was incurred in manual data entry: the scanning of thousands of old sewer plans/profiles, the digitizing of real positions of the manhole covers based on GPS-gathered data, the registration of images with the digital points, all leading ultimately to the creation of a sewer network map. The cost of this data production can be largely attributed directly to human labor.

In a typical municipal GIS, data entry can consume up to 80 percent of the time it takes to implement a GIS project, so if large amounts of data must be created, make sure you allow ample time in the schedule for that to take place. GIS is a rocket that won't launch without fuel in the tank.

Before you start creating your own data, you should check to see if you can obtain the same quality data more quickly and affordably from elsewhere. Common sources of data include the following:

- Similar or partner organizations
- Local and central governments
- Census and survey organizations
- Commercial data providers

If you obtain digital data from other sources, reformatting and editing are frequently necessary to allow the data to be used with existing datasets. Most GIS software can work directly with a variety of data formats. Figure 7.9 shows the names and acronyms of some commonly used vector and raster data formats.

If your software does not directly support a particular data format, you may be able to use a data conversion utility to allow its use in your system. Many software packages include a variety of data conversion utilities. If your package doesn't include the conversion utility you need, you may be able to purchase it from a data supply company.

Based on your own experience or with the advice of a consultant, you should estimate the number of weeks that it will take to move from data availability to data readiness for each dataset. Given the date of availability, determine the first calendar date at which data could be ready. The data-readiness date will probably be revised based on need during the activity planning that follows. However, it is useful to have a potential data-readiness date in your mind as you start activity planning.

## Programming applications

The development of custom applications with a large number of steps is sometimes required to make an information product. If there are severe time limits on product creation, you may have to use customized application programming to speed up the process. The IPD is the starting point for application development; the "steps to make the product" captured in that document are used to specify the application.

| Vector formats | |
|---|---|
| ARC/INFO coverages | Etak MapBase file |
| ESRI Personal Geodatabase (MDB) | Initial Graphics Exchange Standard (IGES) |
| ESRI File Geodatabase (GDB) | Interactive Graphic Design Software (IGDS) |
| ESRI shapefiles (SHP) | Land-use and land-cover data (GIRAS) |
| Atlas GIS Geo .agf files | Map Information Assembly Display (MIADS) |
| AutoCAD drawing files (DWG) | MicroStation Design Files (DGN) |
| AutoCAD drawing interchange file (DXF) | S-57 |
| Automated Digitizing System (ADS) | Spatial Data Transfer Standard (SDTS) |
| Digital Feature Analysis Data (DFAD) | Standard Linear Format (SLF) |
| Dual Independent Map Encoding (DIME) | TIGER/Line extract files |
| Digital Line Graph (DLG) | Vector Product Format (VPF) |
| Raster formats | |
| Arc Digitized Raster Graphics (ADRG) | ESRI Grid |
| ARC/INFO GRID | IMAGINE®. IMG |
| BIL, BIP, and BSQ | JFIF |
| BMP | JPG |
| DTED (Digital Terrain Elevation Data) | RLC (run-length compressed) |
| ERDAS | SID files |
| GIF | SunRaster files |
| GRASS (Geographical Resource Analysis Support System) | Tag Image File Format (TIFF) |

Figure 7.9 **Commonly used data formats**

You should test the resulting application program thoroughly in a production environment before you consider it ready for deployment in a front-line situation. The development of application programs might be done by you or your staff or outsourced to contractors. If outside contractors are used, you will need to allow additional time for the contracting process.

Based on your own experience or with the advice of a consultant, estimate the application programming time needed for each information product. The time will vary according to the size and complexity of the application required (see figure 7.10). If writing an application is projected to take twelve months, it is wise to break the application into two or more stand-alone pieces that can be done separately. Bear in mind that projects over twelve months old have a high risk of failure as a result of changing technology life cycles.

At this stage of planning, your estimates of how long application programming will take should be considered to be plus or minus 50 percent accurate. A programming activity you expect will take two months may actually take between one month and three months.

## Product demand

Other factors influence the timing of the generation of a product: the rate at which products can be generated, the rate at which products can be used by the organization, and the potential for changes in information product priorities because of multiple data use.

Manage expectations from the beginning. There can be delays as you get up and running. Think about the rate at which the information products generated by the system can be absorbed and used within your organization. You may be thinking of producing two hundred new maps per year, but do existing staff have time to examine and use two hundred maps? You need to go over the high-priority information products and discuss their use with staff involved to ensure that the rate of use matches the proposed rate of generation. The results may be surprising, especially given the work that has gone into information product description. If the demand picture changes, adjust your production rates accordingly.

Sometimes, in the process of inputting data to create high-priority information products, sufficient data is entered to generate a lower-priority information product. This is a happy by-product and should alert the GIS

| Size of application program | Nature of application program | Time needed for development |
|---|---|---|
| Small | No application program needed<br>Modest number of steps required to create information product | Zero<br>One staff month |
| Medium | Straightforward information product required, but a large number of steps | Up to twelve staff months or three months elapsed time |
| Large | Application involving many steps in a time-sensitive situation (e.g., a license permitting process) | Up to 144 staff months or twelve months elapsed time |

Figure 7.10 **Timing for programming information product applications**

planning team to try to identify other potential candidates for multiproduct leveraging. Sometimes it could be beneficial to alter the information product priorities to maximize multiple-data-use potential.

## System acquisition

You must also allocate time for system selection and system procurement. Government procurement procedures may be among the slowest. They can involve any or all of these steps:

- Issuing *requests for information* (RFI) and *requests for proposal* (RFP) (see appendix D)
- Proposal review
- Benchmark testing
- Negotiation of best and final offers
- Timing of budget cycles

Each of these procedures may have its own requirements for delay and acceptance. The amount of time required depends on the organization involved. You should estimate the time needed based on your own experience and after consultation with your organization's budgeting and procurement manager.

Finally, allow time for system implementation and a reasonable break-in period, regardless of the targeted operating efficiency of your GIS. During this period, staff will have to work through a steep learning curve; glitches are inevitable and problems have to be resolved. It may not be possible to reach full production status immediately, so that would affect the immediate rate of production. Learn to manage expectations up front. System break-in will also be facilitated if you can allow a window of relatively low demand at the beginning.

## Training and staff

Time for training and staffing issues should be included in your implementation plan. Training needs vary depending on the types of GIS users that need to be trained.

Within large GIS-using organizations, you will find the following types of users:

- Professional GIS users supporting GIS project studies, GIS spatial data maintenance, and commercial map production operations.
- Desktop GIS specialists supporting general spatial query and analysis studies, simple map production, and general-purpose query and analysis operations.
- Business users who require customized GIS information products to support their specific business needs. These are end users who do not require geographic expertise and use information products to support standard business functions.
- Internet and intranet map server users of simple map products using simple publishing wizards and intranet and Internet browser clients.

All four groups of users require training. In addition, new staff may need to be recruited and brought into the GIS team. Training is a vital part of GIS and a significant budget item. It is an essential part of maintaining and keeping skilled GIS staff. Provisions for this must be included in your time plan.

## Activity planning

Activity planning is a specific plan for information-product delivery.

If you've followed the procedures outlined in this chapter, by now you should have a clear sense of the following:

- Information product priorities (perhaps modified somewhat by multiple-data-use potential)
- Data priorities
- Data input timing
- Application programming timing
- System acquisition timing
- Training and staffing timing

Now you are ready to start the overall activity planning for your GIS. First, revisit the information

| Datasets<br>Information products<br>System staff constraints | | Timeline 2007 | | | | | | | | |
|---|---|---|---|---|---|---|---|---|---|---|
| | | Sep<br>29<br>07 | Oct<br>6<br>07 | Oct<br>13<br>07 | Oct<br>20<br>07 | Oct<br>27<br>07 | Nov<br>3<br>07 | Nov<br>10<br>07 | Nov<br>17<br>07 | Nov<br>24<br>07 |
| **Datasets** | Park biophysical | | | | | *Biophysical* ▇ | ▇ | ▇ | ▇ | |
| | Grizzly bear sighting | | | | | | | *Grizzly bear* ▇ | | |
| | Caribou sighting | | | | | | | *Caribou* ▇ | | |
| | Caribou home range | | | | | | | | | |
| | Caribou telemetry | | | | | | | | | |
| | NTS topography | | | | | | | | | |
| | Black bear sighting | | | | | | | | | |
| | DEM 1:50,000 | | | | | | | | | |
| | Slope 1:50,000 | | | | | | | | | |
| | Aspect 1:50,000 | | | | | | | | | |
| | Park fire history | | | | | | | | | |
| | Bear monitoring database | | | | | | | | | |
| | Human-use database, park and BC | | | | | | | | | |
| | Human-use database, Alberta | ▇ | ▇ | ▇ | ▇ | ▇ | ▇ | ▇ | ▇ | ▇ |
| | Elk home range | | | | | | | | | |
| | Elk encounters aggressive | | | | | | | | | |
| | Elk telemetry | | | | | | | | | |
| | Exotic plant database | | | | | | | | | |
| | Abnormal cow/calf | | | | | | | | | |
| | Waterways process change | | | | | | | | | |
| | Future development | | | | | | | | | |
| | CEAA registry | | | | | | | | | |
| | Cultural resources | | | | | | | | | |
| | Zoning | | | | | | | | | |
| | Mortality data | | | | | | | | | |
| | Speed data | | | | | | | | | |
| | Traffic data | | | | | | | | | |
| | Dominant vegetation | | | | | | | | | |
| **Information products** | #41 Grizzly bear habitat model | | | | | | | *Grizzly bear habitat* | | ▇ |
| | #40 Caribou habitat model | | | | | | | | | |
| | #61 Black bear habitat model | | | | | | | | | |
| | #42 Multi-species habitat model | | | | | | | | | |
| | #47 Bear human conflict | | | | | | | | | |
| | #46 Elk human conflict analysis | | | | | | | | | |
| | #10 Dominant vegetation map | | | | | | | | | |
| | #12 Fuel map | | | | | | | | | |
| | #50 Montane ecosystem diversity | | | | | | | | | |
| | #55 Environmental assessment | | | | | | | | | |
| | #44 Current caribou habitat and fire response | | | | | | | | | |
| | #20 Mountain pine beetle analysis | | | | | | | | | |
| | #38 Transportation corridor analysis | | | | | | | | | |
| | #52 Future MED | | | | | | | | | |
| **Constraints** | System acquisition | | | | | | | | | |
| | Staff training | | | | ▨ | | | | | |
| | System startup | ▨ | ▨ | ▨ | | | | | | |
| | Holiday/sick leave 4 weeks per year | | | | | | | | | |

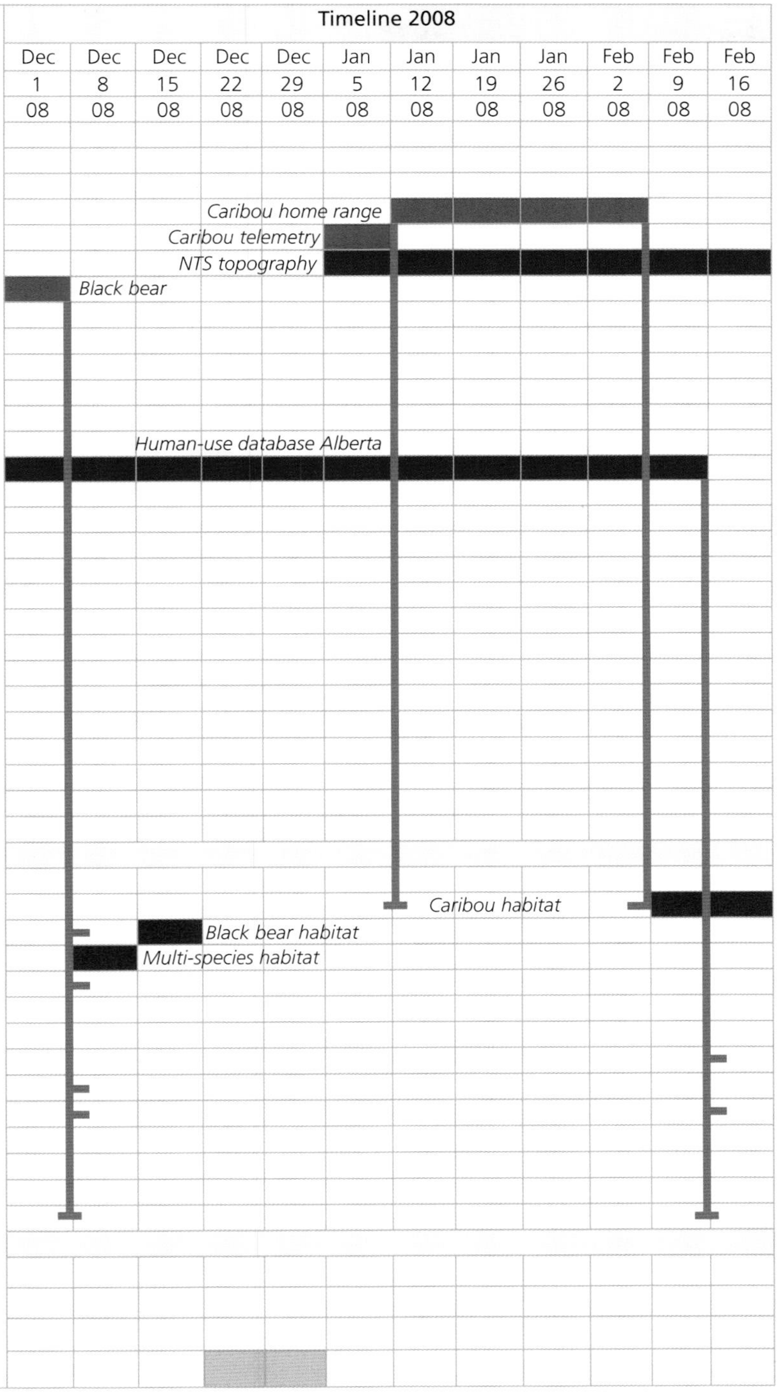

Figure 7.11

**Gantt chart showing a National park's GIS planning for input of datasets (red and green horizontal bars), readiness of datasets for use (blue vertical lines), availability of information products (purple horizontal bars), and system staff constraints (yellow)**

product priorities in order to refine them by answering these questions:

- Will some information products depend on the creation of other information products? If so, the latter must be assigned a higher priority.
- When will it be possible for you to make each information product, given your estimated data-readiness dates (which include both data availability and the time required to input the data)? This is particularly important for the high-priority information products you want to make early.

Use these considerations to revise your information product priorities and establish a second-level priority review.

The next step in activity planning is to use a Gantt chart—essentially an illustrated timeline with dependencies plotted on a linear chart so that one can see which activities are time-sensitive. Gantt charts, like the one in figure 7.11, can help you plan and manage your project effectively. There are many other project evaluation and review techniques and specialist project-management software packages, but this is one of the simplest and easiest to apply. You need to manage your project so that you focus on the tasks that produce results.

Displaying information about activities and their duration, a Gantt chart allows you to schedule and track the activities associated with GIS planning and implementation. Each dataset or information product, system acquisition, or staff activity is a row in the chart, and time periods are columns in the chart. Bars indicate the time necessary to complete each activity, for example, data-loading application, writing break-in period, or staff holiday. Gantt charts make it easy to see when a particular activity will be completed and when other activities relying on its completion can begin. For example, the entry of a particular dataset might be one activity, at the end of which it would be possible to produce a particular information product.

You can use a Gantt chart to document project activities and their duration, establish relationships between your activities, see how changes in the duration of activities affect other activities, and track the progress of your project. You will also use the Gantt chart to schedule hardware, software, and network acquisitions over time, after these have been determined.

Gantt charts can be constructed using ordinary spreadsheet software (such as Microsoft Office Excel) or specialist project-management software from a variety of suppliers. In relatively simple situations, a handmade one will do.

In the left column of your Gantt chart (as in the sample on the previous two pages), first list the name of every dataset you intend to put into your system, followed by the names of the information products you intend to generate in the same time frame. At the bottom, list the constraints—system or staff downtime where nothing can be done in terms of creating information products. These bottom four rows allow time for system acquisition, staff training, system startup, and holidays and sick leave.

The columns on the top of the chart are usually best divided into one-week segments grouped into months and years. You should indicate fiscal years or budget cycles; you can use vertical dotted lines for this. Note that, while our sample (figure 7.11) is just a "snapshot" of the time frame, a Gantt chart for GIS planning usually covers a five-year period.

When you start charting, you are most likely to place activities onto the Gantt chart in the following order:

1. System acquisition and staff training activities
2. Data-input activities—establish when data will be ready
3. Application development activities for any high-priority information product

The order reflects the logic of your planning. Having established when the system will be installed and staff available, you can coordinate the timing of the input of the data with the priority of need for information products. Acquired (bought) datasets tend to require more time for input than datasets generated in house. Usually an in-house dataset (appearing in red on the chart) can be readied more quickly because it originates with the organization and is less likely to require conversion or extensive reformatting. In this case, at the top of figure 7.11, a national park is collecting data about grizzly bear and caribou sightings, two datasets being prepared for use in the space of a week. The park will also buy, or otherwise acquire from elsewhere, datasets like the human-use database Alberta charted in green farther down the list. Work may be needed to make datasets from outside the organization fit the GIS, thus the green lines on this chart may span many more weeks than the red.

Meanwhile, in the category below the list of datasets on the far left, information products await this data readiness. The vertical blue lines on the chart indicate when the datasets they are attached to will be ready for use in creating information products. The "tics" along the blue lines mark the information products (from the column on the far left) that will use a particular dataset. The rows at the bottom of the chart show time dedicated to training, statutory holidays, etc. when staff or system will not be available.

Sometimes what's called an *interim information product* is generated on the way to making another information product, which can be useful by itself or frequently as a dataset for yet another information product. You can plot this out, too: the purple bars next to the blue tics on the chart signify this potential of multiple use. Also occasionally, after you've gotten the first ten or so datasets into the system, you realize you could make some information products of less priority sooner than those of high priority. This is called *multiple data use*, and it affords you the opportunity of adjusting your priorities in order to make the best use of what you can create right away.

Gradually, you build your Gantt chart, taking into account restrictions of staffing and product demand, until you have decided how and when to build each information product. Now you have, for the first time, a date on which you can reasonably anticipate the delivery of the first of each information product. (In chapter 11, through benefit–cost analysis, you'll learn that you should allow one year from the date of the first delivery of each information product to count the benefits that accrue from having that product available.)

Now that you have defined the scope of your system and made a specific plan for information product delivery, in the next chapter you can shift your thoughts to data designing in preparation for setting up a database for GIS implementation.

# Create a data design

*The data landscape has changed dramatically with the advent of the Internet and the proliferation of commercial datasets. Developing a systematic procedure for safely navigating this landscape is critical.*

Now that you know what data you need to make your information products and what it will take to input it all into your database, perhaps a conception of the infrastructure required to support it is beginning to take shape in your mind. But before you get too far in thinking about your conceptual system design as a whole, you'll need to think about how to design the system for data in more detail. The conceptual system design for data comes first because the characteristics of your data determine, in large part, what you'll need from the system architecture.

The issues of data design (in this chapter) and the choice of a data model (in the next chapter) both boil down to two concerns: First, will the data model represent the real world in a way that is useful to you? For example, will it let you describe features, details, behaviors, conditions, and anything else that you need to use in your calculations and analysis? Second, does the use of a particular data model inhibit some of the things you want to do? Does it prohibit the use of other types of data? Is it very complex and slow to execute? Is it scalable? We'll explore data modeling in the next chapter, after first focusing on what you need to know about your data.

## Data characteristics

Part of developing a systematic procedure for creating the conceptual system design for data is having a thorough understanding of the characteristics of your data. These characteristics include each dataset's scale, resolution, map projection, error tolerance, and how the data affects the intended information products. Sometimes you'll need to create multiple versions of the same datasets at different scales or resolutions to generate the map output specified by the IPD. These will all be stored as individual layers in your database.

## Scale

Scale is the relationship between the distance on a map and the corresponding distance in the real world. If a map has a scale of 1:24,000, then one inch on the map is equal to 24,000 inches (2,000 feet) on the ground. Map scale can also be expressed as a statement of equivalence using different units, for example, one inch = two thousand feet. The scale of data reflects resolution and its relative accuracy on a map: the larger the scale, the more detailed the dataset shown. Map scale numbers are counterintuitive: the lower the number, the higher the resolution (and the larger the scale). So 1:6,000 data is significantly higher resolution than 1:100,000 data.

Features drawn in large scale (e.g., 1:6,000) show greater map detail because they are more closely representing the real-world features. On a small-scale map (e.g., 1:100,000) the features are usually generalized or aggregated. Both are useful and serve a purpose.

Consider figure 8.1. A small-scale dataset shows the river on the map as a single, gently curving line. A large-scale dataset shows a smaller part of the river as a polygon depicting the banks and the width of the river.

What scale or scales to set up in your GIS database (i.e., how high a resolution of data to acquire) is a critical factor in the system design. If the scale of primary data is too large, the data volume could overwhelm the computational processing resources. This becomes especially significant when you're trying to build quick-response systems.

If the scale is too small, the database might not contain the details needed, and so would not be able to perform the best analysis or reliably provide the specified information products. The "native" format of your source data (the format in which it comes to you), as well as your budget for computing power, will advise this process.

Once you've chosen the appropriate scale for your GIS database, you may need to convert some data to this common scale, either in advance or in real time, as one of the steps required to create information products to fit with other data.

A good rule of thumb is to avoid changing scale by more than two and a half times in either direction. As in figure 8.2, if you start with a 1:50,000 scale dataset and reduce the scale two and a half times (multiply 50,000 times 2.5), your scale will be 1:125,000. Thus, if you create information products from source data that has a scale smaller than 1:125,000, you may run into data profusion and legibility problems. If you start at 1:50,000 and go two and a half times larger (divide 50,000 by 2.5), your maximum scale will be 1:20,000.

In some cases, you may need to store source data at more than one scale in the database, such as when applications will be performed at both small and large scales. Sometimes you may want to store basemap data acquired

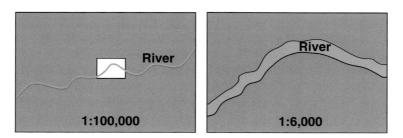

Figure 8.1 **Dataset in small scale (left) and in large scale (right)**

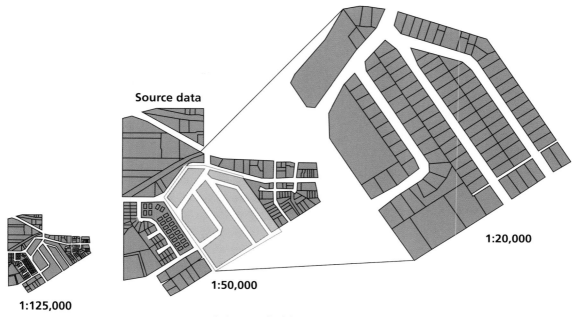

Source data

1:125,000

1:50,000

1:20,000

Figure 8.2   **Minimum (left) and maximum (right) scale**

from external sources at the native scale in which it was received. Although a GIS does not typically store the scale of the source data as an attribute of a dataset, scale is a useful indicator of accuracy, which is why you note scale in the IPD. All users of the data must understand that true spatial analysis—like when you're using geographic overlay functions to derive new information—is only as accurate as its highest resolution layer. If more than one scale is represented in the database, it should be well-documented in the metadata. Note that if the different scales are from different sources, they may not agree.

Scale influences the cost as well as the accuracy of the resulting database. For example, the number of map sheets needed to cover the same area in your database increases exponentially with the scale. Therefore, mapping at 1:6,000 is sixteen times more expensive than mapping at 1:24,000. As the number of sheets needed for your application increases, so does the cost. And because scale does introduce such a significant effect on cost, you must take a close look at the actual needs as specified in

the IPDs. Don't build a rocket to Mars if all you need is one to the moon. The purpose of the application will determine the appropriate scale.

## Resolution

Consider resolution defined here as the size of the smallest features that can be mapped or sampled at a given scale. The resolution of a map is directly related to its scale. As map scale decreases, resolution diminishes and feature boundaries must be smoothed, simplified, or not shown at all. There will be a minimum polygon size and line length you can represent at a given scale. Features below these resolutions are merged into surrounding data, converted to a point, or deleted. In figure 8.3, you can see that a two-acre polygon is visible at a large scale of 1:24,000, but the same polygon appears as a point at the small scale of 1:500,000. Resolution also determines the distance between sample points in a grid or lattice format (for example, satellite imagery).

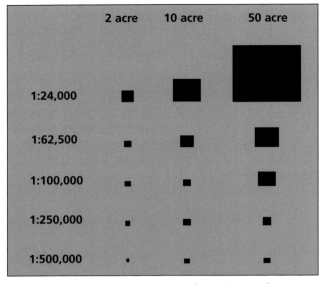

Figure 8.3 **Resolution related to scale**

Like scale, your data must have the minimum resolution necessary to create your information products. You do not necessarily need the highest resolution available. For example, a city's land-parcel data must be high resolution, but a Web application showing interstate travel routes would have to be small scale. Keep in mind that resolution also contributes to data error. Your information product descriptions include error tolerance and will help you determine the required resolution.

## Map projection

The choice of a map projection is another crucial step in the GIS database design process. As part of the conceptual system design for data, you need a basic understanding of map projections in order to determine the one best for your needs.

Paper maps are perhaps the most common source of geographical data in the world. Because the planet Earth is spherical and maps are flat, getting information from the curved surface to the flat one requires a special mathematical formula called a *map projection*. A map projection simply converts Earth's three-dimensional surface to the flatlands of paper—a decidedly two-dimensional space. The process of flattening the earth creates map distortions in distance, area, shape, or direction. The result is that all flat maps have some degree of spatial distortion.

The type of projection used determines the degree and type of distortion found on the map. A specific map projection can preserve one property at the expense of the others, or it can compromise several properties with reduced accuracy. You should pick the distortion that is least detrimental to your database when selecting a projection type. Today's GIS programs offer an array of projection choices, but read the supporting documentation and "help" files before making any database decisions or attempting to reproject any data.

Datums are another important map aspect related to projection. A datum provides a base reference for measuring locations on Earth's surface. It defines the origin and orientation of latitude and longitude lines and assumes a shape for the globe on which they fit. The most recently developed datum is the World Geodetic System of 1984 (WGS84). It serves as the framework for satellite-based location finding worldwide (i.e., the Global Positioning System—GPS).

There are also local datums that provide a frame of reference for measuring locations in a particular area. The North American Datum of 1927 (NAD27), the North American Datum of 1983 (NAD83), and the European Datum of 1950 (ED50) are local datums in wide use. As the names suggest, NAD27 and NAD83 are designed for best fit in North America, while ED50 is intended for Europe. A local datum is not suited for use outside the area for which it was designed. Maps of the same area but using different datums (e.g., NAD27 and NAD83) will result in the same features showing up in different locations on the map—clearly an unacceptable result.

To effectively use spatial data from a map, you need to know the projection of that map and the datum. Often, input maps are in different projections, requiring a conversion or coordinate transformation. Your GIS software should support changing your data's projection and datum.

The amount of data distortion you'll experience due to map projection is related to scale. The larger the geographic area covered by the map (the smaller the scale), the more distortion from projection you will experience. When you see the actual scale varying at different points on a map, that is the result of map projection, and you can use it as a guideline for distortion.

Unfortunately, people put out data without defining the projection. For more information on map projection, including how to figure out what the projection is and what to do if your data is not lining up, see "Further reading" at the back of the book.

## Error tolerance

Understanding the types of error you may encounter in developing and using your GIS is very important but

frequently overlooked in the GIS planning process. Error, because it is related to resolution and scale, is also directly linked to cost: reducing error costs money. Everyone involved in designing and using the GIS must have a sound understanding of what error means and how much is acceptable or unacceptable. This threshold will cost a certain amount. Some error is tolerable as long as the usefulness of the information product is maintained.

When people in your organization request an information product, they rightfully expect to receive benefit from using it. They expect it to save staff time, increase the organization's effectiveness, or contribute new value to the enterprise. The product's benefit is lost if there is so much error that it isn't useful. Worse still, the product could become an extra cost if someone makes a wrong decision based on error-ridden data.

As laid out in chapter 6, the four types of error are referential, topological, relative, and absolute. To review, *referential* error denotes error in label identification or reference. For example, in the case of a sewer-management application, are the correct street addresses on the correct houses? Are the correct sewer segment numbers on the correct sewer segments? *Topological* error occurs when there is a break in a needed linkage, for example, where polygons are not closed or sewer networks are not connected. *Relative* error is inaccuracy in the positioning of two objects relative to one another. For example, in a sewer-management application, imagine the roadway is thirty feet wide. The sewer maintenance crew needs to know where to excavate. It is important to know, relative to the property and the roadway, where the sewer is located. *Absolute* error, on the other hand, refers to the misidentification of the true position of something in the world. Absolute error becomes an issue when you are bringing different maps from different sources together in a graphical or topological overlay or combining GPS reading and maps.

Error can affect many different characteristics of the information stored in a database. Map resolution, and hence the positional accuracy of something, applies to both horizontal and vertical dimensions. The positional accuracy depends on the scale at which a map was created.

Typically, maps are accurate to roughly one line width or 0.5 millimeters. For example, a perfectly drawn 1:3,000 map could be positionally accurate down to 1.5 meters, while a perfectly drawn 1:100,000 map could only be positionally accurate down to 50 meters.

Figure 8.4 shows the relationships at play when determining a suitable map scale. Consider the minimum area to be measured and the amount of tolerable error. The expected percentage error in area measurements is derived from the minimum area mapped and the map's scale.

In the error tables from the short case study that follows, you can see further how map scale, the minimum size area you need to map, and error tolerance are related to one another. As you are developing your conceptual system design for data, keep these relationships in mind.

For example, if you decide to map your entire database at 1:24,000 (because that is what you have readily available, and twenty of your thirty information product requests require this level of accuracy), you will end up creating several information products with little or no value. This will result in unmet user expectations and perhaps discredit the entire GIS. It is important to understand error and be able to effectively communicate its consequences to the people in your organization.

| Given information | Resulting information |
| --- | --- |
| Minimum area, percentage error in area | Map scale |
| Minimum area, map scale | Percentage error in area |

Figure 8.4  **Error table**

# Case study: Determining the required positional accuracy

The concept of error tables is confusing for many people, so let's go over it again using a simple example. Marcella works at a city's economic development department attempting to lure businesses in the warehousing and distribution industry to locate in her city. These businesses typically require good rail and highway access plus relatively level land parcels of twenty-five acres or more. Marcella needs a map that identifies these types of sites with plus or minus 5 percent error in area. (If she provides inaccurate information to new businesses, she won't get very far.) Marcella has requested that map as her information product.

If you were in the role of planning the conceptual system design for data for the city's GIS, you would need to review her information product description and determine the minimum scale for mapping parcels in order to fulfill Marcella's request. She can determine the minimum scale—and you can check her IPD—by using the two types of error tables that follow (figures 8.5 and 8.6):

- Map scale for a given area and error tolerance—shows the scale at which the map must be created given the minimum area that must be measured and the percentage error that is tolerable.
- Percent error in area measurement for a given area and map scale—shows the percentage error in area measurement that can be expected as a result of the minimum area being mapped and the map scale.

These tables are used to show the resulting scale or percentage error if values for minimum area and its incumbent information (figure 8.4) are given. They assume 0.5 mm positional accuracy of mapping and an average case distribution of error.

First, Marcella must convert her minimum site size from acres to hectares. There are 2.471 acres in a hectare, so 25 acres is approximately 10 hectares. To determine the

| Map scale for a given area and error tolerance | | | | | |
|---|---|---|---|---|---|
| Minimum area (ha) | % error in area measurement | | | | |
| | 1 | 3 | 5 | 8 | 10 |
| 0.01 | 1:100 | 1:300 | 1:500 | 1:800 | 1:1,000 |
| 0.1 | 1:300 | 1: 900 | 1:1,500 | 1:2,400 | 1:3,000 |
| 1 | 1:1,000 | 1:3,000 | 1:5,000 | 1:8,000 | 1:10,000 |
| 10 | 1:3,000 | 1:9,000 | 1:15,000 | 1:24,000 | 1:30,000 |
| 100 | 1:10,000 | 1:30,000 | 1:50,000 | 1:80,000 | 1:100,000 |
| 1,000 | 1:30,000 | 1:90,000 | 1:150,000 | 1:240,000 | 1:300,000 |
| 1 hectare (ha) = 10,000 m² = 2.471 acres | | | | | |

Figure 8.5 **Determining appropriate scale**

| Percent error in area measurement for a given area and map scale | | | | | |
|---|---|---|---|---|---|
| Minimum area (ha) | Map scale | | | | |
| | 1:1,000 | 1:5,000 | 1:10,000 | 1:50,000 | 1:100,000 |
| 0.01 | 10.0 | 50.0 | INVALID | | |
| 0.1 | 3.3 | 16.6 | 33.3 | | |
| 1 | 1.0 | 5.0 | 10.0 | 50.0 | |
| 10 | | 1.6 | 3.3 | 16.6 | 33.3 |
| 100 | | | 1.0 | 5.0 | 10.0 |
| 1,000 | INSIGNIFICANT | | | 1.6 | 3.3 |
| 1 hectare (ha) = 10,000 m² = 2.471 acres | | | | | |

Figure 8.6 **Expected error**

appropriate scale, she will use the map scale for a given area and error tolerance table (figure 8.5).

She finds her minimum area in the first column of the table. Next, she finds her error tolerance (5 percent) along the top row of the table. The intersection of 10 hectares and 5 percent error is 15,000. The minimum map scale needed to create Marcella's information product is therefore 1:15,000.

Checking over her calculations using the table in figure 8.6, you find that by using maps at a scale of 1:15,000 or larger, Marcella's application will deliver the required positional accuracy.

## Data standards and conversion

In this section, you'll learn the importance of reviewing your existing data with an eye toward spotting new software capabilities that can help you in your all-important tasks of identifying data sources, developing data standards, and determining data-conversion requirements associated with your data.

### Digital data sources

From the early days of GIS until about fifteen years ago, most GIS databases were created with data converted from paper form—the slow and laborious process of digitizing paper maps. By now, more of what exists in the physical world has been measured and much of that data is now finding its way—in digital form—into the marketplace of information. Some of this data can be bought from commercial vendors for a fee, while other data is available for zero or nominal fees from public agencies.

Determining what datasets meet your requirements and sifting through them takes time—even knowing where to look and how to search can be a challenge. The good news is that the Internet and World Wide Web have become invaluable tools for locating and acquiring digital data. On the Internet, you will find a staggering array of map, tabular, and image data. Some of the best data is actually free, particularly from international, national, regional, and local governments.

In some countries, much data is available at little or no cost if you know where to search. Data portals, such as www.census.gov or www.geodata.gov, are emerging as good places to begin searching for reliable data. From private data vendors, prepackaged processed data is available for a wide range of applications. Maybe your own organization is a source of digital data. Access to this world is wonderful—in fact, sometimes acquiring data is a cost-saver compared to creating data yourself—but no matter how easy data is to get, there is no shortcut around the imperative of recognizing its pedigree. There is no substitute for knowing how accurate and reliable your data is.

When determining whether or not to acquire digital data, you must be able to assess the history and quality of the dataset. If you do not know the data's content, source, age, resolution, and scale, consider it useless for your purposes. You should expect to receive some metadata in the form of a data dictionary or data quality report from the provider or vendor. The metadata should provide pertinent background information about the data. Digital data can speed the process of developing your GIS, but only if you first understand what you're buying or downloading.

## Technology standards

Standards in technology usually refer to an agreed-upon set of guidelines for interoperability. Insofar as technology standards facilitate the effective sharing of application programs and data between offices, agencies, and the public, setting the standards to be met becomes one of the important requirements of a successful GIS. There are several standards to consider: operating system standards, user interface standards, networking standards, database query standards, graphic and mapping standards, and data standards. Here our focus is on standards regarding data, including digital data exchange formats.

Standards bring order to the seemingly chaotic development process and should be agreed on early in the GIS project. This applies to large enterprise-wide systems especially. Standards allow applications to be portable and more accessible across networks.

Along with the benefits, however, come the costs. Most smart managers realize that implementing standards costs time and money up front: to develop and implement standards, to train staff in meeting the standards, and to retrofit existing applications. As a conscientious manager, it is your duty to consider the true benefits and costs of your program and to communicate these to upper management so that funds will be forthcoming.

Another cost, aside from time and money, may come in the form of compromise in acceptable data quality and error tolerance. For example, if you establish a standard for positional accuracy that is plus or minus 40 feet, which is adequate for 95 percent of your applications, the usefulness for the other 5 percent of your applications will be compromised. You must develop data standards by taking into consideration the requirements associated with your information products, as well as the current standards and any anticipated standards that may be coming into effect in related departments or organizations.

The current, or established, data standards in your organization, if any, probably have been developed through informal arrangements, continuation of past practices, and the need to deliver information products. Most likely, they are undocumented and inconsistently applied. Existing standards are often out of date and fail to take advantage of the most recent technology.

Determining established and anticipated data standards is part of the conceptual design process. Again, much of the information you need will be in the IPDs. The GIS team, representing all participants, needs to arrive at a consensus on the following standards related to data:

- Data quality standards (i.e., the appropriate map scale, resolution, and projection for source material)
- Error standards (referential, topological, relative, and absolute)
- Naming standards (layers, attributes)
- Documentation standards (minimum amount of metadata required for each dataset)
- Digital interchange standards

In the United States, national data standards are being developed as part of the National Spatial Data Infrastructure. Take these into consideration as you develop your system. After the GIS team completes its formulation of your set of standards, you may find it useful, as some organizations do, to formally adopt and publish them.

## Survey capabilities

The GIS database can now accept measurements from survey instruments of all kinds in three dimensions and execute all the traditional survey computations necessary to adjust those measurements and create coordinate points with known levels of error. Least-squares adjustment fit of disparate data can be conducted to get the best value for a point. Coordinate geometry (COGO) measurements can

be included with the survey measurements and treated in the same manner. You can also add coordinates derived from GPS stations to the survey measurement database. These survey measurements and computations are carried out within the geodatabase in the same coordinate space as other vector and raster data.

The surveying data flow from field to fabric is greatly improved. Now one optimized operation can handle the process of moving from fieldwork station measurements through data processing of survey computations, to COGO and computer-aided design (CAD) systems for drafting and design, into GIS systems for integration with other data—all within one geodatabase in one coordinate space.

With a significant new capability, you can integrate the survey measurements with the location of GIS features on the map, making the link between coordinates established from survey measurements and points on features. Thereafter, the features can be moved to their correct positions and stored in the database that way. Snapping tolerances, configuration algorithms, and batch processing of adjustments can be selected. All this enables you not only to improve the accuracy of the existing GIS database but also to add whole new GIS features defined by survey measurements. Display of error ellipses can provide measures of error of the new feature locations. The tolerance to relative error and absolute error (expressed in IPDs) can now be quantitatively compared to the accuracy of feature placement.

## Topology

Topology, an arcane branch of algebra concerned with connectivity, has always benefited the GIS industry, never more so than now. Since the earliest days of GIS, topology has been used to identify errors in the vector fabric of the database. Specifically, it could identify when polygons were not closed or when lines overshot the junction, when there were breaks in networks, when names had been incorrectly linked to features, or when two names had been assigned to one feature or no name had been assigned to a feature that ought to have a name. Creating a topologically correct dataset was a significant step forward in establishing the accuracy of a GIS database. It was essential before the days of inexpensive computer monitors (cathode ray tubes), when digitizers were working blind and errors were frequent.

Topology is back with us again after an absence of a few years, faster because of computer speeds, but still in the same role: as an excellent tool for establishing spatial integrity and for error identification and editing. Topology is useful not only in identifying and correcting errors but also in spatial analysis, performing in an hour tasks (like checking for connectivity of street segments) that used to take GIS technicians days of pouring over maps.

The big difference in the current versions of topology is that they operate in three dimensions. In these multi-layered topologies, coincident or intersecting features or parts of features in one layer can be intelligently linked topologically with those from another layer.

In working with a geodatabase, technicians establish rules to control the allowable spatial relationships of features within a feature class, in different feature classes, or between subtypes. For example, lot lines must not have dangles; buildings must be covered by owner parcels, etc. A topology is itself a type of dataset in a geodatabase that manages a set of rules and other properties associated with a collection of simple feature classes. The feature classes that participate in a topology are kept in a feature dataset so that all feature classes have the same spatial reference. A topology has an associated cluster tolerance that can be specified by the data modeler to fit the precision of the data.

You can apply topology to a limited area, which in today's very large databases gives considerable flexibility.

Consider the advantages of such focused topology in error identification. Creating a topological rule does not ensure that it will not be broken, but does ensure that the error will be identified.

Areas of the map that have been edited and changed but not checked for topological consistency according to the rules are called *dirty areas*. When the dirty areas are checked they are said to be *validated*. Note that any errors found are stored in the database. These errors can be fixed using editing tools in the GIS; they can be left in the database as errors; or they can be marked as exceptions to the rule. This means you don't have to validate an entire coverage before using the database.

The editing tools for fixing errors have broad applications. Editing can be done on two feature classes at once. Features can easily be merged and split. Features in one class can be constructed based on the geometry of selected features in another class.

In summary, topological editing tools enforce spatial integrity constraints across multiple feature classes. The arrangement whereby the rules are established in a separate dataset, rather than being embedded in the data, allows for more flexibility within an organization.

The applications of these capabilities are substantial. Imagine, for example, incorporating new construction that changes the location of an associated road. The topological differences between the road centerline and the school district can then be identified and resolved. Now imagine this on a much larger scale. A city in Canada, for example, wanted to integrate all the features mapped on a citywide CAD system into a GIS for the city, potentially a time-consuming and therefore expensive process. The ability to use multilayered topology greatly facilitated this process, raising efficiency and reducing costs considerably. Continually available in the geodatabase, topology is a desirable tool to ensure accurate data in all layers as features, layers, and relationships continue to be added to or amended in the GIS.

## Temporal data

Geographic information systems have been poor at handling temporal data in the past, at best providing multiple static overlays. This is changing with the development of software that can keep track of events happening at different times, either in the same place or in different places. Roughly, it works this way: a simple event—designated with the ID of the object, the time, the place, and, if necessary, the status of the object—places a dot in space at a time in a certain condition. Several simple events can be linked to form a track.

The software also handles complex events, each of which includes additional information about the nature of the object being tracked. A dynamic complex event could be tracking a plane of a certain model, flight number, number of passengers, fuel load, age of aircraft, and name of pilot. Complex stationary events can be envisaged resulting from the use of traffic sensors.

Currently, the software handles moving points or points over time, as well as lines and polygons, all in a similar manner. Examples of what lines might represent in a GIS handling temporal data would include military fronts or weather fronts. Polygons might stand for satellite footprints or oil slicks or temperature maps or precipitation maps.

The software allows for the mapping of these temporal events in geographic information systems. The data can be dynamically presented—played forward or backward. Real-time or near-real-time tracking of data is possible now. Data rates will depend on the communication links available, server speeds, and network speeds. Real-time tracking may include emergency response systems, threat detection, fleet tracking, or satellite tracking systems. A wide range of symbology can be employed, changing as the status of the event changes (as a hurricane intensifies, for example). With each playback, a histogram is available showing the number of events occurring over time, and this can be used for analysis of the events themselves

(e.g., frequency of enemy shelling) or to determine the playback time or repeated playback times for further analysis. All of the displays can be animated for use on a media player and have plug-and-play capability with your own animation engine.

It is possible to show temporal events (single or multiple) in the form of a clock. The clock wizard creates a circular chart, or clock, of temporal data, which can be used to analyze patterns of the data that may be missed when viewing the data on a table or map. Temporal data that illustrates specific aspects of the analysis, such as the nocturnal patterns of animal movement, can be produced simply by modifying the clock bands, changing colors, and using classes and legend settings.

Users can also create and apply preset or custom actions and query temporal data based on location information, feature attributes, or a combination of the two.

## Cartography

While GIS can produce elegant and beautiful maps (see next page), the process has often been cumbersome, particularly when multiple maps had to be created. This state of affairs is rapidly changing.

Now multiple maps can be made from a single geodatabase with a consistency of content and feature selection. This allows frequent updates to be cost-effective, as they are done once rather than on numerous files. Automation is achievable in the higher qualities of map sophistication rather than only in the lower mass-produced cartography. This use of intelligent cartography rather than "brute-force" cartography is starting to be applied to large-scale mapping operations.

You can anticipate more sophisticated allocations of symbology as well. Take the conceptually straightforward task of legend placement, for example: the rule could be, "place a legend somewhere over water or white space on the page such that it is no closer than 1.2 cm from either

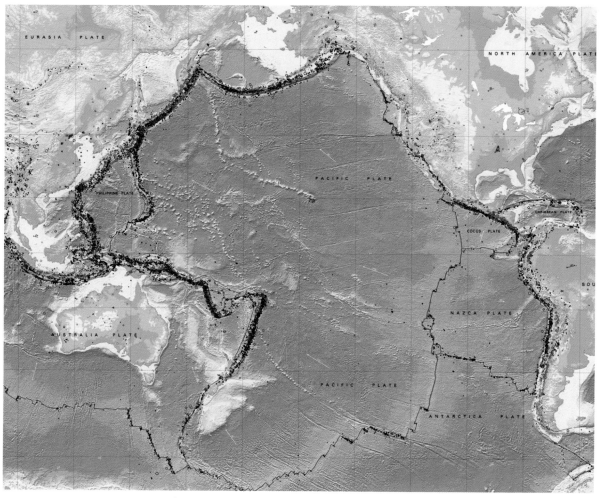

Figure 8.7 **GIS map of volcanoes, earthquakes, impact craters, and plate tectonics**

Courtesy of the USGS, Smithsonian Institution, and U.S. Naval Research Laboratory.

a coastline, the edge of the page, or another element." Such a task is easy to define even now.

However, mapping applications do not yet work with sufficiently refined notions of the shape of an object. Neither are they able intelligently to move objects like legends relative to coastlines. The main issue is the quality of the result. Yet quality is improving as computing power improves, along with the ability of displacement algorithms to displace complex geometries against other complex geometries.

Process models for intelligent map creation have not been especially well defined as a process or as a structure for handling the process. For example, to "construct a base map from a variety of GIS data layers," a mapmaker must know what procedures are needed for each layer in the map, which features are to appear, how to symbolize them, how text is placed for them, and what the priorities are for displaying the features (their relative importance). As problems go, this is complex and has several dimensions that must be simultaneously accounted for. Creating a process model for a map could be useful. To do so, you would have to assign a sequence to the set of operations used to construct the map. You would base that sequence on the interdependent relationships that exist between the data both logically and spatially. This model, in an interactive software modeling environment, would allow a mapmaker effectively to match data sources to layers, which are then used as inputs to the model, and then "run" the model. Such a model is modestly difficult to construct to work for one edition of a given map, but in a subsequent edition things may have changed and, therefore, the model must be flexible enough

to evaluate the data and then make the appropriate choices in processing the data or constructing a map.

Automated page layout, text placement, generalization, and publishing continue to grow and to evolve. Automation of generalization is possible if models can be created to move from one known map design to a second known map design at a different scale. The intelligent cartographic production of high-quality maps from a single geodatabase is becoming available for a growing array of map types in many industries.

## Network analysis

A new data structure for networks in geodatabases is being developed that will allow for much more realistic modeling of network connectivity for the purposes of routing and tracing. This data structure fully supports multimodal

### New data structure for networks

The new data structure for networks in geodatabases takes advantage of the object-relational data model (see chapter 9). Network connectivity can be based on geometry using a very rich connecting model, as well as database relationships such as air-flight relationships between airports or bus-route relationships to bus stops. These database relationships can be thought of as "virtual pathways" that allow for multimodal routing. This means that virtual people, commodities, or ideas can be transported by road, rail, ship, or airplane, transferring between each mode at known transfer points.

Turns are modeled as features, allowing them to be conflated between different feature classes. Turns can also be modeled as "implicit" turning movements, taking into account turning angles.

Networks are made of junction, edge, and turn elements derived from the geodatabase feature classes and object relationships. Elements have any number of attributes, such as travel time for cars, buses, emergency vehicles, heavy trucks, costs, restrictions, slope, number of lanes, pipe diameter, and so on. These attributes can be calculated from field values found in geodatabase tables or from a script. Attributes can be "dynamic," meaning they are calculated on demand. A dynamic attribute might query a recycling data structure containing current traffic conditions downloaded from the Web.

Network datasets are versioned to support planning requirements and multiuser editing. Networks are incrementally built, meaning that only edited portions of the network are rebuilt rather than requiring a full rebuild on each edit.

networks, such as those found in transportation (car, bus, bike, rail, shipping, air routes) and hydrology (stream channels, roadways, wastewater, basins).

The true value of the network structure is that it allows a flexible and extended query capability for the production of information products based on the network. With this query capability, commands take the form of instructions (set off by quotation marks, below) that can be almost as elaborate as you want to make them. The information products that are possible because of this extensive flexibility include the following:

- Shortest path. "Find the least-cost path (time, distance, etc.) through a series of stops." (Stops are network point locations.)
- Closest facility. "Given one location, find the closest (time, distance, etc.) facility (ATM, hospital, coffee shop, etc.)."
- Traveling salesman. "First find the optimal sequence to visit sets of stops, then run a shortest path."
- Allocate. "Build a shortest-path tree to define a 'service area' or a 'space-time defined space.'"
- Origin/destination matrix (OD matrix). "Build a matrix of cost between a set of origins (O) and destinations (D)." OD matrixes are used extensively in many network analyses (such as Tour, Location/Allocation, etc.). Matrixes are represented as a network.
- Vehicle routing. The core route optimizer. "Given a fleet of heterogeneous vehicles, in terms of capacity, available hours of service, cost to deploy, overtime costs, etc., and a set of heterogeneous customers, both vehicles and customers with time window constraints, find the optimal vehicle/customer assignment and route for the vehicle."
- Location/Allocation. "Simultaneously locate facilities and assign (allocate) demand to the facilities."
- Optimal path. "Find the optimal path through a set of connected edges." (Garbage trucks, newspaper delivery.)

- Tracing. Works on a directed network, where "flows" in one direction, such as water, electrons, wastewater, etc., can be handled. Tracing tasks can be thought of as a general query: "select what's upstream and downstream, find cycles, trace both up and downstream, or find dangles."

## Data conversion

In order to get information from different sources into your GIS, you will use one or more data conversion processes that translate data from one format to another. A variety of methods are available. The one you choose will depend on the format and quality of existing data, the format of data from outside sources, and the standards you have set. Your basic options are to develop the data in-house, have the data prepared by an outside contractor, or reformat some existing digital data.

Usually in-house database development is accomplished by means of one or more of the following methods:

- Digitizing
- Scanning
- Keyboard input
- File input
- File transfer

Using data prepared by an outsource contractor is common in situations where the database must be developed rapidly, there is little or no in-house capability, or ongoing maintenance and further database development are not anticipated. When using an outside contractor for this crucial step (remember the "garbage in, garbage out" rule), take a close look at past experience with the vendor, its familiarity with the software and hardware you are using, and the availability of updates. Other GIS users with similar types of applications and database requirements are good sources of information about commercial vendors.

As the sources of digital spatial data proliferate, so does the practice of reformatting existing digital data into a format usable by your GIS. Currently, software built by Safe Software and ESRI is available that allows users to easily integrate multiple data formats (from open or proprietary sources) into their GIS. It is now possible to directly read at least sixty-five spatial data formats, export more than fifty data formats, and even diagram and model your own spatial data format.

*Interoperability* is the term used to refer to this capability of systems or components to perform in multiple environments or to exchange data with other systems or components. Figure 8.8 lists some of the formats supported by the ArcGIS interoperability extension. (You'll find a key to the terminology used in this chart at the bottom of page 91.)

A potentially far-reaching capability is "schema change" carried out during the transformation procedures. This allows algorithms for classification change to bring two datasets into the same schema and avoid the discontinuities at the join, particularly at administrative boundaries. This will greatly facilitate large area/national/continental/global database building from local/regional inputs.

Nevertheless, each data conversion method takes time, brings an associated cost, and may degrade information content. The development of digital data exchange formats and the proliferation of conversion and translation software have made sharing data easier, but you may still encounter problems reformatting data from other systems. Don't assume that the data is easy to use because it is in a digital form.

At times you will find that the cost of reformatting data into something usable is not cost-effective. For example, polygon data from one type of software may be only graphic, with no associated attributes or topology (CAD data, for example). The cost of rendering this data into something suitable for your work may be greater than the cost of in-house digitizing from hard copy. (There is an interchange format to get data from CAD systems called DXF.)

Another potential difficulty is that you may not get adequate documentation for determining the accuracy, currency, source, or anything else about the data. This means you'd have no way of verifying whether the digitized data would meet your needs. Even if you are desperate for the data and believe the source to be credible, you should use such data only with extreme caution. Consider the following as a useful way to think of the integrity of data: 80 percent of data equals 20 percent of problems; 20 percent of data equals 80 percent of problems.

| ArcGIS data interoperability extension—supported formats | | | | | | |
|---|---|---|---|---|---|---|
| Format name | Identifier | Data import | Data export | Direct read | Browse tree | Options on open |
| Adobe Illustrator (EPS) | IEPS | No | Yes | No | No | No |
| Autodesk AutoCAD DWG/DXF | DWG | Yes | Yes | Yes | No | Yes |
| Autodesk MapGuide SDL | SDL | Yes | Yes | Yes | Yes | No |
| BC Electronic Submission Framework (ESF) FTA GML | ESF FTA | Yes | Yes | Yes | No | No |
| BC Electronic Submission Framework (ESF) RESULT GML | ESF RESULTS | Yes | Yes | Yes | No | No |
| BC MOEP | MOEP | Yes | No | Yes | No | No |
| CGDEF ComGraphix Data Exchange Format | CGDEF | Yes | Yes | Yes | Yes | Yes |
| CITS/QLF Data transfer Format (QLF) File | QLF | Yes | Yes | Yes | Yes | No |
| Comma Separated Values (CSV) | CSV | Yes | Yes | Yes | No | Yes |
| Danish DSFL | DSFL | Yes | No | Yes | Yes | Yes |
| Danish DSFL (XML format for Danish DSFL) | XDK | Yes | No | Yes | No | No |
| Danish UFO | UFO | Yes | Yes | Yes | Yes | No |
| DB2 Database (Attributes Only IBM) | DB2 | Yes | Yes | No | No | Yes |
| DB2 Spatial (IBM) | DB2SPATIAL | Yes | Yes | Yes | No | Yes |
| dBASE III (DBF) | DBF | Yes | Yes | Yes | No | No |
| Delaware DXF Submission | DELAWARE DXF SUBMISSION | Yes | No | Yes | No | No |
| Design Files (DGN; Bentley/Intergraph) to v8 | IGDS | Yes | Yes | Yes | No | Yes |
| DLG USGS (Digital Line Graph) | DLG | Yes | No | Yes | Yes | No |
| EPS (Encapsulated PostScript) | EPS | No | Yes | No | No | Yes |
| ESRI ArcInfo Coverage | ARCINFO | Yes | Yes | Yes | No | No |
| ESRI ArcInfo Export (EGO) | EGO | Yes | Yes | Yes | Yes | Yes |
| ESRI ArcInfo Generate | ARCGEN | Yes | Yes | Yes | No | Yes |
| ESRI Geodatabase (MDB) 9.0/3.3 personal | GEODATABASE MDB | Yes | Yes | No | No | No |
| ESRI Geodatabase (SDE) 9.0/3.3 enterprise | GEODATABASE SDE | Yes | Yes | No | No | No |
| ESRI Geodatabase (XML) | GEODATABASE XML | Yes | No | Yes | No | No |
| ESRI GML | ESRI GML | Yes | Yes | Yes | Yes | No |
| ESRI PC ARC/INFO Coverage | ARCINFO | Yes | No | Yes | No | No |
| ESRI Shape | SHAPE | Yes | Yes | Yes | No | No |
| ESRI Spatial Database Engine v3.x/ArcSDE 8.x | SDE3D | No | Yes | No | No | No |
| Facet XDR | FACET | Yes | Yes | Yes | Yes | No |
| FME Feature Store File (FFS) | FFS | Yes | Yes | Yes | Yes | Yes |
| GDMS Dataset | GDMS | Yes | No | Yes | No | No |
| GenaMap | GENAMAP | Yes | No | Yes | Yes | No |
| GEODESYS StruMap | STRUMAP | Yes | Yes | Yes | Yes | No |
| Geographix CDF (WhiteStar) | WHITESTAR | Yes | Yes | Yes | Yes | No |
| GeoMedia Access Warehouse (Intergraph) | FMQ SQL | Yes | Yes | Yes | No | Yes |
| GEOost Names Server | GEONET | Yes | No | Yes | No | No |
| GML v2 | GML2 | Yes | Yes | Yes | Yes | No |
| GPX - GPS (XML) | GPX | Yes | No | Yes | Yes | No |
| IDRISI Vector Format | IDRISI | Yes | Yes | Yes | Yes | No |
| Intergraph MGE | MGE | Yes | Yes | Yes | No | Yes |

Figure 8.8 **Current data interoperability capabilities**

| | | | | | | |
|---|---|---|---|---|---|---|
| ISO8211 | ISO8211 | Yes | No | Yes | No | No |
| Laser Scan IFF - Internal Feature Format | IFF | Yes | Yes | Yes | Yes | No |
| MapInfo MID/MIF | MIF | Yes | Yes | Yes | Yes | No |
| MapInfo TAB | MAPINFO | Yes | Yes | Yes | Yes | No |
| Mercator MCF | MCF | Yes | Yes | Yes | Yes | No |
| Microsoft Access Database (attributes only) | MDB | Yes | Yes | Yes | No | Yes |
| MicroStation Geographics | GO | Yes | Yes | Yes | No | Yes |
| ODBC Database (attributes only) | ODBC | Yes | Yes | Yes | No | Yes |
| Oracle 7 Database (attributes only) | ORACLE DB | Yes | Yes | No | No | Yes |
| Oracle B/Bi/9i Database (attributes only) | ORACLE DB | Yes | Yes | No | No | Yes |
| Oracle Bi/9i Spatial (Obkect) | ORACLEBi | Yes | Yes | Yes | No | Yes |
| Oracle Spatial (Relational) | ORACLE | Yes | Yes | No | No | Yes |
| Oracle SQL Loader (attributes only) | SQLLDR | No | Yes | No | No | No |
| OS (GB) MasterMap (GML 2) | DNF | Yes | No | Yes | Yes | No |
| OS (GB) NTF Products | NTF | Yes | No | Yes | Yes | No |
| PenMetrics GRD | GRD | Yes | Yes | Yes | No | Yes |
| PHOCUS PHODAT | PHOCUS | Yes | No | Yes | Yes | No |
| PostGIS Database | POSTGIS | Yes | Yes | Yes | No | Yes |
| PostgreSQL Database | POSTGRES | Yes | Yes | Yes | No | Yes |
| Raster Image (PNG/GIF) | PNG | No | Yes | No | No | No |
| REGIS | REGIS | Yes | Yes | Yes | Yes | No |
| S-57 (ENC) Hydrographic Data Format | S57 | Yes | No | Yes | Yes | No |
| SAIF (Spatial Archive and Interchange Format) | SAIF | Yes | No | Yes | Yes | No |
| SDTS (Spatial Data Transfer Standard) | SDTS | Yes | No | Yes | Yes | No |
| SLF (Standard Linear Format) | SLF | Yes | No | Yes | Yes | No |
| SVG (Scalable Vector Graphics) | SVG | No | Yes | No | No | No |
| Swedish KF85 | KF85 | Yes | Yes | Yes | Yes | No |
| Swedish MASIK | MASIK | Yes | Yes | Yes | No | No |
| TIGERLine | TIGER | Yes | No | Yes | Yes | No |
| TOP10GML | TOP10GML | Yes | No | Yes | Yes | No |
| VML (Vector Markup Language) | VML | No | Yes | No | No | No |
| VPF Reader (Vector Product Format) Database | VPF DB | Yes | No | Yes | No | Yes |
| VRML (Virtual Reality Modelling Language) | VRML | No | Yes | No | No | No |
| WFS (Web Feature Service) | WFS | Yes | No | Yes | No | Yes |
| XML (generic) | XML | Yes | Yes | Yes | No | Yes |

| Key |
|---|
| **Data import:** The ability to import data in this format to a pGD8 using Simple Import tool. |
| **Data export:** This format is available as an FME-supported data source when using Simple Export tool. |
| **Direct read:** The ability to view format directly through the ArcCatalog Browse tree or by creating a connection via the Interap Datasources node in ArcCatalog. |
| **Browse tree:** The ability to view format directly through the ArcCatalog Browse tree or the Add Data dialog box in ArcMap without creating a connection via the Interap Datasources node. |
| **Options on open:** Some of the formats have default options (or settings) that are available through the FME Automatic translator. You need to create a connection to the dataset via the Interap Datasources node to access these settings. |

Figure 8.8 (continued)

# Choose a logical data model

*The new generation of object-oriented data models is ushering in a host of new GIS capabilities and should be considered for all new implementations. Yet the relational model is still prevalent, and the savvy GIS manager will be conversant in both.*

Ideally at this point in the GIS planning process, you understand the data elements needed to produce your information products so well that you have identified by name any logical links required between them. You know where your data is going to come from; you can picture its limitations as well as its dimensions.

You are ready for the next step—deciding how you're going to structure the data according to one of three logical data models: relational, object-oriented, or object-relational. You will be modeling the organization of the data after one or the other of them—whichever allows your data to be stored and manipulated most effectively to create your information products. Each model affords certain characteristics that would help or hinder you in setting up this management structure for your particular database. You'll compare what you know about your data (and what you need to do with it) against what you learn about these models to see which one is the best match.

The system's end users aren't directly concerned with this data modeling. But for you, the GIS leader, it becomes a significant concern at this juncture because the tools to manage your database—with which to add, store, delete, change, and retrieve your data—are software applications. Therefore, the model you choose for the organization of your database will factor into your decision on what software system to recommend to manage it.

The crux of the issue is that a logical data model must "describe" a complex version of the real world in a database. Such a model not only represents the data in computer logic but also describes the data in terms the computer can virtually "understand"—the model sets up its version of the real world with all its rules and orders that your data must follow. How much it will cost to build and use such a database will depend on how closely you want to model reality.

Determining the best logical model and then building it requires a decision, and now is the time to start thinking about it. Once you've examined the three types of logical data models, you can compare the advantages and disadvantages of each using the table in figure 9.3. Another table, figure 9.4, lists some basic situations alongside the capabilities characteristic of the model needed to handle them. Finding a situation that resembles yours, you may find it useful to consider the model(s) suggested for it. Just remember, though, there's no substitute for thoroughly understanding your options.

Those charged with choosing, describing, then building the conceptual database design will find the more thorough examination of the relational and object-oriented models—and tips on how to structure your database after them at chapter's end—of particular interest.

## Types of logical data models

Essentially, data becomes useful when it's put together into the information you need to do your work. Putting it together becomes easier after it's been logically linked with the data associated with or related to it and then stored that way. Basically, each type of logical data model describes its own distinctive computer logic behind how to store this virtually connected data in the state of readiness required for GIS to create information from it.

The relational database model stores collections of tables that are associated with each other based on fields they share in common (e.g., tables that contain the same column storing values for a single attribute). In an object-oriented model, instead of as rows and tables, data is stored as objects or instances of a class (a group sharing the same set of attributes and behaviors). For an even newer model, the object-relational, GIS software enhances the structure of the relational model with some capabilities of the object-oriented model.

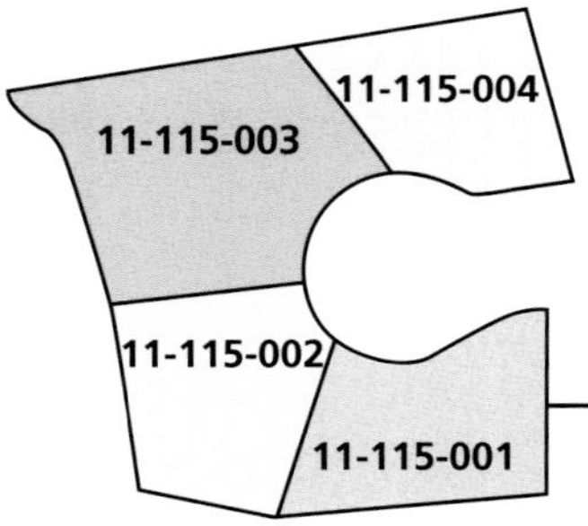


| Parcel-No. | Owner |
|---|---|
| 11-115-001 | Brown, D |
| 11-115-002 | Greene, J |
| 11-115-003 | Smith, L |
| 11-115-004 | Hester, D |

| Parcel-No. | Zoning | Legal-Area |
|---|---|---|
| 11-115-001 | R1 | 12,001 |
| 11-115-002 | R2 | 15,775 |
| 11-115-003 | COM | 19,136 |
| 11-115-004 | R1 | 13,005 |

Figure 9.1 **Tables linked by a common field**

## The relational data model

Currently, the vast majority of geospatial digital data in the world is stored using relational data models. In a database set up as a relational data model, the data is stored as collections of tables (called *relations*) logically associated with each other by shared attributes. The individual records are stored as rows in the tables, while the attributes are stored as columns. Each column can contain attribute data of only one kind: date, character string, numeric, and so forth. Usually, tables are normalized—calibrated to one another—to minimize redundancy. Storing spatial data in a relational database is greatly facilitated by using search engines such as SDE by ESRI, which is software that allows the GIS to read spatial data stored in common relational database management systems (RDBMS), such as Oracle.

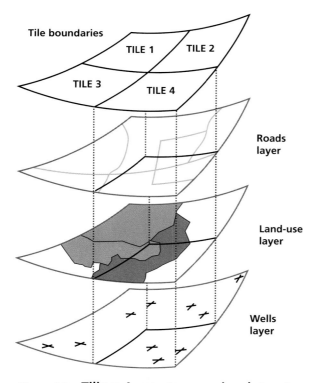

Tile boundaries

TILE 1  TILE 2
TILE 3  TILE 4

Roads layer

Land-use layer

Wells layer

Figure 9.2  **Tiling: A way to organize datasets**

A GIS links spatial data to tabular data. In figure 9.1, you can see the links (shaded) between the spatial data displayed on the map (e.g., parcel numbers) and the table containing attributes about features on the map. A separate but related table uses the common Parcel-No. attribute column to link to the table showing owner information. There could be many additional tables available for use in GIS analysis and thematic display all linked back to one another by a thread of common fields.

Relational data models use a fixed set of built-in data types, such as numbers, dates, and character strings, to segregate different types of attribute data. This offers a tightly constrained but highly efficient method of describing the real world. Relational models execute and deliver results quickly, but require sophisticated application programming to model complex real-world situations in a meaningful way.

Consider the task of dispatching an emergency vehicle. Finding the quickest route requires detailed information about the direction and capacity of each street at different times of the day and the types of signals and change controls at each intersection. These complex variables require a large number of interacting tables, which the relational model makes possible. The strength of relational tables is that they simplify the real world and give swift and reliable answers to the queries that they can handle.

When you develop your logical data model using the relational approach, you may need to consider the layering and tiling structure of your data, also known as the *map library*. (There is a newer approach that uses seamless databases, but it doesn't work under the relational model. For that you need an object-oriented approach.) In this structure, a relational library of map partitions (or tiles) organizes geographic data into datasets of manageable size in an intuitively navigable tile system (see figure 9.2).

To set up the organization of data in accordance with the relational model you must consider all the factors involved in building the data layers of the map library: map units and projection, storage precision, attribute columns for the layered features, data sources and intended uses, logical linkages, data accuracy, and standards. Here is where planning pays off. Most of this information can be found in the MIDL (chapter 7). (For more on the relational approach to the conceptual database design, see page 101.)

## The object-oriented data model

Newer than their relational counterparts, object-oriented data models allow for rich and complex descriptions of the real world in a data structure that users find easy to understand. Objects can be modeled after real-world entities (like sewers, fires, forests, building owners) and can be given behavior that mimics or models some relevant aspect of their behavior in the real world. One simplistic way of thinking about the difference between this and the relational model is that the object stores the information about itself (all its attributes) within itself instead of in a bunch of related tables.

An object model of a street network, for instance, uses lines depicting streets. Each street segment shows behavior that models its real-world actions, such as traffic flowing in a particular direction, with the number of cars per hour able to traverse it at any given hour of the day or night.

### Objects

Objects represent real-world entities such as buildings, streams, or bank accounts in the virtual reality of the computer. Objects contain properties (attributes) that define their state and methods that define their behavior. Objects interact with one another by passing messages that invoke their behaviors.

### Attributes

Attributes are the properties that define the state of an object, like the category of a street, the name of a building's owner, or the peak capacity of a storm drain.

### Behaviors

Behaviors are the methods or the operations that an object can perform. For example, this virtual street may "know" how to calculate the increase in time needed to travel its length as rush hour approaches, or an account may know how to subtract money from its balance when a withdrawal is made. These behaviors can also be used to send messages to other objects, communicate the state of an object by reporting current values, store new values, or perform calculations.

### Encapsulation of behavior

By means of *encapsulation*, the essence of the object-oriented model, an object encapsulates (or encloses within itself) attributes and behaviors. The data within an object can be accessed only in accordance with the object's behaviors. In this way, encapsulation protects data from corruption by other objects, and also masks the internal details of objects from the rest of the system. Encapsulation also provides a degree of data independence, so that objects that send or receive messages do not need to be modified when interacting with an object whose behavior has changed. This allows changes in a program without the cost of a major restructuring, as would be the case with a relational structure.

### Messages

Objects communicate with one another through messages. Messages are the act of one object invoking another object's behavior. A message is the name of an object followed by the name of a behavior the object knows how to carry out: "property/subdivision," for example. The object that initiates a message is called the *sender*, while the object that receives the message is called the *receiver*.

### Relationships

Relationships describe how objects are associated with each other. They define rules for creating, modifying, and removing objects. The kinds of relationships that can be used in the object-oriented data model, including inheritance, association, aggregation, and composition, are described on pages 105–107.

### Classes

A class is a way to group objects that share the same set of attributes and behaviors into a template. Objects of a particular class are referred to as *instances* of that class. For example, the land parcel where you live is just one of many parcels that exist in your city, but each could be thought of as a unique instance. Unique as each one is, all these parcels share certain useful characteristics, like building type or zoning code; these shared characteristics are expressed as *classes*.

Determining the classes that you will need is an important step in your database design, allowing you to then diagram the relationships you need in your data model. (More on relationships and class diagrams starting on page 105.)

### The object-relational data model

The object-relational data model is the most recent development in the domain of logical data models. In such a system, GIS software extends the relational database to incorporate object-oriented behaviors that manage business logic and data integrity. Expressed in terms of subject matter experts and business users, this model blends well with other enterprise business systems. Data is not encapsulated, and remains in standard business tables supporting standard enterprise integration and management.

The object-relational model brings advantages of speed (important in large databases), the ability to handle complexity, and the database-building integrity of object-oriented designs. This model carries with it the additional advantage of supporting an extended form of Structured Query Language (SQL) and the ability to access typical relational database management systems. This alone

can be an important consideration in enterprise-wide systems where other business applications need to access or contribute data to the GIS database.

Object-relational data models incorporate characteristics of both the relational and object-oriented databases. If you recall, the relational model uses tables with a fixed set of built-in data types (for example, numbers, date); in the object-oriented data model, objects have unique attributes, and behaviors are encapsulated within the object. Enter the object-relational model. It extends the relational model by adding into some of the attribute columns a new and richer type of data structure, called the *abstract data type*. Abstract data types are created by combining the basic alphanumeric data types used in the relational model, or by storing a binary representation of the object in a BLOB (Binary Large Object) field.

Abstract data types allow you to add specialized behavior to the relational model. This flexibility in data structure enables the object-relational database model to more closely describe the real world than can the purely relational model.

Object-relational software continues to improve and add more object functionality. Changing rapidly, the object-relational model is becoming better at taking advantage of components of the object-oriented data model.

## Advantages and disadvantages

All these models have advantages and disadvantages, as illustrated in the table comparing them (figure 9.3). How much these characteristics qualify as strengths or weaknesses will depend on your specific needs. In determining what data model is appropriate for your GIS, you must consider the types of functions required to create your information products. For example, if you need to perform a lot of network analysis with complex intersections or junctions, you could choose an object-relational model. If your information products do not require the type of

| Data model | Advantages | Disadvantages |
|---|---|---|
| The relational | <ul><li>Simple table structures that are easy to read.</li><li>Intuitive, simple user interface.</li><li>Many end-user tools (i.e., macros and scripts) are available.</li><li>Easy modification and addition of new relationships, data, and records.</li><li>Tables describing geographic features with common attributes are easily used.</li><li>Attribute tables can be linked to tables describing the topology necessary for a GIS.</li><li>Direct access to data provides fast and efficient performance.</li><li>Independence of data from the application.</li><li>Optimized for GIS query and analysis.</li><li>Large amounts of GIS data are available in this format.</li><li>Large pool of experienced developers, developer tools, textbooks, and consultants.</li></ul> | <ul><li>Limited representation of the real world.</li><li>Limited flexibility of queries and data management.</li><li>Slow sequential access.</li><li>Complex data relationships are difficult to model and often require specialized database application programmers.</li><li>Complex relationships must be expressed as procedures in every program that accesses the database.</li><li>Performance penalty due to the need to reassemble data structures every time the data is accessed.</li><li>Changes in a program may incur the cost of a major restructuring.</li></ul> |
| The object-oriented | <ul><li>Allows complex representations of the real world.</li><li>No need to know the inner workings of an object because encapsulation, combining object attributes and behaviors, makes an object accessible through a well-defined set of methods and attributes.</li><li>Supports multiple levels of generalization, aggregation, and association.</li><li>Maintains history in the database.</li><li>Integrates well with simulation modeling techniques.</li><li>Multiple simultaneous updating (versioning) is possible.</li><li>Using objects that occur naturally, the model has an intuitive feel to it.</li><li>Well-suited for modeling complex data relationships.</li><li>Requires less code in GIS programs, meaning fewer bugs and lower maintenance costs.</li><li>Ensures a high level of data integrity (new data must follow the behavior rules).</li><li>Encapsulation allows for changes in a program without the cost of a major restructuring.</li></ul> | <ul><li>Although object-oriented data models allow complex representations of the real world, complex models are more difficult to design and build. The choice of objects is crucial.</li><li>Import and exchange with other types of databases is difficult.</li><li>Some business applications may not be able to access or contribute to an object-oriented database.</li><li>Large and complex models can be slow to execute.</li><li>Dependent on a thorough description of real-world phenomena (particularly difficult in the natural world).</li><li>Object-oriented databases require the use of object-oriented computer languages for their analysis, but fewer people are trained in such programming.</li></ul> |

Figure 9.3 **Comparing three types of logical data models**

| Data model | Advantages | Disadvantages |
|---|---|---|
| The object-relational | • Fast execution.<br>• Most features of object-oriented databases are available in object-relational.<br>• Uniform repository of geographic data; allows use of legacy and non-GIS databases.<br>• Data entry and editing are more accurate.<br>• Data integrity is high (new data must follow the behavior rules).<br>• Users can work with more intuitive data objects.<br>• Simultaneous data editing (versioning) is possible.<br>• History tracking and remote data replication can be accomplished.<br>• Less need for programming applications to model complex relationships.<br>• Makes possible the close integration with business model databases and the standard backup and support that accompany those models. | • Compromise between object-oriented and relational data models.<br>• Data encapsulation can be violated through direct SQL access to the data.<br>• Limited support for object relationships.<br>• Complex relationships are more difficult to model than when using a pure object-oriented data model. |

Figure 9.3 (continued)

functionality provided by object-oriented capabilities, you might choose the more established relational data model.

Choosing which logical data model is appropriate for your organization is not always a straightforward task. Much has been said about the object-oriented and object-relational data models and how they will continue to affect the traditional relational implementation of GIS. However, this decision should be based on more than the conceptual differences.

Since the 1980s, most GIS databases have been based on the relational data model. But given the difficulty faced by this model in describing the complex behaviors of real-world objects, some GIS software vendors have opted for the object-oriented and object-relational models to support these more complex data structures. Choosing which model is most appropriate for your organization

will in part determine which software you purchase. If a primary need is to model complex data relationships, then you better have a system that supports it. It boils down to the question of which data model is most suitable for the work you want to do. Figure 9.4 describes some typical data modeling situations, along with the logical model characteristics needed to handle them, and suggests data models that would be appropriate.

You always consider costs before deciding what to recommend to upper management, and relative costs may well factor into your assessment of which logical data model will best meet your needs. Comparing costs of your high-priority information products is one standard approach. Set up two categories of costs for each data model, then estimate the costs for developing your priority information products under each category for

| Data modeling situation | Logical model characteristics | Suggested logical data model |
|---|---|---|
| Forest inventory of tree stands, rivers, and roads for forest-harvesting analysis. | Simple relationships between features. | Relational |
| Addition of new forest stand attributes as forest matures. Addition of features such as property boundaries. | Easy modification and addition of new features and attributes as time passes. | Relational |
| Small staff. Need to minimize training and implementation time. | Simple, easy-to-use interface. Database that is simple and easy to design and build. | Relational |
| Enterprise-wide system must connect to existing sales and business partner databases. | Connects well to existing databases. | Relational or object-relational |
| Large business needs to perform suitable site analysis for locating new stores. | Need to use existing demographic data. | Relational or object-relational |
| Need to do real-time flood forecasting along a river system. | Complex representation of real world. | Object-oriented or object-relational |
| Need to simulate traffic flow through a street network during an emergency situation. | Integration with sophisticated simulation models. | Object-oriented |
| Major utility company needs to simultaneously update many parts of its large database as daily additions and repairs are made. | Multiple simultaneous updating (versioning). | Object-oriented or object-relational |
| Database is in constant use in mission-critical, life-dependent situations. | High level of data integrity. | Object-oriented or object-relational |
| Numerous new applications will be developed over time. | Low application development costs once initial model is developed. | Object-oriented |
| Complex analysis of natural resource features in large watershed (e.g., Columbia River Basin). | Fast to execute, particularly for large, complex analysis. | Object-relational |
| Many legacy relational databases and non-GIS databases to be linked to new GIS. | Links well with all types of databases. | Object-relational |
| Water utility needs to model water network, including water mains, laterals, valves, pump stations, and drains. | Complex relationships. Inheritance of attributes and behaviors. | Object-oriented or object-relational |
| Large amount of data maintenance and updating. | High level of data integrity. | Object-oriented or object-relational |

Figure 9.4  **Suggested data models for some typical modeling situations**

each data model. Assign the various costs to either the database creation category or the application programming category. Under the former, include costs of developing and maintaining the database(s) needed to create the information products (e.g., costs of database design, data conversion, ongoing data exchange with legacy systems, staff training, and so on). Within the application category, list the costs of programming the application and any database manipulation required specifically for the information products. Use this approach with actual figures, if such data is available, or with relative rankings if not. What are the real costs of preparing twenty or thirty information products over the life of your system, using each logical data model for comparison? Once you've factored this in, you can make your choice of models and begin work on your conceptual database design. Next we explore the tasks involved in developing a database, specifically under the relational and object-oriented models, and by inference, under the object-relational model insofar as it incorporates pertinent elements of both.

# Designing the conceptual database: Relational model

The layering structure you choose for your map library is important; it will affect database maintenance, data query, and overall performance. You determine the content of each data layer as part of the conceptual database design. How you organize your data layers depends on how you will be using the data. You thought this through when you prepared the master input data list. (After reviewing the terms below, you can revisit your MIDL and make any necessary modifications.) In designing the layers, you'll be taking into account many factors, some of which are defined here.

## Layer

A layer is a logical grouping of geographic features (parcels, roads, wells, etc.) that can also be referred to as a *coverage* or *theme*.

First, review the MIDL to compile your final list of all the necessary layers. Early on, you should finalize the

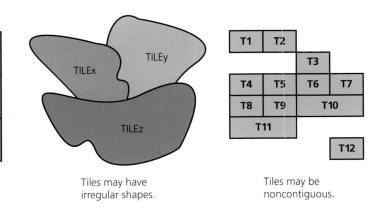

A regular arbitrary grid is a simple, convenient structure, particularly for point or polygon data.

Tiles may have irregular shapes.

Tiles may be noncontiguous.

Figure 9.5 **Tile structure options**

layer-naming convention. Settle on a unique (hopefully, descriptive) name for each and every layer. Once agreed on by the GIS team and published to the entire user group, these layer names are to be adhered to rigorously throughout the rest of the conceptual database design. It's good practice to name layers descriptively so that the contents can be easily recognized.

## Tile structure

Review figure 9.2. The tile structure is the spatial index to the data in your GIS, and another thing that must be finalized before you can proceed with your design. Tiling speeds up access because the system indexes the data geographically, allowing you to search just the area of immediate interest and not the whole thing. Remember, GIS datasets tend to be large, so anything we can do to cut to the chase pays dividends. Once established, tile structure is labor-intensive to change, so think carefully about your tile selection. For example, it is better to frame your tiles using physical objects such as roads rather than on political boundaries that may change over time.

An abstract grid, such as USGS quadrangle boundaries, offers a stable, somewhat standard, tile structure, too. If your IPDs show that your most important applications will need access by quadrangle, then making the same quadrangles your tiling unit could be beneficial.

## Map projection

Use a single coordinate system for all the data layers in a map library. Data can originate from different projections but should be projected into a common coordinate system before being added to the library. This is imperative, since once you're in a mapping display mode, data with different coordinate systems or projections will not even appear in the same space.

## Units (imperial or metric)

Use a single set of map units for your library. Sometimes the map projection and coordinate system you choose determines the units you employ. For example, the state plane coordinate system typically stores data in feet, while UTM stores data in meters.

## Precision (single or double)

The storage precision of x,y coordinate data is important. Review your IPDs to determine what precision is necessary for your organization. Coordinates are either single-precision real numbers (six to seven significant digits) or double-precision (thirteen to fourteen significant digits). The precision you choose also affects your data storage requirements because, as you might expect, double-precision requires more data storage capacity.

## Features (entities)

If you can, organize features on the layers so that points, lines, and polygons are stored in separate layers. For example, you might store parcels (represented by polygons) in one layer, roads (represented by lines) in another layer, and hydrants (stored as points) in yet another. (And just to spice things up, these days we also have cell-based grids representing images.)

Features should be organized thematically as well. For example, roads and streams could both be represented as lines, but it wouldn't make sense to represent them on the same line layer because they are different things and therefore need to be considered independently.

## Attributes

Identify a set of attributes that pertain to the features in each layer. Say, for example, for each well site (a feature represented by a point), you want to know the following attributes: the well's identification number, depth, pipe diameter, type of pump, and gallons per minute. These comprise the data elements that need to be present and available to become part of your information product about this feature, so you will set them up as attribute columns in the layers.

## Intended uses

You also need to know the intended use of the data. For example, if your city's water source comes from a series of public water wells, you should determine if you want only public wells in this layer or if you also want to include private wells. It is important to review your information product descriptions to determine the data requirements for each layer. If, in looking over your IPD, you are reminded that you need information about the public wells only, then you would not include data about private wells as attributes in the layers.

## Logical linkages

When designing your layers, make sure that the logical linkages—between the data layers and any attribute files necessary to make your information products—have been established. It is important to look for linkages that apply

but might not be in place. If you identify logical linkages not currently in the data but required for a product, you have to perform the necessary tasks to set up those links. For example, to link tables you can use a field they share in common. This common field, say "Parcel-No.," is referred to as a *key* when it is contained in both tables and can be used to link them together.

## Source

You must know—and document in the metadata—the source of each data layer. The source information will affect the data standards set for each map library.

## Data accuracy and standards

Data accuracy and standards ensure that the layers in your database will serve as source data for meaningful analysis. For example, earlier we mentioned that all layers in a map library should have a similar resolution. Think of what would happen if you forgot that the resolution of a certain input dataset was only 1:200,000, while all the other datasets in that map library were digitized at a much higher resolution of 1:6,000. In an overlay analysis, using the lower resolution dataset with the rest of the data

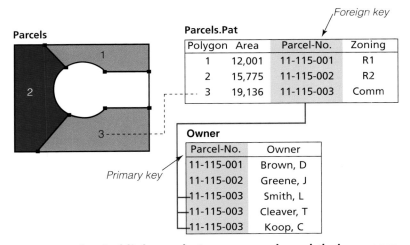

Figure 9.6   **Logical linkages between parcels and their owners**

| Layer name | Real-world object | Feature type | Attribute users need to see |
|---|---|---|---|
| Street | City streets | Lines | Name, class of street |
| Block group | Census block groups | Polygons | Age group population counts, median household income |
| Zone | Land-use zoning | Polygons | Zoning type |
| Land use | Actual activity of land use | Polygons | Activity type |
| Railroads | Main train lines | Lines | Railroad name |
| Sewer complaints | Incident locations | Points | Address, date, and description of incident |

Figure 9.7 **Descriptive documentation of layers**

could profoundly compromise the validity of the resulting output. Worse yet, users unaware of the inaccuracy might base a crucial business decision on erroneous analysis. Making sure this can't happen is incumbent on the GIS leader, and the way to make sure is through rigorous documentation in the metadata.

The matrix in figure 9.7 shows a list of some data layers from a typical municipal government GIS. It shows the layer name, the real-world objects represented by the name, the type of feature, and for each layer the attributes users need to see in their information product. You need to develop a matrix, probably much longer than this one, that describes all of the layers in your design. Keep

in mind that it's not unusual for layer counts within an established GIS in a large municipal setting to number in the hundreds.

In addition to meeting standards for data accuracy, you should make sure that the system you purchase adheres to the main IT standards of interoperability in general, shown on the bottom half of figure 9.8. The figure shows the main standards being used today, the ones from the more frequently used sources; you should know they exist and be familiar with some of the options of GIS standards (at top) as well.

Standards become increasingly important as systems get larger. An enterprise system needs to adopt standards

| Geographic information systems standards | |
|---|---|
| Metadata | FGDC content standard for digital geospatial metadata, ISO 19115 |
| Data content | FGDC framework model, ArcGIS data models |
| Spatial data format | SDTS, GML, VPF, KML, shapefile, ISO-S57 |
| Web-based spatial services | WMS, WFS, WCS, CS-W |
| Spatial data management | Simple features specification for SQL, OLE/COM, CORBA, ISO 19125:1,2 ISO 13249:3 |

| Information technology standards | |
|---|---|
| Web services | XML, WSDL, UDDI, SOAP |
| Network protocols | NFS, TCP/IP, HTTP |
| Software API | JAVA, .NET, CORBA, COM, SQL |
| Emerging standards | Security: GeoXACML |

Figure 9.8 **Standards relevant to interoperability**

so that any part of it can use the control database and write broadly used applications. The implications for regional, national, and global GIS are obvious. Granted, standards are not a mature part of the technology yet, but a lot of work is going on by different groups and various countries as this issue continues to develop.

# Designing the conceptual database: Object-oriented model

When modeling your data structure after the object-oriented approach, you use the concept of class as a way to group objects that share the same set of attributes and behaviors—a very different template than the layering in the relational model's map library. Determining the classes that you need to organize your data is an important beginning step in this, a very different conceptual database design model, which offers a new way of thinking about objects.

Objects stand for real things, but once they are part of a class they become more flexible than the real thing—like a bank account that can substract money from itself. Objects are somewhat like capsules of data and behavior all rolled into one. Once you group each class into a template, the objects within it become instances of that class, retaining their uniqueness. Being part of a class, however, offers advantages of its own. Classes can be nested to any degree, and *inheritance*—gaining attributes and behaviors from another class—will automatically accumulate down through all the levels. The resulting tree-like structure is known as a *class hierarchy.*

Once you determine the classes, you can chart all the other ways objects can be associated with each other—in *relationships,* another important concept in the object-oriented model. Determining the classes that you need enables you to diagram the relationships you need; these *class diagrams,* in turn, allow you to diagram your database design.

## Relationships

Relationships describe how objects are associated with each other. They define rules for creating, modifying, and removing objects. Several kinds of relationships can be used in the object-oriented data model, including the following:

- Inheritance allows one class to inherit the attributes and behaviors of one or more other classes. The class that inherits attributes and behaviors is known as the *subclass.* The parent class is referred to as the *superclass.* In addition to the behaviors they inherit, subclasses may add or override inherited attributes and behaviors. A superclass is referred to as a *generalization* of its subclasses, and a subclass is a *specialization* of its superclass. For example, a house is a specialization of a building, and a building is a generalization of a house. A house class can inherit attributes and behaviors of the building class, such as number of floors, rooms, and construction type.

- An *association* is a general relationship between objects. Each association, in turn, can have a *multiplicity* associated with it, which defines the number of objects associated with another object. For example, an association might tell you that the object "owner" can own one or many houses. *Aggregation* and *composition* are specialized types of associations.

- Aggregation is a particular type of association. Objects can contain other objects, so aggregation is simply a collection of different object classes assembled into an aggregate class, which becomes a new object. These new composite objects are important because they can represent more complex structures than can simple objects, without losing the integrity of the simple object. For example, a building object can be aggregated with a sign object. But if you delete the sign, the building still remains.

- Composition is another specialized form of association. This is a stronger association relationship, in which the life of the contained object classes controls the life of the container object class. For example, a building is composed of (or contains) a foundation, walls, and a roof. If you delete what the building contains—its foundation, walls, and roof—you automatically delete the building, but not its sign.

## Class diagrams

Class diagrams are used to diagram the conceptual database design according to the object-oriented model. They help you map the relationships that you need in a data model by illustrating the classes and relationships in your database. The following four class diagrams show you how to diagram classes, attributes, methods, and their relationships. The diagrams are a standard notation for expressing object models and are based on the Unified Modeling Language (UML), the emerging standard.

To review, a class is a set of similar objects. Each object in a class has the same set of attributes and behaviors (or put another way, the same set of defining properties and method or performance capabilities). In figure 9.9, the class named "Parcel" has attributes of feature-polygon, size, cost, and zoning, and it can perform these behaviors (or methods): calculate tax value, split parcels, and merge parcels.

Inheritance or generalization is the ability to share object properties and methods with a class or superclass. Inheritance creates a new object class by modifying an existing class.

Associations represent relationships between classes, as said earlier. The specialized types of associations, aggregation, and composition merit further discussion.

Aggregation is an asymmetric association in which an object from one class is considered to be a *whole* and objects from another class are considered to be *parts*. Object classes can be assembled to create an aggregate class. For example, the aggregate class "Property" can be created by aggregating the "Land parcel" class and the "Dwellings" class (figure 9.10).

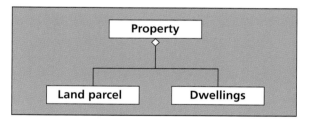

Figure 9.10 **Property as aggregate class**

Composition is a stronger form of aggregation in which objects from the whole class control the lifetime of objects from the subordinate class. If the object that makes up the whole is deleted, the subordinate objects that compose the whole are also deleted.

In figure 9.11 you have a "Network" class of water features with subordinate classes of "Stream" and "Canal." When you delete Network, the objects that compose it (Stream and Canal) are also deleted.

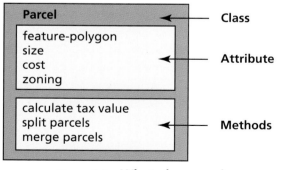

Figure 9.9 **What *class* can do**

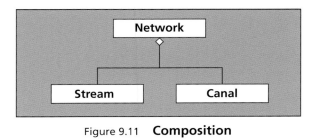

Figure 9.11 **Composition**

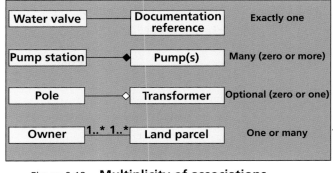

Figure 9.12 **Multiplicity of associations defined**

Multiplicity defines the number of objects that can be associated with another object. In figure 9.12 (which uses a notation device from the UML), we see that a water valve can have exactly one documentation reference and vice versa. In contrast, a pump station can have many pumps associated with it, but each pump can have only one pump station. While this might seem obvious, the rule system that this suggests is what gives object-oriented modeling its strength.

Consider the next line in figure 9.12: a pole can have zero or one transformer, but a transformer does not have the option of zero poles. Finally, we see that an owner can own one or many land parcels, and a land parcel can be owned by one or many owners.

# Determine system requirements

**10**

*Getting the system requirements right at the onset is what separates the adults from the children in successful GIS planning.*

Now you will design a technology system that can handle the data and functionality you've specified. In chapter 9, you learned about creating the conceptual system design for your data; here you will create the conceptual system design for technology. Typically, these two planning processes are carried out at roughly the same time because understanding the functionality you need helps you identify the technology required for it. In conceiving of a system design for technology, the focus is on defining a set of technologies (hardware, software, networking) that will adequately support the demand for system functions in creating information products as needed. This is also the time and place to consider the implications of distributed GIS and Web services.

The chapter's objective is to describe the relationships between the basic components of a technology system, in order to help you think about GIS within the context of your own particular organization's specific needs. Each GIS project is factually unique, from a hardware, software, data, networking, or personnel perspective, and so both the system design and the approach to configuring it must be tailored to fit. This chapter guides you through one among several ways of planning a system technology. Every organization is different—there is no recipe for integrating GIS into the workplace—so you must exercise your own professional judgment when presenting your recommendations to management.

First, we set the stage for software selection. Then, after examining some architectural alternatives, a detailed example (a three-year "case study" of the fictional City of Rome) will illustrate an approach to identifying platform and network loads during peak operations. Finally, platform sizing and pricing models will show you a way to estimate the cost of the selected hardware, information you will need to include in your preliminary design document. Documenting your overall concept is an important step if you are to proceed with planning for software and hardware procurement and for the GIS implementation that follows.

## Software selection

In concert with other system components, software programs orchestrate the computer operations necessary to input the datasets and make the information products. By adding up these functions—and highlighting those most crucial to your workflows—you can determine the functionality you need from a software program. The results of this summary and classification will give you the function requirements, which you can provide to the software vendor after your proposal is approved.

Basically, your plan must envisage software that does all the things you need it to do, and performs very reliably the things you need done well and most often. So you must specify and quantify those functions first, rather than assume that every GIS program will have them. You can buy the latest software available, but you're wasting your money if it is missing a key bit of required functionality. Or what if it lacks speed and efficiency in the execution of some key function? That can be equally critical. For instance, when you know you'll often need crucial data from the public works department, you'll steer clear of a software program that does not easily import data from there. Summarizing the type and number of functions you need, and then classifying them according to workflow and frequency, will keep your planning on track as you consider software selection.

### Summarizing the function requirements

This summary is simply a list showing each function alongside the number of times a software program will be called on to perform it in a given year. In chapter 6, you identified the functions required to get data into the

system and to generate each identified information product. You already listed these function requirements, on the master input data list and in the individual information product descriptions. Your job at this point is easy: review the IPDs and summarize the number of times that each specific function will be used to produce the full set of information products in a year. Add to this summary the additional data input functions identified in the MIDL (things like data import and conversion functions). The result is called the *total function utilization*; a summary not only naming the particular functions to be invoked but also quantifying how many times in the first year each function will be performed (see page 50 for more on functional use).

For planning purposes, you may want to forecast ahead, especially if you anticipate your organization's need for certain information products changing over time. Refer back to the calculations for a five-year span in chapter 6 and include every function that you foresee being invoked at any time during that period, including all of the datasets that will be input in the first five years (typically all of them), plus any other basic system capabilities.

Another option is to estimate each function's use on a year-by-year basis. Such summaries—for year one, year two, year three—can be useful, especially if you expect to require limited functionality in the early years of a system and a higher level as your organization grows over time.

### Classifying system functions

Classifying system functions is a way of highlighting those most crucial to your operation, so that you can select software with the capabilities that meet your specific needs. One glance at the function utilization summary (under "Frequency of use" on pages 50 and 51) tells you that the functions used most frequently are the ones that carry out basic system chores. Whatever your workhorse functions are, consider them essential to your system's operation. Typically, you'll find one or a small coterie of data manipulation and analysis functions that have an extremely high frequency of use. These functions are essential; your system relies heavily on them. These are *class 1* functions. The software you ultimately select must be able to perform them and perform them well. Any system that does not offer optimally suited and operationally efficient class 1 functions should be automatically disqualified from consideration.

Recognizing the least-used functions is just as straightforward. Take a look at them in figure 10.1, clustered along the bottom on the right side. These rarely used functions can be critical to individual operations nonetheless, so they deserve a place in your system. Classify those that need to be present, but not necessarily efficient, as *class 3* functions.

Those remaining (in the middle of the graph) provide important functionality and are heavily used: class 2 functions. During benchmark testing of systems prior to a major procurement, class 2 functions are always thoroughly tested. They must be in place and they must be efficient.

Document the classifications of functions required by your system overall, including the GIS and the frequency of their use. When you're ready to procure your system, you can provide vendors with this document—your list of objective criteria to support software selection. Note that only the functions on this list should be considered during procurement. This will help to keep you focused.

The figures you work with in planning are estimates, so don't be surprised when you discover they were off

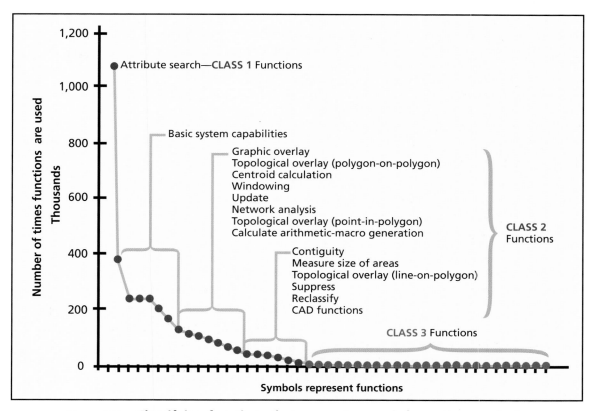

Figure 10.1   **Classifying functions that generate your information products**

by 20 or 30 percent. You should expect variations in the methodology and information product timing over the five-year plan and accept this with equanimity. Recognize that some give is already built into the planning process—your technology design can accommodate a plus or minus 30 percent change in functional requirements. The objective is simply to avoid being 200 or 300 percent wrong and wasting thousands or even millions of dollars on systems that aren't even close, which is the track record of those who charge ahead without thinking about where they're going.

## Interface and communication technologies

You already know the datasets by name and relationship, having traced their source in your MIDL; now it's time to get even better acquainted. Determining an adequate system interface and network communication configuration requires your understanding of where the major datasets in your and other organizations are maintained and stored, and how well they can travel to you and from you.

### Choosing a system interface

You will probably need to link many of your organization's existing databases to your GIS. If you were to call on these datasets often, you would need each visit to be a quick trip and each conversation to be a free-flowing exchange. The determining factors for choosing a system interface are frequency and speed of access, and whether the data formats involved are compatible.

Take note of whether your GIS requires such frequent, repeated, high-speed access to major databases. Ideally, these would be two-way links that "talk to each other" easily: you're getting data and sending different data. Not every linkup will be a marriage made in heaven, though. Consider the city information systems folks who want to link their utility billing records to the GIS parcel database. If the

two databases are stored in different formats, then to allow for this linkage you may need special interface software or a custom software interface, which requires programming. For your preliminary design document, you'll need to estimate in time and money how much the programming will cost.

You might consider using replication software or translation functions as an interface to the data sources. Establishing certain procedures to support frequency of data transfer is another possibility. Sometimes, all this discussion of database technology makes organizations realize they are using dated technology, and triggers an organization-wide migration to a new standard database platform on which all applications, including the GIS, will successfully operate. In fact, GIS itself might be chosen as the integrating software. More and more it is.

And possibly, less and less will custom interfaces be required, as the new service oriented architecture (SOA) takes hold. The SOA strategy is for each business unit to provide Web services; in other words, the interface between business systems or departments would be through standard Web service protocols, rendering custom interfaces unnecessary.

### Network communications

Network connections provide the communications link that allows you to both access data and distribute it throughout the organization. In a typical municipality, for example, a centralized server stores the data. City employees carry on with their workflows, getting the data they need from the server through their desktop computers. The network was probably configured to allow for these existing workflows. But in doing its job of producing information products that streamline workflows, GIS will change how some things operate.

Whether you're thinking about a GIS in only one department or throughout the organization, implementing it is likely to have a major effect on the existing network. Be aware that GIS requires moving big data and

## Data capacity and data-transfer rates

GIS data is often characterized by large file sizes and shared through a network, which is simply a group of connected computers linked for the purpose of sharing. Largely, the purpose of a technology system for GIS is to move data quickly from here to there and have it arrive in the same shape it left in. Network bandwidth facilitates the former (data transfer from server to user), while the latter (processing) is left to CPUs or central processing units (often held on servers). Data is dependent on these components for quick travel.

In planning to implement a GIS, you need to consider your organization's requirement for both data capacity provided by the storage technology and data-transfer rates determined by the available bandwidth or network capacity for network traffic. Data capacity is how much data can be stored; at the moment, it is measured in gigabytes, terabytes, or petabytes (or even exabytes, zertabytes, and yottabytes). A server is capable of storing large amounts of data, but like your own desktop computer, the server can hold only as much data as its disk space permits. A small municipality may require only 40 to 80 gigabytes of disk space to meet its data storage requirements. Large data repositories, like the one maintained by the U.S. Census Bureau, may have the capacity to store data in the terabytes.

Regardless of how much data can be stored, its size is useless if it cannot be put into motion and shared with many users in a reasonable amount of time. This is where data-transfer rates come into play, or how fast data traffic can be sent by the server over a network. Adequate network bandwidth capacity must be available to support these data transfer loads at their peak.

Note that data traffic rates on the network are measured in bits per second. When translating the data volume stored on one storage disk to data traffic over a network, the formula is 1 megabyte equals 10 megabits (includes 2 bits of network protocol overhead for every 8 bits of data). Fifty-six Kb/sec is the same as 56,000 bits/sec; so 10 Mb/sec is the same as 10,000,000 bits/sec. Thus, a 10 Mb/sec local area network or LAN can support the transfer of nearly 180 times more data per second than a 56 Kb/sec wide area network or WAN.

This is often a misunderstood issue because of misinterpretation of communication units. But the devil is in these very details, especially as you approach planning for a big enough network bandwidth. Really understanding what the data-transfer rates mean is a critical dimension of GIS planning. Data-transfer speed is always the same (the speed of light), only the bandwidth, or throughput capacity, is different. Throughput capacity is very important; as cumulative network traffic approaches 50–75 percent of throughput capacity, significant communication delays will occur due to frequent collisions at higher transmission rates.

complex (big) applications over a network that must allow for such heavy traffic. Providing shared communication segments that work like city roadways, networks can support only one communication packet at a time. So in order for a network to accommodate multiple communications during peak traffic loads, these data packets must wait in line. It is frustrating for end users to know that the data is on the server, but they must wait several minutes for its retrieval and regeneration. With the newer technology, such traffic delays are experienced only when cumulative network traffic exceeds roughly 50–75 percent of the available network capacity. Beyond 75 percent, however, the network becomes a system performance bottleneck, and users suffer under lengthening wait times like urban drivers stuck in rush hour traffic.

Couple high-data loads with frequently used applications, and you've got enough to choke undersized network connections or render them too slow. Advancements in technology have created GIS servers intended specifically to minimize data transfer loads. Instead of simply sending all the data, these servers do work on the data and dispense the results only.

With such servers running the applications themselves, your GIS users may be able to access data through the existing network or after some slight updating. Or you may have to adopt an entirely new networking system. You can find out—predict the bandwidth suitable for your GIS—by using the information about your data and specific needs, with the approach provided later in this chapter. Make sure your calculations take into consideration the growth of your organization. One way to be vigilantly careful is to anticipate the highest possible numbers—in all your calculations—and then add 20 percent to be safe.

There are two basic network types: local area networks (LANs) and wide area networks (WANs). LANs support high-bandwidth communications over short distances. They provide high-speed access to data typically within a building or other localized environment, such as a campus. WANs support communications between remote locations. For example, a file server in a city office building shares data with its field offices through a WAN. Using a different protocol, WAN technology usually has a much lower bandwidth than the LAN environment and is more expensive due to the cost of constructing the communications infrastructure for data transmission over long distances. The Internet, in essence, is a global WAN.

## Client-server architectures

Most commonly, transferring data over a network is accomplished by some form of client-server technology: the client requests data for an application and the server delivers data to the application. The transfer of information relies on a common language that permits this two-way street between the sender and the receiver, called a *communication protocol*. The type of client-server architecture chosen for a system will dictate which communication protocol is used.

The four basic types of client-server architectures are described below, along with the protocols associated with them. Most often you'll find the "heavy" users who want to make their own information products within the first two architectures, which support data transfer between the data server and the application client. The last two architectures—transferring map display from application server to display client—usually don't need as much bandwidth as the first two because there is less data to transfer. (Fewer bits of data are needed to display an information product than to create it.)

### Central file server with workstation clients

A central file server shares data with computer workstations across the network. The application software resides on the workstations, which perform both data query and map rendering functions. With its high demand for bandwidth, this type of configuration is best deployed over a LAN, which offers greater bandwidth over shorter distances (i.e., on campus, within a local organization). Common disk mounting protocols associated with this network architecture are NFS (UNIX—network file services), SMB (Microsoft Windows—server message block), and CIFS (Windows—common Internet file services). All of the disk mounting protocols are standard TCP/IP protocols.

## Central DBMS server with workstation clients

A central DBMS (database management system) server also shares data with computer workstations across the network (figure 10.2). The application software resides on the workstations, where map rendering is processed. The DBMS retrieves data from the server, but transfers only the data required to support the client display. Compared to the previous configuration, this type significantly reduces demands on the network. Yet, because it still requires the transfer of large quantities of data between the DBMS server and the client application, this configuration is also best deployed over a LAN. (Search engines compress the data before shifting it to the workstation client, which decompresses it.) The standard TCP/IP protocols apply.

## Centralized application processing with terminal clients

In this configuration (figure 10.3), the data and application software are both stored and run on servers located in the computer facility. The terminal workstations remotely display and control applications executed on the terminal servers. These are the "dumb" terminals that first brought computing to the people. The only data transferred from the server to the terminal is the resulting display environment, which significantly reduces network bandwidth requirements. This type of architecture lends itself well to WANs. Common protocols associated with this network architecture are RDP (Windows—remote desktop protocol), ICA (Citrix—independent computing architecture), and X.11 (UNIX—Open Windows display protocol).

## Web transaction processing with browser or workstation clients

Application software and data files reside on servers located in the computer facility. The map server provides information products—data and maps—to Web

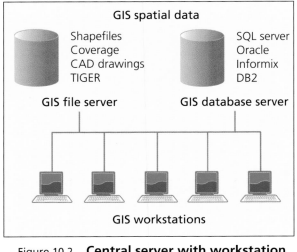

Figure 10.2  **Central server with workstation clients**

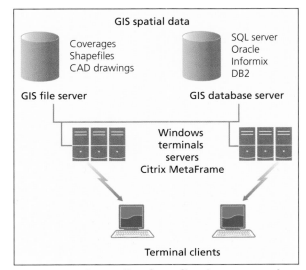

Figure 10.3  **Centralized application processing with terminal clients**

browsers or other "thin" clients (e.g., Java applications) via the Internet or a secure local intranet. This architecture (figure 10.4) allows a single application process to provide simultaneous support to a large number of random GIS user transactions. The protocol associated with this network architecture is HTTP (Hypertext Transfer Protocol).

Every communication architecture has its own advantages and disadvantages. If the information products must be generated quickly through a WAN—for example, to create a locator map for emergency response—then a centralized application with terminal clients is viable. If application performance is not critical, but the ability to share the information with a large population of users is, then Web transaction processing is appropriate. A central file or database server with workstation clients used to be necessary for users requiring high-performance access to large datasets that they must check out, edit, and then check back. But these days, terminal servers can provide almost the same high performance computing as desktop. Keep in mind that many organizations use a combination of all four architectures to meet the demands of their user community.

## General issues of network performance

Networking is a specialized and quickly evolving field; some issues related to network performance are outside the scope of this book. The following discussion about networking capacities is intended to give you an overview of network traffic considerations, not a working knowledge of the intricacies of network engineering.

You can use the volume of data transferred and network bandwidth capacity to identify the network transport contribution to expected user application wait times. A typical workstation GIS application might require up to 1 MB of spatial data that must be pulled over the network to generate a new map display or do an analysis. In contrast, a similar application deployed as a Web service or in a

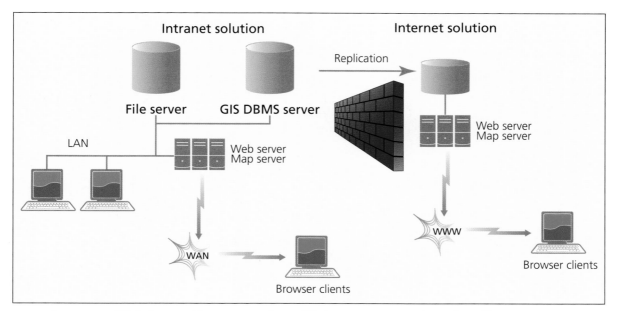

Figure 10.4 **Web transaction processing with browser or workstation clients**

terminal environment might require just 100 KB of data to support the same display or analysis.

Figure 10.5 compares the network time needed for the data transfer under various configurations. It measures the total transfer of data (network traffic) in megabits (Mb) that must be transmitted and factors in data compression percentages and traffic overhead that would typically be deployed under each client-server configuration. The transport time required to transfer this data is calculated for five standard bandwidth solutions. This chart illustrates how different client-server configurations affect the time it takes to transfer data.

The first two client-server communication options in the chart are examples of a central data server with workstation clients. In this case, the full 1 MB of data and traffic overhead is transferred from the server to the workstation to meet the demands of the application. The next two options represent Web transaction processing, and the last, centralized application processing with terminal-client solutions. These latter three configurations make use of the data and application software on central servers located in the computer facility. While 1 MB of data is needed to generate the information product, the results are transferred from

the server facility to the terminal clients as a display only, which reduces the amount of data required for transfer to 100 KB. Traffic is different for each protocol (see figure 10.8).

Of course, the third weighty factor to consider in configuring system architecture is user needs. It is imperative to design a system that supports peak user workflows. Also, networks should always be configured with enough flexibility to provide special support to power users whose data transfer needs exceed typical GIS-user bandwidth requirements. Figure 10.6 provides recommended design guidelines for network environments based on the expected client loads. These guidelines establish a baseline for configuring distributed LAN and WAN environments.

## Determining system interface and communication requirements

Now that you have a preliminary understanding of interface and communication technologies, you can think about the best configuration for your organization's system. Keeping in mind that you can find much of the

| Client-server communications | | Network traffic transport time (seconds) | | | | | | |
|---|---|---|---|---|---|---|---|---|
| | | Wide area network (WAN) | | | | Local area network (LAN) | | |
| | | 56 Kbps | 1.54 Mbps | 6 Mbps | 45 Mbps | 10 Mbps | 100 Mbps | 1 Gbps |
| Data | File server to GIS desktop client (NFS/CIFS) | 893 | 32 | 8.33 | 1.11 | 5.00 | 0.5 | 0.05 |
| Data | GIS database server to GIS desktop client (TCP/IP) | 89 | 3.2 | 0.83 | 0.11 | 0.5 | 0.05 | 0.005 |
| Display | Web server to GIS desktop client (HTTP) | 18 | 0.6 | 0.17 | 0.02 | 0.1 | 0.01 | 0.001 |
| Display | Web server to browser client (HTTP) | 9 | 0.32 | 0.08 | 0.01 | 0.05 | 0.005 | 0.0005 |
| Display | Windows terminal server to terminal client (ICA) | 5 | 0.18 | 0.05 | 0.01 | 0.03 | 0.0028 | 0.0003 |

*Best practices*

Figure 10.5   **Network time needed for data transfer within various configurations, 2004**

| Local area networks bandwidth | Concurrent client loads | | | |
|---|---|---|---|---|
| | File server | SDE servers | Windows terminals | Web products |
| 10 Mbps LAN | 2–4 | 10–20 | 350–700 | 150–300 |
| 16 Mbps LAN | 3–6 | 16–32 | 550–1,100 | 250–500 |
| 100 Mbps LAN | 20–40 | 100–200 | 3,500–7,000 | 1,500–3,000 |
| 1 Gbps LAN | 200–400 | 1,000–2,000 | 35,000–70,000 | 15,000–30,000 |
| Wide area networks bandwidth | Concurrent client loads | | | |
| | File server | SDE servers | Windows terminals | Web products |
| 56 Kbps modem | NR | NR | 2–4 | 1–2 |
| 128 Kbps ISDN | NR | NR | 5–10 | 2–4 |
| 256 Kbps DSL | NR | NR | 10–20 | 5–10 |
| 512 Kbps | NR | NR | 20–40 | 10–20 |
| 1.54 Mbps T-1 | NR | 1–2 | 50–100 | 25–50 |
| 2 Mbps E-1 | NR | 1–3 | 75–150 | 40–80 |
| 6.16 Mbps T-2 | 1–2 | 6–12 | 200–400 | 100–200 |
| 45 Mbps T-3 | 10–20 | 50–100 | 1,500–3,000 | 700–1,500 |
| 155 Mbps ATM | 30–60 | 150–300 | 5,000–10,000 | 2,500–5,000 |

Figure 10.6 **Network design guidelines based on peak user workflows**

information you will need for determining your system interface and communication requirements in the IPDs and MIDL, start asking the following questions about your proposed system:

- What external databases, if any, are planned for use within the system and what format are they in?
- What records need to be accessed? How frequently? How quickly?

If any external databases that you plan to connect to your GIS applications are stored in an incompatible format, you may need interface software in order to access them. The storage formats of all these datasets are identified in your MIDL. The records needed, the frequency of access, and the wait tolerance are given in the IPDs. Make a note of these databases and how often and how quickly your system will need to access them, so you can plan for obtaining the required interface software.

Next ask these questions about your proposed system:

### What are the wait tolerances of the information products?

Review the wait tolerances specified in the IPDs. Information products with low wait tolerances, such as emergency-service applications, will require a software technology solution that maximizes user productivity or one that takes advantage of the new interoperability technology.

### Where is the data located?

Think about the location of the databases planned for use with the GIS and review these data sources, listed in the MIDL. Ideally, all the data would be stored in one central database in a standard environment. In the real world, however, datasets are often stored on different servers throughout the organization. If this is the case and access to a dataset impedes the creation of your information products, you may find a solution in server technology, which facilitates access not only to databases but also to software and ready-made applications.

### Where are the data handling locations (user sites), and what is the data handling load (peak user workflows) at these locations?

This information is crucial in determining how to tie users together through the network, and you already have it: you pinpointed the location of all sites expected to make use of the GIS data while determining the scope of the system (chapter 7). You also identified the number of users and the peak user workflows at these locations (page 64). You have gauged the traffic at rush hour—where it's coming from and where it's going. Now you need to assess if your organization has the communication infrastructure to handle all this.

### What is the current network configuration?

Using your information product display requirements from the IPDs, along with the data handling loads (peak user workflows), estimate the total volume of data (in megabits or Mb) that must be transmitted for your high-priority information products, paying particular attention to those with a low wait tolerance. Compare this demand with the existing bandwidth and traffic volumes for each segment of the network that will be used. Do you see a bottleneck in the making? Network access is vital to building and sharing information products—do not underestimate what your organization may need to accommodate the introduction of a GIS.

Your objective is to get a rough idea of what fits. Remember, you are merely seeking logical approximations intended to get your estimates within range. Your job is to identify the criteria required to make your system operate effectively, but you are not expected to be a systems administrator. So don't hesitate to consult with your network administrators, vendors, or others trained in this field and ask for their opinion. There are

many different ways to configure a system. There might be more than one configuration option that could work well in your organization.

## Distributed GIS and Web services

Distributed GIS, which allows more than one person to be working on the same data in separate locations, is becoming an increasingly larger dimension of new GIS installations. Now that digital data is more available and the price of technology is decreasing, the distributed model is becoming more and more attractive. Several steps allow you to evaluate your initial assumptions and better understand the options and likely costs. The main concepts, which the case study will illustrate, are peak usage and peak bandwidth loads, which enable you to assess bandwidth suitability, wait times, batch processing, platform sizing, and costs.

First review what you already know at this stage. For each department and business-process workflow, you have determined the degree of complexity of the information product and the number and size of datasets used. The same is true for the total number of users who will be making the information product, and, of those, the number that will be working concurrently. These can be brought together in a list that, for each site in your organization, summarizes the total number of users and the number of high-complexity and low-complexity concurrent users, and the peak Web usage expressed in number of requests per hour at each site. This is the same list identified for each user location in figure 7.6.

To show how you might use such a list to model your own system design, we built a realistic "case study" of a fictional city that we call Rome. This example illustrates one way (among several alternative methods) of estimating the platform sizing and the network bandwidth requirements of the system architecture configuration under consideration. (After walking you through this detailed analysis, we'll pick up again on several more factors to consider at this stage of planning, continuing on page 148.)

## Platform sizing and bandwidth requirements

The calculations of the size of computers needed and the availability of communications bandwidth required are based on estimates of the number of peak users on the system at any one time. Rules of thumb have been developed based on assumptions about the amount of work being done by each user and the volume of data being handled at a given time. You can use these "rules" or methods for platform sizing, using performance models like the one below; they translate the number of peak users into the number of CPUs (processor cores) for different types of system architecture. (Platform memory is assumed to be 2 gigabytes per server core.)

The initial system design for the City of Rome, supporting the initial year 1 and year 2 hardware selections, was conducted in 2004. The user workflows implemented by this typical city and the corresponding 2004 hardware capacity sizing models are summarized in figure 10.7.

You can apply these same guidelines, developed from much experience, to predicting the amount of, and planning big enough bandwidth for, the data traffic volume your network will have to support. Guidelines

for these network loads for various workflows are given in figure 10.8. Note that desktop client/server workflows use megabits per second per user, while Web services use megabits per Web product.

The network traffic guidelines factor is based on the type of architecture involved. We cover five architectures here:

1. File server client—a standard GIS desktop client accessing data from a file server data source.
2. Database client—a standard GIS desktop client accessing data from a DBMS data source (as used in the City of Rome). Application interface with the data schema is provided through a search engine (such as SDE) supported either on the DBMS server or the GIS desktop.
3. Terminal client—access to GIS desktop software executed on a Windows terminal server (used in the City of Rome).
4. Browser client—a browser client accessing a standard Web image map service (used in the City of Rome)
5. Web GIS client—a GIS desktop client accessing a standard Web image map service.

For each of these, we've accepted certain assumptions regarding the average size of data per query, including the percent of compression applied. (The network load factors are based on average display complexities, and heavier than average display complexity will result in higher data transfer requirements.) The network load factors can be

| Platform | Performance per CPU | Memory |
|---|---|---|
| GIS file server | 30 clients/CPU | 2 GB/CPU |
| Database server | | |
| Web transaction loads on the data server | 1,600 transactions per hour equivalent to 1 data server client | |
| Internet Web server | File server data source 6,000 transactions per hour/CPU | 1 GB/CPU |
| | Database server data source 12,000 transactions per hour/CPU | |
| Windows terminal server | File server data source 6 GIS desktop clients/CPU | 2 GB/CPU |
| | Database server data source 7.5 GIS desktop clients/CPU | |

Figure 10.7 **Capacity planning models, 2004**

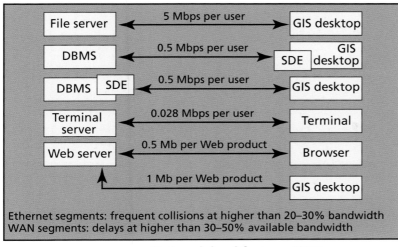

Figure 10.8   **Network load factors, 2004**

used to estimate peak traffic loads expressed in megabits per second: Mbps per user for client workflows and per query for Web products.

With these network load factors in hand, having already identified where your data sources, computers, and users are located, you may be able to estimate the platform sizing and network bandwidth required for your organization's GIS implementation for the first year and beyond. Let's take a run through how you might do that over time by experiencing how the planner for the City of Rome did it, starting in 2004.

## City of Rome case study

With the figure 10.7 and 10.8 guidelines in hand, put yourself in the shoes of the GIS planner for a large organization—a city—and follow along as this case study uses a simple method for determining platform sizing and network suitability for your system design plan. Later, with your own list in hand, you can use information you've already gathered to see if the method works for you in selecting a platform and in analyzing network bandwidth requirements based on projected user workflows. The

results of your own analysis, perhaps like the one here, will provide a foundation for your hardware costs and documenting infrastructure implementation requirements. This will become a crucial part of presenting your plan to management in your final report.

## In the beginning: Year 1 and year 2

During the requirements assessment, the city department managers identified specific requirements needed to support their business operations. The first task is to collect these requirements for both year 1 and year 2 and show peak user loads projected for each business workflow. You will also need to identify the user locations and network connectivity to support your system loads analysis.

### Year 1 user locations and network connectivity

It is proposed that the GIS take advantage of the existing city communication structure for its first year. All GIS users will be linked to the central GIS DBMS with search engine capabilities on the server so they can use the existing city system network configuration and bandwidth.

Some will link via Windows terminal servers and others through Web services. Figure 10.9 lays out the user locations and network communications that exist at the start, the site configuration for 2004: year 1. This is the baseline reality from which GIS will launch.

## Estimating user requirements

The numbers indicating the user requirements for the first year of GIS in the City of Rome are listed in figure 10.10. In the role of Rome's planner, you will be using these values later on, for comparison, in projecting how your system might grow as the city's needs change and grow, next year and the year after. You will also use these numbers to estimate network traffic requirements during peak business operations. Tables like the one on the next page, in which you estimate the usage by department, are useful for planning purposes because you need to get department managers to sign off on the designs before going further in assessing the platform capacity and bandwidth needed.

Since you want to plan a system that is scalable—one that will grow smoothly as your users' needs grow—you must anticipate that growth so you can begin with network bandwidth and platform sizing suitable for expanding. So now you must estimate your organization's user requirements for the second year of GIS in Rome.

In the same kind of table, make your estimates for the second year. Perhaps assuming that new departments will need access to the GIS; special requirements could emerge, such as a firewall between the central computer and the police computer. Plan for operations to be extended to cover 911 emergency services and connections with vehicles; additional remote sites will need to be serviced.

With all this, you'll need to consider an extended architecture for the second year. What are your options for increasing system capabilities to meet Rome's increasing needs? All this is likely to confirm your opinion that, in planning the first year, you are wise to establish a system that is scalable, one that can grow as the organization

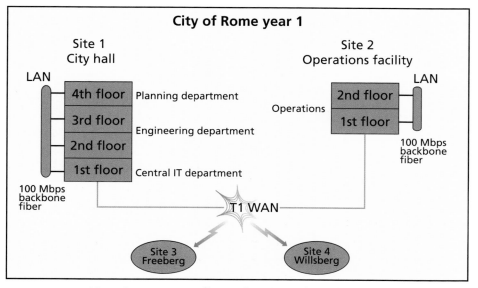

Figure 10.9    **Year 1 system configuration: User locations and network communications**

| City of Rome - year 1 | | | | Total users | Peak usage | | |
|---|---|---|---|---|---|---|---|
| | | | | | Processing complexity | | Web req/hr |
| Department | Workflow | IPD | User type | | High | Low | |
| **Site 1 - City hall** | | | | | | | |
| Planning | Zoning | 1.0 | Planner | 20 | | 8 | |
| | | 1.1 | Web services | | | | 2,600 |
| | Permits | 1.2 | Inspector | 20 | | 10 | |
| | | 1.3 | Appraiser | 15 | 8 | | |
| | | 1.4 | Supervisor | 2 | | 2 | |
| | | 1.5 | Web services | | | | 600 |
| Engineering | Sewer backup | 2.1 | Engineer | 4 | | 3 | |
| | | 2.2 | Web services | | | | 800 |
| | Electrical breaks | 2.3 | Electrician | 13 | 6 | | |
| | | 2.4 | Supervisor | 2 | 1 | | |
| | | 2.5 | Web services | | | | 600 |
| | Highway repair | 2.6 | Field engineer | 10 | | 4 | |
| | | 2.7 | Contracts | 4 | | 4 | |
| City hall totals | | | | 90 | 15 | 31 | 4,600 |
| **Site 2 - Operations** | | | | | | | |
| Operations | Cleanup program | 3.1 | Ops. staff | 4 | | 2 | |
| Operations totals | | | | 4 | | 2 | |
| **Remote field offices (WAN)** | | | | | | | |
| Site 3 - Freeberg | Inspection | 4.1 | Field engineer | 40 | | 30 | 600 |
| Site 4 - Willsberg | Inspection | 4.1 | Field engineer | 30 | | 20 | 600 |
| Remote totals | | | | 70 | | 50 | 1,200 |
| City totals | | | | 164 | 15 | 83 | 5,800 |

Figure 10.10   **Year 1 user requirements**

grows. Just be sure that you are reflecting the objectives of the needs of the departments concerned.

## Year 2 user locations and network connectivity

It has been decided that a central computing environment will be maintained through the second year of GIS in Rome, and GIS operations will be extended to three additional remote sites and mobile operations with access through the city's Internet connections. The system will have its needed firewall for the police department data (see figure 10.11). The city database is replicated in the police department so the department can use it in combination with their confidential data to serve their office staff and, through wireless connections, to serve their vehicles independently.

The operations building is currently served from city hall over a T1 WAN connection, and now the mayor has proposed that the 911 emergency services be located there in year 2. The city hall GIS data server hosts the emergency services data, to which emergency services desktop clients have terminal access only indirectly, through the city hall Windows terminal server farm (WTS) that runs their low-complexity desktop applications. Emergency Web services are supported out of city hall on the enterprise Web server farm over the city Internet connection. Emergency vehicles will access the 911 Web services over wireless Internet connections to the city hall Web services. Remote site 3 and 4 are connected by T1 to the WAN; while sites 5, 6, and 7 are connected to the Web server at city hall over T1 connections.

The year 2 user requirements table that follows (figure 10.12) summarizes the increase in the number of users in both the high-complexity and low-complexity categories. Compare the increases in the peak number of requests per hour over the Web from year 1 to year 2. Total desktop users have more than doubled, the total remote desktop users have tripled, and the number of Web server requests per hour has doubled. (Figure 10.13 summarizes these increases.)

## User requirements summary

Next we will summarize year 1 and year 2 user requirements to support our analysis. Figure 10.13 identifies peak usage for each user department, by location, for each of the two years. It also represents peak user loads for year 1 and 2 based on requirements identified by each department manager. These are the same user loads identified in the earlier year 1 and year 2 user requirements tables, but providing them in a compressed format here makes sense for two reasons: (1) it's simply easier for managers to sign off on the requirements if they can compare estimates for the two planned years side by side, and (2) you will be using this summary to complete the network bandwidth suitability and platform loads analyses.

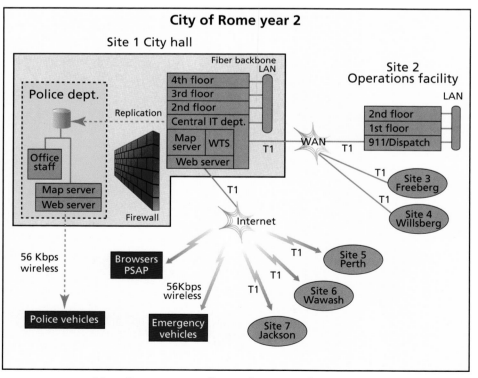

Figure 10.11 **Year 2 system configuration: User locations and network communications**

| City of Rome - year 2 | | | | Total users | Peak usage | | Web req/hr |
|---|---|---|---|---|---|---|---|
| | | | | | Processing complexity | | |
| Department | Workflow | IPD | User type | | High | Low | |
| **Site 1 - City hall** | | | | | | | |
| Planning | Zoning | 1.0 | Planner | 25 | | 15 | |
| | | 1.1 | Web services | | | | 2,600 |
| | Permits | 1.2 | Inspector | 25 | | 15 | |
| | | 1.3 | Appraiser | 20 | 10 | | |
| | | 1.4 | Supervisor | 5 | 2 | | |
| | | 1.5 | Web services | | | | 900 |
| Engineering | Sewer backup | 2.1 | Engineer | 5 | | 3 | |
| | | 2.2 | Web services | | | | 1,000 |
| | Electrical breaks | 2.3 | Electrician | 13 | 6 | | |
| | | 2.4 | Supervisor | 2 | 1 | | |
| | | 2.5 | Web services | | | | 1,900 |
| | Highway repair | 2.6 | Field engineer | 11 | | 7 | |
| | | 2.7 | Contracts | 4 | | 4 | |
| City hall LAN totals | | | | 110 | 19 | 44 | 6,400 |
| Police (Firewall) | Patrol schedule | 5.1 | Administration | 10 | | 3 | |
| | Crime analysis | 5.2 | Detectives | 10 | 5 | | |
| | Special events | 5.3 | Traffic | 10 | | 3 | |
| | | 5.4 | Web services | | | | 100 |
| Remote patrols | Patrols | 5.4 | Patrol officers | 20 | | | 100 |
| Police network totals | | | | 50 | 5 | 6 | 200 |
| **Site 2 - Operations** | | | | | | | |
| Operations | Cleanup program | 3.1 | Ops. staff | 4 | | 2 | |
| 911 | Response | 3.2 | Call takers | 50 | | 30 | |
| | | 3.3 | Web services | | | | 4,000 |
| Remote vehicles | Dispatch | 3.4 | Drivers | 30 | | 30 | |
| Operations totals (WAN) | | | | 84 | | 62 | 4,000 |
| **Remote field offices (WAN)** | | | | | | | |
| Site 3 - Freeberg | Inspection | 4.1 | Field engineer | 45 | | 30 | 515 |
| Site 4 - Willsberg | Inspection | 4.1 | Field engineer | 60 | | 40 | 685 |
| Remote field office (WAN) totals | | | | 105 | | 70 | 1,200 |
| **Remote field offices (Internet)** | | | | | | | |
| Site 5 - Perth | Inspection | 4.3 | Field engineer | 10 | | 2 | 40 |
| Site 6 - Wawash | Inspection | 4.3 | Field engineer | 50 | | 40 | 840 |
| Site 7 - Jackson | Inspection | 4.3 | Field engineer | 60 | | 20 | 420 |
| Remote field office (Internet) totals | | | | 120 | | 62 | 1,300 |
| City totals (excluding police private network) | | | | 419 | 19 | 238 | 12,900 |

Figure 10.12   **Year 2 user requirements**

## Bandwidth suitability analysis

To assess whether the available bandwidth is adequate for the use proposed, we'll use the network load factors provided in figure 10.8 and the user requirements summary in figure 10.13 to estimate peak network traffic requirements. The GIS peak traffic projections along with our bandwidth recommendations will be provided to the network administrator to support appropriate planning of enterprise network bandwidth capacity needs (GIS traffic is only part of the overall enterprise traffic over the WAN connections).

Applying these considerations to your analysis would allow you to calculate the estimated peak traffic (Mbps) and compare it with the bandwidth available in the proposed network architecture. Figure 10.14 provides a summary of peak user loads on the network. (This analysis is strictly for GIS planning and, at this point, does not take into account other users on the network.) In your analysis, first determine the peak user workflows supported by each network connection. Using the user requirements summary chart (figure 10.13) as a source, you transfer peak user loads to the appropriate network connections, which include the city hall backbone, WAN, and Internet connections; the operations WAN connection; and the WAN and Internet connections to each remote office.

| City of Rome | Year 1 | | | | Year 2 | | | |
| | Total users | Peak usage | | Web req/hr | Total users | Peak usage | | Web req/hr |
| | | Processing complexity | | | | Processing complexity | | |
| Department | | High | Low | | | High | Low | |
| Site 1 - City hall | | | | | | | | |
| Planning | 57 | 8 | 20 | 3,200 | 75 | 12 | 30 | 3,500 |
| Engineering | 29 | 7 | 11 | 1,400 | 31 | 7 | 10 | 2,900 |
| City hall LAN totals | 86 | 15 | 31 | 4,600 | 106 | 19 | 40 | 6,400 |
| Police (firewall) | | | | | 104 | 15 | 39 | 200 |
| Remote patrols | | | | | | | | |
| Police network totals | | | | | 104 | 15 | 39 | 200 |
| Site 2 - Operations | | | | | | | | |
| Operations | 4 | | 2 | | 4 | | 2 | 2,000 |
| 911 | | | | | 50 | | 30 | 2,000 |
| Remote vehicles | | | | | 30 | | 30 | |
| Operations totals (WAN) | 4 | | 2 | | 84 | | 62 | 4,000 |
| Remote field offices (WAN) | | | | | | | | |
| Site 3 - Freeberg | 40 | | 30 | 600 | 45 | | 30 | 515 |
| Site 4 - Willsberg | 30 | | 20 | 600 | 60 | | 40 | 685 |
| Remote field office (WAN) totals | 70 | | 50 | 1,200 | 105 | | 70 | 1,200 |
| Remote field offices (Internet) | | | | | | | | |
| Site 5 - Perth | | | | | 10 | | 2 | 40 |
| Site 6 - Wawash | | | | | 50 | | 40 | 840 |
| Site 7 - Jackson | | | | | 60 | | 20 | 420 |
| Remote field office (Internet) totals | | | | | 120 | | 62 | 1,300 |
| City totals | 160 | 15 | 83 | 5,800 | 415 | 19 | 234 | 12,900 |

Figure 10.13  **2004 user requirements summaries for year 1 and year 2**

A separate network supports police operations, which include remote patrol traffic distributed over twenty individual dial-up connections (figure 10.15). You would analyze the police network backbone and dial-up connection this way: the total one hundred hits per hour from remote patrol officers results in peak loads of five transactions per hour over their twenty wireless connections.

Transferring the peak network load summaries to the charts on the next two pages (figure 10.16 and figure 10.18) completes the network suitability analysis. You combine desktop users in one column and translate the Web traffic to requests per second. To estimate peak traffic, apply the network load factors for each user workflow.

Basically, in conducting a bandwidth suitability analysis you are translating the peak user loads based on departments to peak user loads over the network connections. What bandwidth will serve Rome in its first year with GIS? Let's walk through the year 1 network suitability analysis step by step. Go back to the city hall network loads analysis chart (figure 10.14) and add up the numbers of high- and low-complexity users next to the row called "City hall backbone" (15+31=46 users). This total, 46, is the peak load of year 1 desktop users. Web requests per second are generated from Web requests per hour; by dividing the Web requests per hour from this analysis by 3,600 (4,600/3,600=1.28). These are the

| Network loads | Year 1 peak loads | | | Year 2 peak loads | | |
|---|---|---|---|---|---|---|
| | High | Low | Web req/hr | High | Low | Web req/hr |
| **Site 1 - City hall** | | | | | | |
| City hall backbone | 15 | 31 | 4,600 | 19 | 44 | 6,400 |
| City WAN connection | | 52 | 1,200 | | 132 | 5,200 |
| City Internet connection | | | | | 62 | 1,300 |
| **Site 2 - Operations** | | | | | | |
| WAN connection | | 2 | | | 62 | 4,000 |
| **Remote field offices (WAN)** | | | | | | |
| Site 3 - Freeberg | | 30 | 600 | | 30 | 515 |
| Site 4 - Willsberg | | 20 | 600 | | 40 | 685 |
| **Remote field offices (Internet)** | | | | | | |
| Site 5 - Perth | | | | | 2 | 40 |
| Site 6 - Wawash | | | | | 40 | 840 |
| Site 7 - Jackson | | | | | 20 | 420 |

Figure 10.14   **City hall network loads**

| Network loads | Year 2 peak loads | | |
|---|---|---|---|
| | High | Low | Web req/hr |
| **Police network** | | | |
| Police network backbone | 5 | 6 | 100 |
| Police dial-up connection | | | 5 |

Figure 10.15   **Police department network loads**

numbers (46 and 1.28) that you see at the top of the first two columns in figure 10.16.

To calculate estimated peak traffic for city hall desktop users in Mbps, multiply the number of desktop users in the first column by the appropriate network load factor from figure 10.8 (46 x 0.5=23), assuming that the city hall GIS desktops in Rome are connected to a DBMS server, (which is a good assumption unless file servers are specifically required). The city hall Web server responds to public browser requests about their activities. So multiply the city hall Web requests per second from figure 10.16 by the network load factor for Web servers to browsers (1.28 x 0.05 = 0.64). These are the numbers (23 and 0.64) that you see in the middle two columns of figure 10.16.

The total Mbps peak usage of the city hall backbone is the sum of the Mbps calculation for desktops and Web requests usage you have just made (23 + 0.64 = 23.64). The capacity of the city hall backbone is 100 Mbps;

therefore, the GIS demand can be met on the physical installation now in place.

## Recommended year 1

Now you're ready to make your recommendations for the network bandwidth that should be available for the city in its first year of GIS (figure 10.17).

Clearly from figure 10.16, the existing WAN connection (T1) bandwidth is inadequate, so you recommend a T2 (6 Mbps). Similarly, the T1 connection to the remote site at Freeberg will experience delays at higher utilization rates (optimum use is below 30 to 50 percent of total capacity), so you recommend an upgrade to a T2 on that link as well. The network administrator will need to consider these recommendations in light of other enterprise communication requirements to establish comprehensive infrastructure planning requirements.

| Year 1 network suitability | Peak load summary | | Estimated peak traffic | | | Existing bandwidth Mbps | Upgrade to: Mbps |
|---|---|---|---|---|---|---|---|
| | Desktop users | Web req/sec | Desktop Mbps | Web Mbps | Total Mbps | | |
| Site 1 - City hall | | | | | | | |
| City hall backbone | 46 | 1.28 | 23 | 0.64 | 23.64 | 100 | |
| City WAN connection | 52 | 0.33 | 1.456 | 0.17 | 1.62 | 1.54 | 6 |
| Site 2 - Operations | | | | | | | |
| WAN connection | 2 | | 0.056 | | 0.06 | 1.54 | |
| Remote field office (WAN) | | | | | | | |
| Site 3 - Freeberg | 30 | 0.17 | 0.84 | 0.08 | 0.92 | 1.54 | 6 |
| Site 4 - Willsberg | 20 | 0.17 | 0.56 | 0.08 | 0.64 | 1.54 | |

Figure 10.16    **Year 1 network suitability analysis**

| | |
|---|---|
| City hall WAN connection (T1) | Upgrade to T2 |
| Freeberg WAN connection (T1) | Upgrade to T2 |
| City Internet connection (T1) | Upgrade to T2 |
| Note: City hall backbone is close to limits. | |

Figure 10.17    **City of Rome year 1 network upgrade recommendations**

## Recommended year 2

Having conducted the network suitability analysis on year 2 using figure 10.18, you are ready to assess the network bandwidth necessary for the city's second year with a GIS. You see that peak traffic will considerably increase in the second year, putting pressure on both the city hall backbone and the terminal server connections, when you take into account the percent utilization delay factors. Assuming that the year 1 upgrades are in place, you recommend that the city hall backbone be upgraded to a gigabit switch for year 2 (figure 10.19). This switch will not be expensive because the existing backbone is on fiber.

The WAN connection, already a T2, will be under stress with 132 users, so you'll consider upgrading it to a T3 (45 Mbps).

The WAN connection from the operations facility and the new Internet connection from city hall should be established on a T2 (6 Mbps) to accommodate peak traffic, as should the connections to the remote sites at Willsberg and Wawash.

These recommendations will have a significant impact on the costs of GIS communication in the City of Rome—we will discuss how to take such things into account in the cost model, in the next chapter.

## Wait tolerance assessment

You have already defined a wait tolerance for each of the information products, in the IPDs. Now you can review the architecture and assess whether it will deliver response times within the wait tolerances. This is a balancing act. Clearly, the time taken for disk access, application CPU processing, and video display will determine wait tolerance on a stand-alone workstation. In distributed processing, however, the collected response times of each of the following components will be involved: disk access, server

| Year 2 network suitability | Peak load summary | | Estimated peak traffic | | | Existing bandwidth Mbps | Upgrade to: Mbps |
|---|---|---|---|---|---|---|---|
| | Desktop users | Web req/sec | Desktop Mbps | Web Mbps | Total Mbps | | |
| **Site 1 - City hall** | | | | | | | |
| City hall backbone | 63 | 1.78 | 31.5 | 0.89 | 32.39 | 100 | 1,000 |
| City WAN connection | 132 | 1.44 | 3.696 | 0.72 | 4.42 | 6 | 45 |
| City Internet connection | 62 | 0.36 | 1.736 | 0.18 | 1.92 | 1.54 | 6 |
| **Site 2 - Operations** | | | | | | | |
| WAN connection | 62 | 1.11 | 1.736 | 0.56 | 2.29 | 1.54 | 6 |
| **Remote field office (WAN)** | | | | | | | |
| Site 3 - Freeberg | 30 | 0.14 | 0.84 | 0.07 | 0.91 | 6 | |
| Site 4 - Willsberg | 40 | 0.19 | 1.12 | 0.10 | 1.22 | 1.54 | 6 |
| **Remote field offices (Internet)** | | | | | | | |
| Site 5 - Perth | 2 | 0.01 | 0.056 | 0.01 | 0.06 | 1.54 | |
| Site 6 - Wawash | 40 | 0.23 | 1.12 | 0.12 | 1.24 | 1.54 | 6 |
| Site 7 - Jackson | 20 | 0.12 | 0.56 | 0.06 | 0.62 | 1.54 | |
| **Police network** | | | | | | | |
| Police network backbone | 11 | 0.03 | 0.308 | 0.01 | 0.32 | 100 | |
| Police dial-up connection | | 0.001 | | 0.001 | 0.001 | 0.056 | |

Figure 10.18  **Year 2 network suitability analysis**

| City hall backbone (100 Mbps) | Upgrade to 1 Gbps |
|---|---|
| City WAN connection (T2) | Upgrade to T3 |
| City hall Internet connection (T1) | Upgrade to T2 |
| Operation facility WAN (T1) | Upgrade to T2 |
| Willsberg Internet connection (T1) | Upgrade to T2 |
| Wawash Internet connection (T1) | Upgrade to T2 |
| Note: Monitor network utilization during first year of operation. | |
| Note: Selectively upgrade network when bandwidth utilization exceeds recommended levels. | |

Figure 10.19 **City of Rome year 2 network upgrade recommendations**

CPU processing, network communications, application CPU processing, and video display. However long those operations take will determine the total response time for a particular application query. With current CPU technology, most application processing and server processing takes less than two seconds. But with distribution processing involved, the data transport time over the network is key—quite possibly the primary determinant of network transaction performance.

So let's see how this plays out in five combinations of server-to-client transmissions, referring back to figure 10.5 (on page 117). Using that chart, you can determine the network traffic transport times for each of the five server-to-client connections.

Again, client-server performance numbers provide the network traffic transport time for each bandwidth. The backbone in city hall, where servers support applications being run on Windows clients, has a network transport time of 0.05 seconds. The Windows terminal servers to terminal clients over a T1 WAN have a network transport time of 0.2 seconds; or if a T2 WAN was installed, a 0.05 second transport time. The Web-server-to-browser clients in PSAP units and remote sites experience a network transport time of 0.32 seconds over a T1 connection, and 0.08 seconds over a T2 connection. A network transport time of 18 seconds applies to the connection from Web server to emergency vehicles and police vehicles over 56 Kbps wireless transmission.

To assess whether your configuration performs within the wait tolerance you specified for each information product, you can add up all the response times that apply to it. (Of course, you must also consider how much other software applications performing on these shared network resources will affect available bandwidth, which we are not taking into account here.)

**Batch processing**

In any system, some functions are done in a batch processing mode. These include data loading, database administration, data backup, replication services (for the police), reconcile-and-post operations (for the engineering department), and some automated map production. In Rome, these functions will be performed in the IT department in city hall, but they will still make demands on the CPU. While this can be scheduled in off-peak hours, the best practice is to plan for at least one batch process consuming a dedicated CPU on the server during peak processing loads. (Batch processes executed on a separate client—workstation, etc.—may require much less than one server CPU: in some cases, such as automated map production scripts, one server CPU can support up to five concurrent client batch processes.)

## Platform sizing

Now you're ready to assess how many CPUs the whole system will require, which will tell you the platform sizes required. The performance or capacity planning model, figure 10.7 (on page 120), will help in this process. In compiling performance models, keep in mind that when a typical desktop client accesses a data server, for example, a certain percentage of the processing is carried out on the desktop and a certain percentage is carried out on the server. The resulting process load distribution determines how many desktop clients can be supported simultaneously by one server CPU. Clearly, the nature of the desktop and the software being used affect this distribution of effort. So for these performance models, assume that all CPUs are the same (3,200 Mhz, as in the Intel Xeon 3200 Mhz). For general planning purposes, we also assume these will scale in a linear fashion.

The city hall system deployment for year 1 and year 2 will be supported by a central GIS database server, a Windows terminal server farm, and a Web server hosted in the central IT department data center. Peak user loads for each of these platforms are identified in figure 10.20.

The police department network will be supported by a separate GIS database server and a Web server to support police vehicle reporting services (figure 10.21).

The number of CPUs required and the required platform configurations are generated in the platform sizing analysis that follows. In year 1, the city GIS database has peak loads of fifteen high-complexity users and eighty-three low-complexity users. Based on CPU performance models (figure 10.7), we know that a single data server CPU with search engine can support thirty concurrent desktop users. Figure 10.22 summarizes the platform sizing analysis.

Web transaction loads on the same data server can be included with standard desktop clients through a simple conversion: one desktop client equivalent to 360 Web requests per hour (each Web client generates six displays per minute). Batch processing will also be done on this computer, with four batch processes envisaged in the first year: database loading, database administration, data backup, and reconcile-and-post operations for the engineering department. A single CPU can handle these batch requirements, if an eight-second response time is adequate.

So as not to interfere with what clients expect from system performance, only one batch process will be allowed on the server during peak loads. Web loads affect the CPU, too. The resulting total load—144 GIS-related users on the city GIS database in year 1—requires 4.4 CPUs. Because processors come in two CPUs per box,

| Server platform | Year 1 peak loads | | Year 2 peak loads | |
|---|---|---|---|---|
| | High | Low | High | Low |
| GIS database server | 15 | 83 | 19 | 234 |
| Windows terminal server | | 52 | | 194 |
| Web server | Requests per hour 5,800 | | Requests per hour 12,900 | |

Figure 10.20  **City hall platform loads summary, 2004**

| Server platform | Year 1 peak loads | | Year 2 peak loads | |
|---|---|---|---|---|
| | High | Low | High | Low |
| GIS database server | | | 5 | 6 |
| Web server | Requests per hour 0 | | Requests per hour 200 | |

Figure 10.21  **Police department network platform loads summary, 2004**

| Year 1 | | | | | | | | | |
|---|---|---|---|---|---|---|---|---|---|
| Data server capacity | Peak desktop | | Batch load 1 | Web load | Total load | Per-CPU factors | CPU sizing estimate | Estimated pricing | |
| | High | Low | | | | | | Intel | UNIX |
| City GIS database | 15 | 83 | 30 | 16 | 144 | 30 | 4.8 | $55,000 | $68,750 |
| City Web services | | | Requests per hour 5,800 | | | 12,000 | 0.5 | 12,000 | $12,000 |
| WTS farm | | 52 | | | 52 | 7.5 | 6.9 | $80,000 | |

| Year 2 | | | | | | | | | |
|---|---|---|---|---|---|---|---|---|---|
| Platform sizing | Peak desktop | | Batch load 1 | Web load | Total load | Per-CPU factors | CPU sizing estimate | Estimated pricing | |
| | High | Low | | | | | | Intel | UNIX |
| City GIS database | 19 | 234 | 30 | 36 | 319 | 30 | 10.6 | $160,000 | $200,000 |
| City Web services | | | Requests per hour 12,900 | | | 12,000 | 1.1 | 12,000 | 12,000 |
| WTS farm | | 194 | | | 194 | 7.5 | 25.9 | 156,000 | |
| Police GIS database | 5 | 6 | 30 | 1 | 42 | 30 | 1.4 | 12,000 | $12,000 |
| Police Web services | | | Requests per hour 200 | | | 12,000 | 0.02 | $12,000 | |

Notes:

Storage pricing estimates: volume of data (GB) + 50% (database indexing) X $ per GB at RAID level required.

a.  Batch load: batch process in replication takes full CPU = 30 clients

b.  Web load: divide requests by factor of 360 = number of equivalent clients

c.  Per-CPU factors: number of clients/requests per CPU

d.  CPU pricing estimates: use hardware pricing model 2004 provided

   Note that SPECrate_int2000 specification indicates current technology CPUs.

   Choose next highest even CPU number for intermediate values, e.g., 4.8 use 6

   WTS farm and Web services can be used most efficiently in units of 2 CPU, e.g., 6.9 = 2x4 @ $12,000 = $48,000.

Figure 10.22   **Platform sizing analysis, 2004**

you would recommend a six-CPU server platform to support this load.

You will estimate terminal server performance in the same manner. In the first year, there are fifty-two low-complexity users. Using the performance model rule of 7.5 users per CPU (from figure 10.7), you know that 6.9 CPUs are required. Therefore, four dual-processor servers will support the terminal server farm configuration here.

In figure 10.22, you estimated that Web services will have 5,800 peak requests per hour in the first year. With the performance rules of 12,000 requests per hour per map server CPU accessing a DBMS data source, the demand could be met by 0.5 CPUs.

Year 2 presents a different picture. Referring to figure 10.22, you see that use of the city GIS database server now totals 253 concurrent users (19 high-complexity plus 234 low-complexity users). With the addition of

replication services for the police department and automated map production, batch-processing must handle a greater level of activity. While these bigger loads can be fit into the business operations schedule and scheduled for off-peak times, they still make significant CPU demands. A single batch process on the server consumes a server CPU, which is equivalent to supporting thirty concurrent desktop clients. Web data server loads have increased to 36 equivalent users, for a total load of 319 users on the city's central data server, requiring 10.6 CPUs. You would recommend a 12 CPU server platform to support this load.

The police department has a separate secure database and services eleven office staff users and batch processing including replication, for a total load of forty-two equivalent users, requiring 1.4 CPUs. One dual-processor server (two CPUs) will support this.

Terminal server loads are significantly extended in year 2. The additional servers in city hall and in the police department must support a total of 194 concurrent users now. At 7.5 per CPU, this requires 25.9 CPUs, but you can get this from thirteen dual-processor servers (two CPUs each) configured in a Citrix-Windows terminal server farm.

You estimate a total of 12,900 peak Web requests per hour for year 2; 12,000 per hour can be accommodated per CPU accessing the city hall database, leading to a demand for 2.2 CPUs. This Web environment would be supported with two dual-processor servers (two CPUs each). The police department provides its own secure Web services to its vehicles over 56 KBps dedicated dial-up lines. This is a modest use but still requires 0.02 CPU, and therefore one dual-processor server (two CPUs).

## Costs

These server requirements and related costs (in 2004) are summarized in the final columns of the same server sizing chart (figure 10.22). The costs for servers are taken from the 2004 hardware pricing model—figure 10.23—since the year 1 and year 2 analyses were completed in 2004. You can estimate the type and number of desktop and browser units you will need by assessing the total number of users at each level of processing complexity.

Software license costs for all systems depend on the level of complexity of the software and the number of concurrent users. You can calculate cost from the analysis already completed.

Storage costs vary according to the level of security required and the volume of digital data. Take a look at figure 7.8 to review the amount of disk space various

| Hardware pricing model 2004 | | | |
|---|---|---|---|
| Performance | | Operating system | |
| CPU | SPECrate_int2000 | Intel | UNIX |
| 2 | 34 | $12,000 | $12,000 |
| 4 | 58 | 30,000 | 30,000 |
| 6 | 73 | 55,000 | 68,750 |
| 8 | 88 | 80,000 | 100,000 |
| 10 | 109 | 120,000 | 150,000 |
| 12 | 130 | 160,000 | 200,000 |
| 14 | 150 | 200,000 | 300,000 |
| 16 | 171 | 240,000 | 360,000 |
| 18 | 188 | 280,000 | 420,000 |
| 20 | 206 | 320,000 | 480,000 |
| 22 | 223 | 360,000 | 540,000 |
| 24 | 240 | 400,000 | 600,000 |
| 26 | 258 | 450,000 | 900,000 |
| 28 | 275 | 500,000 | 1,000,000 |
| 30 | 293 | 550,000 | 1,100,000 |
| 32 | 310 | $600,000 | $1,200,000 |

Figure 10.23   **Hardware pricing model used for planning years 1 and 2**

storage options allow for, along with the 2007 prices. Now find the figures on the volume of digital data in the MIDL on page 58. You can estimate cost by adding 50 percent of those amounts to the volume figures to allow for data indexing (at a price per gigabyte dependent on the level of security required).

These are preliminary estimates to provide platform sizes and communications bandwidths, which allow you to make your first approximations of cost in the benefit–cost analysis to follow in chapter 11. These engineering and pricing models change as technology changes. Nevertheless, this method of accumulation of the costs for hardware, software, and storage will be useful for future years.

For instance, we don't need to solicit reports of benchmark tests and user experiences to see what has to happen in the City of Rome. A straightforward comparison of the technology needs in year 1 and year 2 tells us that there can be a phased implementation strategy

for the acquisition of technology and its deployment year by year. No longer is the paradigm of buying one large computer and expecting it to handle all requirements for the next five years a useful one.

Fortunately, we are planning within the context of not only rapid technology change but also component architecture to accommodate such change: dual-core processors allow you to add CPUs like building blocks as you grow. So plan for them: integrate a strategic plan for technology change with your activity plan for data acquisition and application development, and be aware of the technology life cycles you can anticipate (see figure 10.40 on page 149).

## City of Rome year 3 platform sizing and bandwidth planning

To continue with our fictional case study, let's say that the City of Rome implemented years 1 and 2 in 2005

| Hardware pricing model 2007 | | | | | | |
|---|---|---|---|---|---|---|
| Platform sockets | Single-core sockets | | Dual-core sockets | | Operating system | |
| | Core | SRint2000 | Core | SRint2000 | Intel/AMD | UNIX |
| 1 | 1 | 30 | 2 | 60 | $5,000 | $6,500 |
| 2 | 2 | 60 | 4 | 120 | 10,000 | 13,000 |
| 4 | 4 | 120 | 8 | 240 | 25,000 | 34,000 |
| 6 | 6 | 180 | 12 | 360 | 55,000 | 75,000 |
| 8 | 8 | 240 | 16 | 480 | 80,000 | 115,000 |
| 10 | 10 | 300 | 20 | 600 | 120,000 | 170,000 |
| 12 | 12 | 360 | 24 | 720 | 160,000 | 232,000 |
| 14 | 14 | 420 | 28 | 840 | 210,000 | 310,000 |
| 16 | 16 | 480 | 32 | 960 | 260,000 | 390,000 |
| 18 | 18 | 540 | 36 | 1,080 | 335,000 | 510,000 |
| 20 | 20 | 600 | 40 | 1,200 | 400,000 | 610,000 |
| 22 | 22 | 660 | 44 | 1,320 | 470,000 | 725,000 |
| 24 | 24 | 720 | 48 | 1,440 | 540,000 | 840,000 |
| 26 | 26 | 780 | 52 | 1,560 | 605,000 | 950,000 |
| 28 | 28 | 840 | 56 | 1,680 | 670,000 | 1,060,000 |
| 30 | 30 | 900 | 60 | 1,800 | 740,000 | 1,180,000 |
| 32 | 32 | 960 | 64 | 1,920 | $800,000 | $1,300,000 |

Figure 10.24　**Hardware pricing model for planning year 3**

and 2006, based on the initial design analysis in 2004, and GIS demand grew throughout the city. Changes in technology since the initial 2004 design and a growing interest in expanding GIS operations led to the following year 3 design, which was conducted in 2007.

Technology changes since 2004 include a new and improved Web mapping services software, dual-core socket server technology, and recommendations to take advantage of search engine architecture performance improvements. The new technology promised reduced hardware and licensing costs along with improved user productivity. The updated hardware pricing model is given in figure 10.24.

A new sizing methodology was also introduced that would expand system design planning capabilities. (These new capacity planning models, based on Intel dual-core 3.0 GHz performance, are provided in figure 10.25.) GIS planners can take advantage of these 2007 platform sizing models, which reflect the advances in technology, as well as the 2007 hardware pricing models with their lower cost formulations. The new system architectures will also improve the network load factors that can be used in 2007.

Recent developments in software have made it important to differentiate between architectures with search engines attached to the enterprise DBMS and those with search engines embedded in the workstation (desktop) software, or in the Windows terminal server, either with a "direct connect" to the DBMS. Except in a few cases of nonenterprise geodatabase use limited to coverages and shapefiles, all architectures now employ a search engine, most efficiently in "direct connect" workflows.

Along with the new platform sizing methodology, methods developed from experience can be applied to predicting the amount of, and planning sufficient bandwidth for, the data traffic volume your network will have to support. Guidelines for these network loads (megabits per second per user, or megabits per Web product) are given in figure 10.26. The Web traffic network throughput was changed in the updated models to account for more complex information products being deployed in Web solutions.

With these factors in hand and the knowledge already established of where data sources, computers, and users are located, we can estimate platform sizing and network

| User workflow | 2007 capacity planning model per core SPECrate_int2000 = 30 | | | |
|---|---|---|---|---|
| | Service time (sec) | Capacity per core | | |
| | | Displays/min | Displays/hr | Peak users |
| **GIS data server (desktop user productivity = 10 displays per minute)** | | | | |
| File data source | 200 displays/min per 100 Mbps network interface card | | | |
| Database server with direct connect client | 0.060 | 1,000 | 60,000 | 100.0 |
| Database server with search engine | 0.120 | 500 | 30,000 | 50.0 |
| **Web server (Web user productivity = 6 displays per minute)** | | | | |
| ArcGIS server using DBMS with direct connect | 0.580 | 103 | 6,207 | 17.2 |
| ArcGIS server using DBMS with search engine | 0.520 | 115 | 6,923 | 19.2 |
| **Windows terminal server (desktop user productivity = 10 displays per minute)** | | | | |
| Windows terminal server using DBMS with direct connect | 0.540 | 111 | 6,667 | 11.1 |
| Windows terminal server using GIS file data source | 0.600 | 100 | 6,000 | 10.0 |
| Windows terminal server using DBMS with search engine | 0.480 | 125 | 7,500 | 12.5 |

Figure 10.25 **Capacity planning models, 2007**

bandwidth requirements for year 3 still using the "peak user" approach we are familiar with from year 1 and year 2.

## Year 3 requirements

Year 3 exhibits the usual trend in GIS operations. More parts of the organization want to take fuller advantage of GIS capabilities, some for the first time, some in addition to ongoing usage, and some to take advantage of software advances that did not exist previously.

The police department wants to take advantage of new capabilities for replicating selected parts of the database rather than incurring complete replication every night. It also wants to double its use of GIS for crime analysis and introduce two new information products for police dispatching and optimal routing of patrol officers. Several major improvements are required in the operations facility. The fire and ambulance dispatch needs a 911 In-Vehicle Routing Display. Using ArcGIS Tracking Analyst, the snow clearing operations will be aided by GIS in their scheduling and vehicle tracking of one hundred snowplows.

The engineering department intends to use GIS for work order optimizing in both the engineering and field operations and for work reports to improve workflow. Two additional field offices (Petersville and Rogerton), both with large staffs, have asked to be added to the GIS. In city hall, the business development department wants to use ArcGIS Business Analyst for its site selection process—taking advantage of the net application service from NatureServe and Flood Zone Analysis of serviced

land using FEMA Web services—to calculate emergency response time for a variety of proposed business sites. Both the business development department in city hall and the remote field offices (now on the Internet) expect an increase in the number of requests per hour on their Web services.

The year 3 increases in GIS activity are summarized in figure 10.27, with the new activity highlighted in red.

Comparing the workloads of year 3 and year 2, figures 10.27 and 10.12 make the increases clear. In city hall, the engineering department has added five peak users. The business development department accounts for an additional eighteen peak users: those to be involved in site selection (eight), analysis of flood endangered land (eight), and the calculation of emergency response capability for potential business development (two). The police department has assigned an additional ten detectives as peak users in crime analysis; managing the police dispatch service will require an additional three peak users. In the operations facility, the fire and ambulance dispatch will need thirty more peak users, and scheduling for snow clearing adds another four.

The two new remote field offices, Petersville and Rogerton, represent 120 peak users combined. When added to the peak users already on the system (figure 10.12)—66 + 70 + 182 = 318—they make a total of 318 remote desktop users accessing the Windows terminal server, 24 users accessing the police network production server, and an overall total of 404 desktop users on the city enterprise data server. The anticipated increase in Web requests per hour of 2,000 provided by the business

| Client platform | Data per query | | Traffic per query | | Kbps traffic per user | |
|---|---|---|---|---|---|---|
| | KBpq | Adj KBpq | Kbpq | Mbpq | 6 dpm | 10 dpm |
| File server client | 1,000 | 5,000 | 50,000 | 50.000 | 5,000 | 8,333 |
| Search engine client | 1,000 | 500 | 5,000 | 5.000 | 500 | 833 |
| Terminal client | 100 | 28 | 280 | 0.280 | 28 | 47 |
| Web browser client | 100 | 100 | 1,000 | 1.000 | 100 | 167 |
| Web ArcMap client | 200 | 200 | 2,000 | 2.000 | 200 | 333 |

Figure 10.26 **New network load factors**

| City of Rome - year 3 | | | | Total users | Peak user workflow | | | Server IMS |
|---|---|---|---|---|---|---|---|---|
| | | | | | Desktop | | Business Analyst | |
| Department | Workflow | IPD | User type | | High | Low | | |
| **Site 1 - City hall** | | | | | | | | |
| Planning | Zoning | 1.0 | Planner | 25 | | 15 | | |
| | | 1.1 | Web services | | | | | 2,600 |
| | Permits | 1.2 | Inspector | 25 | | 15 | | |
| | | 1.3 | Appraiser | 20 | 10 | | | |
| | | 1.4 | Supervisor | 5 | 2 | | | |
| | | 1.5 | Web services | | | | | 900 |
| Engineering | Sewer backup | 2.1 | Engineer | 5 | | 3 | | |
| | | 2.2 | Web services | | | | | 1,000 |
| | Electrical breaks | 2.3 | Electrician | 13 | 6 | | | |
| | | 2.4 | Supervisor | 2 | 1 | | | |
| | | 2.5 | Web services | | | | | 1,900 |
| | Highway repair | 2.6 | Field engineer | 11 | | 7 | | |
| | | 2.7 | Contracts | 4 | | 4 | | |
| | Work orders | 2.8 | Managers | 4 | | 3 | | |
| | Work reports | 2.9 | Field units | 10 | | 2 | | |
| Business development | Site selection and NatureServe | 6.1 | Planners | 10 | | | 8 | |
| | FEMA flood zone, serviced land | 6.2 | Planners | 10 | | | 8 | |
| | Emergency response, time, etc. | 6.3 | Planners | 2 | | | 2 | |
| | Web services | 6.4 | | | | | | 2,000 |
| City hall LAN totals | | | | 146 | 19 | 49 | 18 | |
| IT department | Public | | Web services | | | | | 17,600 |
| Police (Firewall) | Patrol schedule | 5.1 | Administration | 10 | | 3 | | |
| | | 5.5 | Web services | | | | | 200 |
| | Crime analysis | 5.2 | Detectives | 20 | 15 | | | |
| | Special events | 5.3 | Traffic | 10 | | 3 | | |
| Remote patrols | Police dispatch | 5.4 | Traffic | 10 | | 3 | | |
| | Patrols/routing | 5.6 | Patrol officers | 20 | | | | 200 |
| Police network totals | | | | 70 | 15 | 9 | | 400 |
| **Site 2 - Operations** | | | | | | | | |
| Operations | Cleanup program | 3.1 | Ops. staff | 4 | | 2 | | |
| 911 | Response | 3.2 | Call takers | 50 | | 30 | | |
| | | 3.3 | Web services | | | | | 4,000 |
| Remote vehicles | Fire and ambulance dispatch | 3.4 | Schedulers | 30 | | 30 | | |
| | Routing | 3.5 | Drivers | 30 | | | | |
| Snow clearing | Scheduling | 3.6 | Engineers | 4 | | 4 | | |
| | Snowplows | 3.7 | Drivers | 100 | | | | |
| Operations totals | | | | 218 | | 66 | | |
| **Remote field offices (WAN)** | | | | | | | | |
| Site 3 - Freeberg | Inspection | 4.1 | Field engineer | 45 | | 30 | | |
| Site 4 - Willsberg | Inspection | 4.1 | Field engineer | 60 | | 40 | | |
| WAN field offices | Inspection | 4.2 | Web services | | | | | 1,200 |
| Remote field office (WAN) totals | | | | 105 | | 70 | | |
| **Remote field offices (Internet)** | | | | | | | | |
| Site 5 - Perth | Inspection | 4.3 | Field engineer | 10 | | 2 | | |
| Site 6 - Wawash | Inspection | 4.3 | Field engineer | 50 | | 40 | | |
| Site 7 - Jackson | Inspection | 4.3 | Field engineer | 60 | | 20 | | |
| Site 8 - Petersville | Inspection | 4.3 | Field engineer | 80 | | 60 | | |
| Site 9 - Rogerton | Inspection | 4.3 | Field engineer | 80 | | 60 | | |
| Internet field offices | Inspection | 4.2 | Web services | | | | | 4,000 |
| Remote field office (Internet) totals | | | | 120 | | 182 | | |
| City totals (excluding police private network) | | | | 589 | 19 | 367 | 18 | |

Figure 10.27   **Year 3 user requirements (new activity highlighted in red)**

137

| Server platform | Year 3 peak loads | | |
|---|---|---|---|
| | High | Low | |
| GIS database server | 19 | 367 | 18 |
| Windows terminal server | | 318 | |
| Web server | Requests per hour 17,600 | | |

Figure 10.28  **City hall platform loads summary, 2007**

| Server platform | Year 3 peak loads | |
|---|---|---|
| | High | Low |
| GIS database server | 15 | 9 |
| Web server | Requests per hour 400 | |

Figure 10.29  **Police department platform loads summary, 2007**

development department and 2,700 by the remote field offices result in a new total of 17,600 requests per hour for public Web services. The police network will have to handle an additional 200 Web requests per hour, for a total of 400 (see figure 10.29).

## Calculating platform size

What size platform could handle these new peak loads? Calculating that might be easier than you think, if you use the platform loads summaries in figures 10.28 and 10.29 and the calculations summarized for analysis in figure 10.30. In figure 10.28, you can see there are 318 peak users using the Windows terminal server. In Rome, this is configured using a DBMS with a search engine located on the terminal server, and reference to figure 10.30 shows that it can handle 11.1 GIS clients per terminal server core. This means that 28.6 cores will be required to support the terminal server.

Unlike central enterprise database servers, terminal servers can be supported using a group of commodity server platforms configured as a server farm. These server farms can be purchased and managed as a group

of server blades, with each server blade supporting multiple processor cores. A typical server blade contains two dual-core sockets—four cores—and each blade costs $10,000 (figure 10.24). Therefore, eight of these can handle the demand for 28.6 cores, for a total price of $80,000 (in 2007).

And how about the platform sizing to accommodate the growing load on the enterprise application server? It must expand to handle 17,600 Web requests per hour. Figure 10.25 tells you that a Web composite server (Web application server and map server on the same platform), using a DBMS with direct connect, can handle 6,207 map requests per hour per Web server core. So 2.8 cores will be enough to handle the City of Rome's expanding public Web services.

The city, considering batch processes and security, would like to support their Web services with two servers to improve availability and provide 24-7 support. One more Web server in the design would be a good investment: to support geodatabase replication services and other potential batch processing loads during peak operations, and to provide services if one server fails.

| Platform sizing | Year 3 | | | | | | | | | |
|---|---|---|---|---|---|---|---|---|---|---|
| | Peak desktop | | | Batch load 1 | Web load | Total load | Per-core factors | Core sizing estimate | Estimated pricing | |
| | High | Low | BA | | | | | | Intel | UNIX |
| City GIS database | 19 | 367 | 18 | 100 | 49 | 553 | 100 | 5.5 | $25,000 | $34,000 |
| City Web services | | | | Requests per hour 17,600 | | | 6,207 | 2.8 | 10,000 | 13,000 |
| WTS farm | | 318 | | | | 318 | 11.1 | 28.6 | 80,000 | |
| Police GIS database | 15 | 9 | | 100 | 1 | 125 | 100 | 1.2 | 5,000 | $6,500 |
| Police Web services | | | | Requests per hour 400 | | | 6,207 | 0.06 | $5,000 | |

**Notes:**
Storage pricing estimates: volume of data (GB) + 50% (database indexing) X $ per GB at RAID level required.
a.  Batch load: batch process in replication takes full CPU = 100 equivalent clients.
b.  Web load: divide requests by factor of 360 = number of equivalent clients. (One Web user = 6 DPM.)
c.  Per-core factors: number of clients/requests per core.
d.  Single- and dual-core socket platforms available at same pricing (use dual-core sockets).
e.  Socket pricing estimates: use hardware pricing model 2007 provided on page 134.
    Note that SPECrate_int2000 specification of 30 indicates current technology (Intel dual core 3.0 GHz).
    When more than 1 socket, choose next highest even socket number for intermediate values, e.g., 5.5 core = 4 dual-core sockets.
    WTS farm and Web services can be used most efficiently in units of 2 dual-core sockets, e.g., 28.6 = 4x8 @ $10,000 = $80,000.

Figure 10.30  **Year 3 platform sizing analysis model**

With a total of 3.8 cores required to support expected peak processing loads, two blade servers, each with two dual-core sockets (four cores per server), would be plenty to meet these year-3 peak processing requirements. At $10,000 each, that's a $20,000 price tag (in 2007).

The primary enterprise data server uses a DBMS with direct connect clients (search engine supported on the client applications). The enterprise data server must support a total of 318 GIS Windows terminal server clients and 86 local desktop clients for a total of 404 peak users, to which must be added the impact of the Web transaction load. Using the factors from the 2007 platform sizing model (figure 10.25), this is calculated by dividing 17,600, the total number of map displays (or requests) per hour, by 360 (one Web user's worth), which gives the equivalent of 49 peak users to be added to make the total 453.

Additionally, replication services for the police department will place onto the enterprise database server a standard load of 100 peak users per replication (including

other batch processing loads such as reconcile-and-post, tracking service packets, maintenance operating or data loading); plus 18 more peak desktop users of ArcGIS Business Analyst—all of which raises this server's total peak user load to 553. According to the 2007 platform sizing analysis model (figure 10.30), a desktop GIS, using a DBMS with direct connect clients, can manage 100 clients per DBMS core, which means you need at least 5.5 cores on the enterprise database server platform. Because these cores must be in a single platform to share the overall load, an 8-core (4 dual-core sockets) platform will be necessary; the 2007 Intel pricing for that was $25,000.

The price for these cores is reducing rapidly as multicore socket technology becomes more available.

## Calculating bandwidth requirements

Again this is very straightforward. The object is to determine the bandwidth required for each segment of the communications network. To do this, you need

139

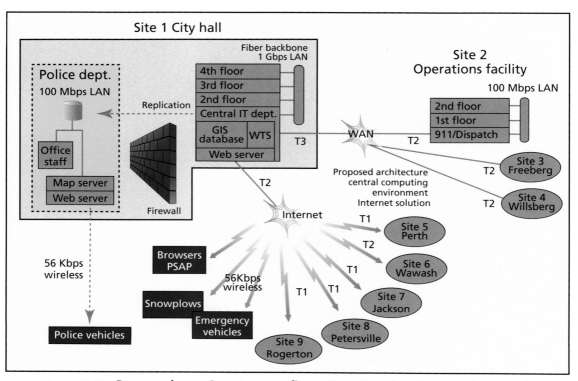

Figure 10.31 **Proposed year 3 system configuration: User locations and network communications updated with year 2 recommendations**

three pieces of information. One is the illustration (figure 10.31) updated with the proposed user locations and network communications proposed in the year 2 recommendations, which illustrates just what has to be connected together and the current bandwidth available.

The second is the number of peak users that will be using each segment (figure 10.32), information we referred to earlier in determining platform sizes. The third piece of information can be found in figure 10.26, the updated network load factors, giving the number of megabits per second consumed by each user in typical system architectures.

The year 3 user requirements (figure 10.27) can be used to identify the peak workflow users multiplied by their factor for architecture from figure 10.26, and gives

the megabit per second traffic in each communication segment (figure 10.33).

Three types of system architecture are involved in Rome. The first is the city enterprise server using DBMS and a search engine, connected to the peak users in city hall by a fiber-optic Ethernet. There are 86 (19+49+18) peak users in city hall. Using the factor table, with 0.833 megabits per second consumed by each user, you can calculate that these 86 peak users make a demand of 71.638 megabits per second on the Ethernet. Given the frequent collisions at higher than 20 to 30 percent of the 100 megabits per second bandwidth available on this link, it is recommended that a giganet fiber-optic switch be put in place to increase the capacity to 1,000 megabits per second. This move would also accommodate the 24 police peak

| Network loads | Year 3 peak loads | | | |
|---|---|---|---|---|
| | High | Low | Business Analyst | Web req/hr |
| **Site 1 - City hall** | | | | |
| City hall backbone | 19 | 49 | 18 | |
| City WAN connection | | 136 | | |
| City Internet connection | | 182 | | 17,600 |
| **Site 2 - Operations** | | | | |
| WAN connection | | 66 | | |
| **Remote field offices (WAN)** | | | | |
| Site 3 - Freeberg | | 30 | | |
| Site 4 - Willsberg | | 40 | | |
| **Remote field offices (Internet)** | | | | |
| Site 5 - Perth | | 2 | | |
| Site 6 - Wawash | | 40 | | |
| Site 7 - Jackson | | 20 | | |
| Site 8 - Petersville | | 60 | | |
| Site 9 - Rogerton | | 60 | | |
| **Police network** | | | | |
| Police network backbone | 15 | 9 | | 200 |
| Police dial-up connection | | | | 10 |

Figure 10.32  **Year 3 network loads**

| Year 3 network suitability | Peak load summary | | Estimated peak traffic | | | Existing bandwidth Mbps | Upgrade to: Mbps |
|---|---|---|---|---|---|---|---|
| | Desktop users | Web req/sec* | Desktop Mbps | Web Mbps | Total Mbps | | |
| **Site 1 - City hall** | | | | | | | |
| City hall backbone | 86 | | 71.638 | | 71.64 | 1,000 | |
| City WAN connection | 136 | | 3.808 | | 3.81 | 45 | |
| City Internet connection | 182 | 4.89 | 5.096 | 2.44 | 7.54 | 6 | 45 |
| **Site 2 - Operations** | | | | | | | |
| WAN connection | 66 | | 1.848 | | 1.85 | 6 | |
| **Remote field office (WAN)** | | | | | | | |
| Site 3 - Freeberg | 30 | | 0.84 | | 0.84 | 6 | |
| Site 4 - Willsberg | 40 | | 1.12 | | 1.12 | 6 | |
| **Remote field offices (Internet)** | | | | | | | |
| Site 5 - Perth | 2 | | 0.056 | | 0.06 | 1.54 | |
| Site 6 - Wawash | 40 | | 1.12 | | 1.12 | 6 | |
| Site 7 - Jackson | 20 | | 0.56 | | 0.56 | 1.54 | |
| Site 8 - Petersville | 60 | | 1.68 | | 1.68 | 1.54 | 6 |
| Site 9 - Rogerton | 60 | | 1.68 | | 1.68 | 1.54 | 6 |
| **Police network** | | | | | | | |
| Police network backbone | 24 | 0.06 | 0.672 | 0.06 | 0.73 | 1.54 | |
| Police dial-up connection | | 0.003 | | 0.003 | 0.002 | 0.056 | |

* Note that the category Web requests per hour has been converted to Web requests per second.

Figure 10.33  **Extended year 3 peak load summary**

141

users, also using a factor of 0.833, and their total demand of 19.992 megabits per second (figure 10.26).

The next segment of concern is the city hall WAN connection that supports the operations facility and the remote sites at Freeberg and Willsberg. There are 66 peak users in the operations facility and 70 more in the field offices. With their communication handled by a terminal server, the factor for the WAN traffic is 0.047 megabits per second per user, which gives a total demand of 6.392 Mbps on the city-hall-to-WAN link. Bearing in mind the delays with traffic higher than 30 to 50 percent of available bandwidth on WAN segments, the existing T2 connection (6 megabits per second) will need to be upgraded to T3 (45 megabits per second). The connections to the WAN from the operations facility building will involve 66 peak users, demanding 3.102 megabits per second, requiring a T2 connection rather than the T1 that currently exists.

Similarly, the remote sites at Freeberg and Willsberg—with 30 and 40 peak users and a terminal server factor of 0.047 resulting in numbers that overload the T1—will require T2 communications. The Internet link between the city hall Web server and the Internet must accommodate all the remote field offices in sites 5, 6, 7, 8, and 9. A total of 182 peak users work at these sites, so factoring in their demand of 8.554 megabits per second, the connection should be a T3 (45 megabits per second).

The individual connections from the Internet to the remote sites are derived from the number of peak users at each site given in figure 10.27, the year 3 user requirements. All of the sites, with the exception of site 5, have peak users that demand more megabits per second than a T1 can handle, and should be upgraded to a T2.

Finally, the load on the city-hall-to-Internet link demanded by IT Web services must be examined. This load comes to 17,800 requests per hour, calculated by adding up the Web services requests (figure 10.29) from city hall (8,400), remote field offices (9,200), and the police department (200). Translated into requests per second (17,600 ÷ 3,600 = 4.944)—and using a Web service to browser network factor of 1.000 (from figure 10.26)—this load of 4.944 Mbps on the network can be accommodated on the T3 now linking the Internet to city hall.

## New detailed approach

All the capacity planning calculations we've done so far have been based on the number of peak users making demands on computer platforms and on communication services. Yet a more detailed approach has been devised by systems architect Dave Peters. He postulates that all users are not the same and can be differentiated based on the number of displays generated by the computer in the process of carrying out the task involved. In the production of an information product, this may translate into the number of steps to make the information product, the degree of function complexity being used within the step, and the volume of data being handled by that function at that time.

In this way, the model establishes platform service times for standard workflow types, service times that can be adjusted based on performance metrics collected during initial application deployment. As a guideline, it can be assumed that the average user with the average task generates ten displays per minute during peak usage. This number may decrease to as few as two for simple tasks or increase to multiples of ten for complex operations. Batch process loads are adjusted to consume a platform core on the primary component server, and can generate appropriate service loads on the remaining affected platform for more discrete platform sizing metrics. Figure 10.34 provides the year 3 analysis using the more detailed approach.

This approach will be of increasing use, particularly in large enterprise systems with a steady workflow and observable repetitive operations, where it will allow platform sizing and bandwidth requirements to be more precisely calculated.

To explore this more detailed method, let's apply it here to Rome year 3, keeping the user requirements exactly the same as the ones shown for the year 3 model (figure 10.27) in the previous analysis. Based on the concept that one unit of work common to all user activity is the display, this finer-grained approach regards the processing components of a computer system involved in producing the display as the "workflow." At the heart of this approach is the effort to identify more specifically the workflow involved in the production of a display. Workflows vary, depending on the software used in conjunction with the hardware involved, from stand-alone workstations to the use of a GIS spatial server, a Web server, or a Windows terminal server. Whether a file data source is employed or a DBMS database (activated in conjunction with a search engine) further differentiates the matter. Direct access architecture takes advantage of

the search engine being located on the client terminal server or Web server. Otherwise the DBMS is used in conjunction with the search engine on the database.

Each type of workflow has an impact on the productivity of the user and on the workload required of a core. The workloads you see in Rome year 3 are fairly typical. You can trace how workflows from the user requirements in figure 10.27 are in conjunction with the workflow types that appear in the 2007 capacity planning models (figure 10.25): public Web services are handled by a Web composite server acting on the DBMS (search engine supported on the Web composite server). The composite server includes the Web application server and the Web mapping server processing loads. The city hall desktops are directly connected to the DBMS with the search engine supported on the client application installed on the desktop. This effective configuration is more efficient

| City of Rome workflow analysis year 3 | | | | | | |
|---|---|---|---|---|---|---|
| Types of workflow | Software technology | Users | DPM/client | DPM | Mbpd | Mbps |
| **Site 1 - City hall** | | Total city ISP traffic = 13.383 | | | | |
| Public Web services | Server | 48.9 | 6 | 293 | 1.000 | 4.890 |
| GIS batch processing services | | 1 | 100 | 100 | | |
| High | Desktop | 19 | 10 | 190 | 5.000 | 15.833 |
| Low | | 49 | 10 | 490 | 5.000 | 40.833 |
| Business Analyst | | 18 | 10 | 180 | 5.000 | 15.000 |
| | | Total city WAN traffic = 6.347 | | | | |
| **Site 2 - Operations facility** | | Total operations facility WAN traffic = 3.080 | | | | |
| Low | Desktop | 66 | 10 | 660 | 0.280 | 3.080 |
| **Remote field office (WAN)** | | Total remote office WAN traffic = 3.267 | | | | |
| Site 3 - Inspection 4.1 | Desktop | 30 | 10 | 300 | 0.280 | 1.400 |
| Site 4 - Inspection 4.1 | | 40 | 10 | 400 | 0.280 | 1.867 |
| **Remote field offices (Internet)** | | Total remote office ISP traffic = 8.493 | | | | |
| Site 5 - Inspection 4.3 | Desktop | 2 | 10 | 20 | 0.280 | 0.093 |
| Site 6 - Inspection 4.3 | | 40 | 10 | 400 | 0.280 | 1.867 |
| Site 7 - Inspection 4.3 | | 20 | 10 | 200 | 0.280 | 0.933 |
| Site 8 - Inspection 4.3 | | 60 | 10 | 600 | 0.280 | 2.800 |
| Site 9 - Inspection 4.3 | | 60 | 10 | 600 | 0.280 | 2.800 |

Figure 10.34 **Year 3 city hall workflow analysis**

143

| City of Rome workflow analysis year 3 | | | | | | |
|---|---|---|---|---|---|---|
| | Software technology | Peak workflow | | | Network traffic | |
| Types of workflow | | Users | DPM/client | DPM | Mbpd | Mbps |
| Site 1 - Police network | | Total city ISP traffic = 13.383 | | | | |
| Police patrol Web services | Server | 1 | 4 | 4 | 1.000 | 0.056 |
| GIS batch processing services | | 1 | 103 | 103 | | |
| High | Desktop | 15 | 10 | 150 | 5.000 | 12.500 |
| Low | | 9 | 10 | 90 | 5.000 | 7.500 |

Figure 10.35    **Year 3 police department workflow analysis**

and less expensive than licensing the search engine on the DBMS. The operations facility and sites 3 and 4 field offices are connected to the city DBMS via the WAN, through the Windows terminal server acting on the city DBMS, again with the search engines on the Windows terminal server. The remote Internet field offices at sites 5 through 9 also use thin terminal clients accessing GIS desktop applications supported on the Windows terminal server with direct connection to the city DBMS.

The police department has its own data server and composite Web server platforms. The Web composite server supports the remote police patrols and uses a public Web services type of workflow over their private network. The GIS batch processing service is used to support data replication from the city hall database.

The use of the workflows in platform selection is based on assumptions about the size of the displays being produced, the number of users (productivity) per workflow, and the demands on the core of each component of the workflow in the process of producing the display. These assumptions are as follows:

- A display is considered to be a standard unit of work undertaken by a GIS for a specific workflow.
- The term *display* refers to the screen content in front of the user after an operation has been performed or a unit of system loads generated by an average user for a particular workflow.

- The *size* of the display refers to the traffic involved expressed in megabits.
- Display size depends on the complexity of the data and display resolution.
- The efficiency of the transportation protocol and the data compression used are also factors that contribute to display traffic volume.
- For planning purposes, using this approach, we assume that typical displays require 50 megabits of traffic from a file data source, or 5 megabits of traffic from a data source when a search engine is used.
- Experience has shown that Web browser traffic is typically 100 kilobytes (1 megabit) per display.

Within this concept, network load factors for the new model are represented in figure 10.36. The new network load factors represent traffic in terms of map displays and Web products, where an average desktop user generates ten map displays per minute. (Note that the information is the same as in figure 10.26; figure 10.36 is simply an expanded graphic representation.)

The number of users (productivity) per workflow will vary from organization to organization and task to task. You can make adjustments for such variation, using this more detailed approach, and that's part of its charm. For planning purposes, the default productivity rates used are as follows:

- A display every 6 seconds for a power user (10 displays per minute)

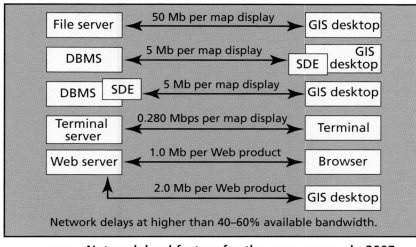

**Figure 10.36** **Network load factors for the new approach, 2007**

Values from Dave Peters, "System Design Strategies," 2007. Used with permission.

- A display every 10 seconds (6 displays per minute) for a Web user

The number of users per workflow is taken directly from the year 3 user requirements (figure 10.27), calculated by department, information product, and user type. Similarly, the number of requests per hour for Web products is taken from the year 3 user requirements and translated into number of requests per minute for use in platform sizing.

The number of seconds of service time per workflow is the summation of the time in seconds invoked in each component of the supporting hardware configuration. A stand-alone workstation is self-contained. A workstation direct connection to a DBMS (search engine supported on the client workstation) makes demands on the server using the search engine and the DBMS (90 percent of the load on the client workstation and 10 percent on the database server). Similarly, a GIS desktop terminal client application (search engine on the terminal server) making a direct connection to a DBMS supports about 90 percent of the processing load on the Windows terminal server, with approximately 10 percent of its work handled within

the DBMS. A GIS composite Web server supports the Web application requesting display services from the GIS server, which can use a direct search engine connection that includes additional DBMS query loads performed on the data servers.

The times are expressed in seconds per display. The component service times required to produce an average map display are identified by workflow to quantify hardware platform computer requirements.

It becomes very useful to remember that the summarized average service time for a workflow is made up of the individual service times in each step on each piece of hardware used in the workflow. These individual service times can be observed over a period of time, and the planning model can be adjusted in light of the measurements obtained.

The service times will depend on the information handling capacity of current cores, capacities illustrated in the 2007 capacity planning models (figure 10.25). On the left, you see the various types of workflows encountered in Rome. Next comes the service time for each, along with the capacities per core. Moving to the right, you'll note the 2007 estimates, with a per-core SPECrate_int2000 that equals

30. A fully detailed model, provided by Peters, includes all practicable forms of workflow and all current cores, with calculated SPEC rates and the displays per core used in system costing, and is published in his current white paper, "System Design Strategies" (www.esri.com/systemdesign). You will find the most frequently encountered workflows in figure 10.25, however, including the ones found in Rome.

## New approach to platform sizing

Working from this (figure 10.25) and the workflows identified in year 3 user requirements (figure 10.27), you can calculate the city production server requirements, as illustrated in figure 10.28, year 3 platform loads. At city hall, the public Web services workflow fields 17,600 requests per hour, which translates into (17,600/60) 293 displays per minute (figure 10.34). Assuming a user requests 6 displays per minute, this equals 48.9 users at peak workflow. To these must be added the GIS batch processing services invoked by the police department replication, which will put a standard load of 100 displays per minute per replication

on the server, resulting in a total of 398 displays per minute at peak workflow (see figure 10.37). Power users in the planning department ("High"), engineering department ("Low"), and business development department ("Business Analyst"), numbering 19, 49, and 18, respectively, all use search engine enabled workstations. Each power user demands 10 displays per minute, resulting in the 190, 490, and 180 displays per minute required of the server.

The wide area network (WAN) traffic connecting the site 2 operations facility and the sites 3 and 4 remote field offices, all with their client-side search engine capability, are connected via the Windows terminal server to the city DBMS. These make a combined demand of 660+300+400 = 1360 DPM on the server. The remote Internet field offices at sites 5 through 9—a total of 182 peak users with 10 displays-per-minute requirements—are similarly connected to the Windows terminal server, using its search engine to facilitate connection to the DBMS. This results in a total of 318 peak users demanding 3,180 displays per minute from the Windows terminal server and from the DBMS.

| Server loads | Software technology | Peak workflow | | Per-core factors DPM | Core sizing estimate | Total sockets | Estimated pricing | |
|---|---|---|---|---|---|---|---|---|
| | | Users | DPM | | | | Intel | UNIX |
| Windows terminal server using DBMS with direct connect | Desktop | 318 | 3180 | 111 | 28.6 | 16 | $80,000 | |
| Web composite server using DBMS with direct connect | Server | 48.9 | 393 | 103 | 3.8 | 2 | 10,000 | $13,000 |
| DBMS with direct connect client | DBMS | | 4433 | 1,000 | 4.4 | 4 | 25,000 | 34,000 |

Notes:
Storage pricing estimates: volume of data (GB) + 50% (database indexing) X $ per GB at RAID level required (see figure 7.8).
a. Batch load: batch process takes full Web mapping server core (100 DPM).
b. Per-core factors: number of displays/server core.
c. Platform pricing estimates: use hardware pricing model 2007.
  Note SRint2000 specifications shows vendor benchmark for performance baseline core.
  Choice of single- or dual-core sockets (dual-core sockets provide best value).
  Windows terminal server and enterprise application server best supported by two-core socket platforms
  (4.6 = 2x2 dual-core sockets @ $10,000 = $20,000).

Figure 10.37  **Year 3 city hall refined platform sizing analysis**

| Server loads | Software technology | Peak workflow | | Per-core factors DPM | Core sizing estimate | Total sockets | Estimated pricing | |
|---|---|---|---|---|---|---|---|---|
| | | Users | DPM | | | | Intel | UNIX |
| Web composite server using DBMS with direct connect | Server | 0.6 | 106 | 103 | 1.0 | 2 | $10,000 | $13,000 |
| DBMS with direct connect client | DBMS | | 346 | 1,000 | 0.3 | 2 | 10,000 | 13,000 |

Figure 10.38  **Year 3 police department refined platform sizing analysis**

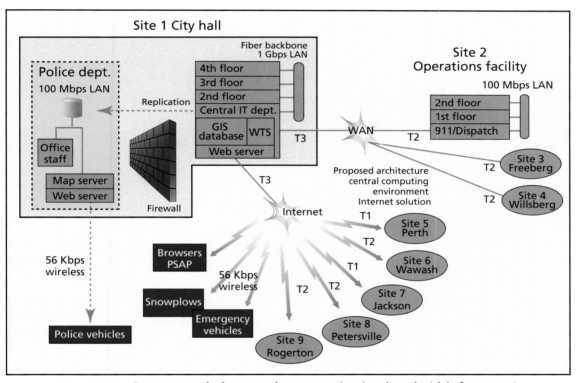

Figure 10.39  **Recommended network communication bandwidth for year 3**

You can find these loads on the server summarized in figure 10.37.

Assuming client-side search engines, the Windows terminal server using direct access to the city DBMS has a per-core factor of 111 DPM. (Note: this calculation uses the 2007 capacity planning models for a per-core SPECrate_int2000 equals 30.) Therefore, if one core can handle 111 (a number factoring in the peak workflow expressed by 3,180 displays per minute), then the core sizing requirement is 28.6 cores or 8 server blades.

The Web server for public Web services handles 48.9 users with a productivity of 6 displays per minute per client, resulting in a requirement of 293 displays per minute, to which are added the GIS batch processing services with 100 displays per minute, for a total Web server load of 396 displays per minute. The per-core factor is 103, or 3.8 cores required. In a high-available configuration, these two dual-core socket servers would provide capacity options for deploying additional batch processing loads such as geoprocessing services, mobile client check-out operations, or general system tuning and maintenance support during peak operations.

Finally, the city DBMS responding to these direct-connect clients is the source of all data, and therefore must feed data for 4,436 displays per minute. The per-core factor is 1,000, indicating a need for 4.4 cores.

The police network workflow analysis was provided earlier in figure 10.35, and the server loads analysis for the police department is included in figure 10.38.

It is evident from the refined platform sizing analysis that the police department's Web service demands remain quite low: 0.6 requests per minute which, assuming 6 displays per minute per client, demands 4 displays per minute. The GIS batch processing replication service makes 1 demand of the standard 103 displays per minute, giving a total load on the server of 107 displays per minute, with a per-core factor of 103 requiring 1.0 cores in a total of 2 sockets (minimum number) at a price of $10,000. The 24 detectives working at a rate of 10 displays per minute on search engine enabled workstations make a demand of 240 displays per minute from the DBMS. Coupled with the Web server demands of 107 displays per minute, this makes the total DMBS demand 347 displays per minute, with a per-core factor of 1,000. This requires only 0.3 cores, but sold at a minimum of 2 sockets, the price will be $10,000.

### New approach to bandwidth suitability

Again, the approach is straightforward. Instead of using network traffic factors based on the peak number of users, the network traffic factor is now based on the displays per minute on each segment of the network. The network traffic factor is based on the assumed size of the displays and the productivity of users (the num-ber of displays per minute by user). These displays per minute for each type of user (workflow) appear in figure 10.34. To the right of this DPM column, the assumed size of the display in megabits per display (Mbpd) is noted. These translate into the megabits per second required on each communication link involved, so you can directly compare them with the capacity in megabits per second of the bandwidth currently installed in your organization.

The recommendations for updating the communication infrastructure to accommodate year 3 GIS requirements are the same as given by the old method and summarized in figure 10.33. The revised values are shown on the Rome year 3 architecture configuration in figure 10.39.

The City of Rome example is just one way of analyzing the technical issues. Other options exist now, and will later, in this dynamic, evolving realm of technology. The approach you choose—related to doing a user needs assessment and to figuring out system requirements and integration recommendations—resides within your good judgment. As with all stages of GIS planning, decisions must be based on the best interests of your organization, and there are many factors to consider.

## Other considerations

Other things to consider at this stage of GIS planning are your organization's existing policies and standards, technology life cycles, and when you're ready, writing a preliminary design document convincing enough to earn you the approval of upper management to proceed to implementation planning.

### Organization policies and standards

Most GIS planners must design their organization's hardware solution and meet software and communication needs within the context of existing policies and prac-tices. If possible, plan to comply with those policies and standards your organization may have adopted regarding system configuration. For example, you must find out if your organization has adopted an operating system standard (e.g., Microsoft Windows XP, UNIX) or if they have a specific processing model (e.g., Web processing), and then document—and be cognizant of—these preferences in the preliminary design report.

Many organizations have a long-established relationship with particular hardware or software vendors. These relationships developed because of the past reliability and suitability of the products and the level of service satisfaction and trust in particular vendors. Your organization may already have established maintenance agreements (common in big enterprise hardware and software deals) or have invested heavily in training for certain products. These issues cannot and should not be ignored. On the other hand, because of normal technology life cycles, no solution can ever be considered permanently set in stone. It is not uncommon for the prospect of an enterprise-wide GIS implementation to invoke major changes in technology standards across the organization. If a change in technology platforms or operating systems is required,

spell out the reasons clearly. Explain how existing capabilities are critically inadequate and list the benefits of the alternatives you're suggesting.

## Technology life cycles

The life cycle of technology, including the rate of technologic change, is a crucial consideration in the acquisition, purchase, or upgrade of new systems. Computer technologies are constantly evolving and becoming more cost-effective (we've all heard of Moore's Law by now). Stay abreast of this and tell senior management about your strategy for keeping the GIS cost-effective. If management knows well in advance that future upgrades will be required, they will be that much more likely to approve funding for regular technology upgrades.

Figure 10.40 shows the life cycles of all of the technologies related to a major GIS implementation. It lays out how many months each technology, in turn, would be considered current, useful, obsolete, then nonfunctional, according to the following definitions. *Current* represents

| Technology | Current | Useful | Obsolete | Nonfunctional |
|---|---|---|---|---|
| Network infrastructure | 24–36 | 37–50 | 51–84 | 84+ |
| Wide area networks* | 12–24 | 25–48 | 49–72 | 72+ |
| Computer | | | | |
| • Server | 12–18 | 19–60 | 61–80 | 81+ |
| • Workstation | 6–12 | 13–48 | 49–72 | 72+ |
| • Desktop | 6–12 | 13–36 | 37–60 | 60+ |
| • Laptop | 6–12 | 13–24 | 25–48 | 48+ |
| • Mobile PDA | 6–12 | 13–24 | 25–48 | 48+ |
| OS software | 18–36 | 37–60 | 61–72 | 72+ |
| Vendor software | 12–18 | 19–36 | 37–60 | 60+ |
| Internet products (browsers, associated products) | 9–12 | 13–24 | 24–36 | 36+ |
| Data | Variable—depends on rate of decay of validity | | | |
| *Internet bandwidth increasing at 300% per year | | | | |

Figure 10.40  **2006-2007 Technology life cycles estimated in months**

the period between major releases with significant functional improvement. *Useful* indicates the length of time that current software will run on this equipment. *Obsolete* shows when new releases of software will not be compatible with the equipment. *Nonfunctional* is defined as the point at which the technology is no longer worth the cost of maintenance and training. Note that networking technology and operating systems have the longest life cycles (up to three years of currency). Contrast this to workstation, desktop, laptop computers, and mobile PDAs, which can be expected to move from current to useful within much shorter periods.

To stay current with technology trends, attend software user conferences, read GIS publications, and establish communication with vendors and industry peers.

## The preliminary design document

At the end of this stage in your GIS planning, after having determined both the data and technology requirements, you will be ready to place your findings into a report. This interim report, the preliminary design document, covers all your conceptual work so far and will mark the transition from system design to implementation planning, system procurement, and implementation. This document is a critical component of your effort: it spells out the requirements for the GIS that must be put in place to meet your organization's needs. It must win you executive approval to move into implementation planning.

The conceptual system design overall—and therefore also this document—is derived from the function requirements identified in the IPDs, the data input requirements as identified on the MIDL, and the conceptual system design for technology (addressed in this chapter). The

planning process has built on itself, with the results from earlier work carried through for use in later stages. At this stage, you will use these results to inform your report and back up your recommendations.

See appendix E for details about how to write the preliminary design document by section in this order: executive summary, introduction, data section, conceptual system design for technology, recommendations, and appendixes. Basically, you will present all the sections, except the first (executive summary) and last (recommendations), in a strictly objective, reportorial style—just the facts. In the first and last sections, however, you can present your recommendations with conviction.

Include as many illustrations and diagrams in the document as you need to make the points. For example, visual representations of map layers help people understand the nature of the data selections, while communication networks in the technology section are most clearly understood in the form of schematic diagrams, examples of which you have seen in the City of Rome case study.

You will circulate your first draft for review and comments to the individuals involved in the GIS database design. When you are implementing a shared database model, representatives from each department intending to use the system must review your plan with a careful eye to ensure that the database concepts overall are consistent and complete.

After this comment period, you will submit the preliminary design document to the GIS committee and senior management for formal approval. Before you can move into the actual implementation planning and procurement, there must be general agreement on the overall system design, and then attention paid to the three issues we'll consider in the next chapter: benefit–cost, migration, and risk.

# Consider benefit–cost, migration, and risk analysis

*The most critical aspect of doing a realistic benefit–cost analysis is the commitment to include all the costs that will be involved. Too often managers gloss over the real costs, only to regret it later.*

Rarely do the benefits from GIS become evident right away, and the initial outlay of money can be substantial. Invariably, GIS brings change—the need to migrate from old systems to new—and change can be unsettling. Also, approaching implementation, the planning team starts feeling the risk of project failure. It's important to supply yourself with information to meet these concerns. Before proceeding with planning the actual launch, you must show whether and when GIS will become cost-effective.

## Benefit–cost analysis and cost models

Your first task at this stage is to do a benefit–cost analysis, with the aid of a cost model, and document both. Benefits have been estimated on an information-product-by-information-product (hence department-by-department) basis, but costs are for the GIS as a whole. The funding source may be enterprise-wide or shared between certain departments or budgets. By and large, each organization will arrive at its own formula, yet benefit–cost calculations are typically for the whole.

Benefit–cost analysis is a technique that allows you to compare the expected cost of implementing a system with the benefits it's expected to bring within a certain period of time. This comparison indicates whether or not your project is financially viable and when you can expect an actual financial return on your initial investment.

A cost model charts all the costs you expect to incur during your GIS implementation, also within a specific planning period. You create the cost model during the first step of these four steps of benefit–cost analysis:

1. Identifying costs by year
2. Calculating benefits by year
3. Comparing benefits and cost
4. Calculating benefit–cost ratios

## Step 1: Identifying costs by year

The focus of benefit–cost analysis is always within the context of a specific time frame, as is a cost model's. To create a cost model for your project, set up a cost matrix that breaks down the five cost categories on the opposite page by the year that the cost will be incurred. Establish columns for each year. List the data that will be available in the first year. Determine the costs associated with the hardware and software needed to produce information products as they are planned year by year. Anticipate the pace of the growth of your system—look ahead at expected demand—and plan accordingly.

What makes the model work as a true gauge of reality is your commitment to include all the costs that will be involved. Surprisingly to the uninitiated, the immediate hardware and software costs typically comprise a relatively small percentage of the overall cost model initially. Staffing, data, and application programming all require significant up-front expenditures. Refer to the cost model components on page 153 and figure your costs for at least the first year; and then estimate your costs for two-, three-, four-, and five-year windows to see what may happen over time.

As you build the cost model, the value of the planning process starts to show (or, as the case may be, its absence is felt). Since you have planned the information products and the data readiness that they depend on, you know such things as whether and when you need a budget for application program development and how big it should be. You've thought about it all, so you can

trust that your expectations are realistic. Unfortunately, not all confidence is so grounded in reality. There have been well-publicized examples in recent years of major GIS technology procurements that failed to specify information products up front, so they did not factor in application programming. As a result, costly delays and other unanticipated expenses ensued. The worst part of instances like these—and there continue to be too many—is that the organizations lose their chance to see what GIS can do for them. Poor planning has doomed the effort before the much-needed new business processes can even be deployed.

## Step 2: Calculating benefits by year

Now shift your focus to the benefits of GIS. Sufficient empirical data now exists to show that you can rely on benefit analysis in GIS to be an economically rigorous reality check on your own planning. For step two of this overall technique of comparison and analysis, recall the major categories of benefits:

- **Savings:** savings in money currently budgeted (i.e., in the current fiscal year) through the use of the new information provided by the proposed GIS (e.g., reductions in current staff time, increases in revenue).

- **Benefits to the organization:** improvements in operational efficiency and in workflow, reduction of liability, increases in revenue and in the effectiveness of planned expenditure (less cost, better results). In my observations of the use of GIS worldwide, this category of benefits stands out as the most significant. (See "The benefit approach" on page 154 for a useful way to quantify these benefits.)

- **Future and external benefits:** these are benefits that accrue to organizations other than those acquiring the GIS or outside the planning time horizon of the work. To date, these benefits have often been underestimated in benefit–cost calculations.

# The cost model

Include in the cost model these five cost categories and their associated components.

## Hardware and software

Estimate the yearly cost of the hardware and software you will purchase. Include workstations (high-end and low-end); servers, including data servers, application servers, blades, terminal servers, Web servers, and map servers; disk drives; CD-ROMs; input devices such as digitizers and scanners; output devices such as laser printers and plotters; and software licenses, including extensions and extra seats. Include maintenance costs for your hardware and software in the cost model, as well as your planned upgrades. The scheduling of incremental technology acquisition is the key to subsequent financial management.

## Data

As the need to generate more and more information products grows, so likely will your database. Depending on the project purpose and scope, data acquisition can easily become a significant expense, particularly over the first five years. The costs are associated with each dataset acquisition, including licensing or royalties as required by year. The costs of data conversion, development, and maintenance are included in staff time.

## Staffing and training

Staffing is probably the largest segment of system cost over time. Recently we have been paying more attention to staff cost in the cost model and simplifying application programming in the process.
Create your estimates for staff time by year for the following:
- Data conversion, including any necessary editing
- Data development, including updates
- Data maintenance
- Application development
- System administration
- Customer support
- Staff training and travel, including the costs of travel required for training and retraining

## Application programming

The cost of writing application programs is mainly borne by your staff and is included in this chapter. In circumstances where you wish to purchase a ready-made application or hire a contract programmer to create what you need, the cost should be included here.

## Interfaces and communications

Finally, calculate the cost of any hardware or software interfaces you need to purchase and any communications networks necessary to support your system. Include hardwiring, hubs, switchers-routers, remote communications equipment (modems, compression DSNs), leased communication lines, software, and site preparation in your calculations.

## The benefit approach

Benefits to organization:

A. Write sentences that describe directly what the information product will do (on the ground).

B. Identify line-item budgets that will be affected by the new information.

C. Identify actual change in operating procedures in subline-item budget that will result from the improved information.

D. Estimate the percentage increase in effectiveness of that expenditure as a result of the new information (quicker, more accurate, less cost, more work accomplished, better results, lower public safety risk, lower risk of damage, reduction in liability, etc.)

Benefit = X percent improvement in effectiveness:

E. As a consequence of all the improvement identified above, there may be potential improvements in other activities (other line-item budget categories). Identify these activities, beginning at step B above, and assess the benefit to them down the list. As these are *consequential* benefits, the estimates for their percentage of increase in effectiveness (in step D) are likely to be modest.

You have already estimated the benefit that will result from having each information product. Your plan also predicts when each information product will be available. The question to be answered now is, when will the benefits from each accrue to the organization? One year after the first availability of the particular information product is the conservative estimate of when the benefits will be realized, even though this will depend somewhat on the nature of the benefit.

## Step 3: Comparing benefits and costs

After you have estimated the costs of system implementation and the benefits that will accrue from having at hand the information products created by the system, you can assess the benefits in relation to their associated costs. This assessment is the crux of the benefit–cost analysis. It will tell you if your implementation is financially feasible and, if so, when you will see a real return on your GIS investment.

You can use graphs like the ones here to visualize costs versus benefits over the life of the project. Note in figure 11.1 where the two lines cross: this is the crossover point to a positive cash flow.

In figure 11.1, with values in nondiscounted dollars, costs are represented by the green line, which peaks early at just under $2 million then falls gradually. Meanwhile, the benefits (the orange line) rise steadily through the early years then level off at a high value over time. The graph shows that implementing this GIS requires a high front-end investment, mainly during the first years, with a positive net effect approximately two years into the project.

You can also examine costs and benefits as a pair of cumulative numbers, side by side over time as in figure 11.2 on page 156. The new benefit or cost incurred each year is added to the previous year's total to give the new number. All numbers have also been discounted (brought back) to their equivalent value for the year 2007 to remove the effects of inflation and reflect the true net present value of money.

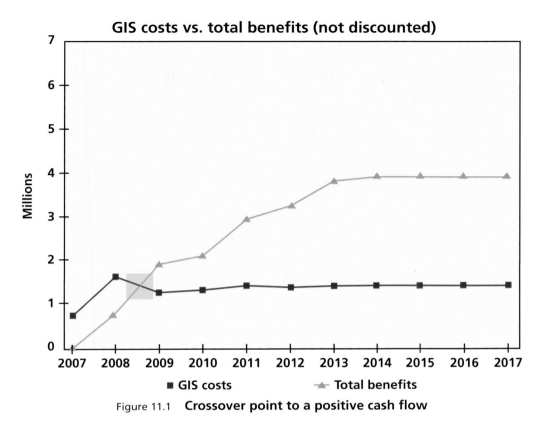

Figure 11.1   **Crossover point to a positive cash flow**

The cumulative benefits first exceed the cumulative costs in 2013. The overall benefits of a well-planned and well-managed system typically begin to outweigh the total costs somewhere between the fourth and the sixth year.

## Step 4: Calculating benefit–cost ratios

For the last step, express all costs identified in your cost model in discounted funds. In benefit–cost analysis, you use discounted costs, as shown in the bottom row of figure 11.3, in order to capture the true value of money. Discounting is most significant when the total dollar value is high or the cost of money is high (high inflation rate). Costs that spread over a period of years into the future must be discounted to the

base year using a discount rate to remove the effects of inflation.

The base year is the current year or the year in which the benefit–cost analysis begins, whichever is the earliest. For example, suppose the base year is 2007 and the cost of a maintenance contract is $100 per year. Because of inflation, a cost of $100 incurred in the year 2012, is less in real terms than a cost of $100 incurred in 2007. Similarly, if $100 of benefit accrues in the year 2012, this is worth less in real terms than a benefit of $100 realized in 2007. To assess investment decisions properly, the benefits as well as costs must be discounted to a common year—the base year—to remove inflation's effects.

As an example, using 4 percent as the current discount rate would mean that $100 last year is worth $96 this year.

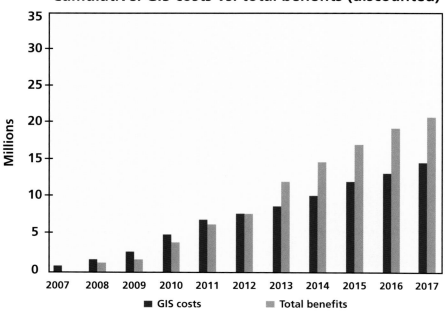

**Cumulative: GIS costs vs. total benefits (discounted)**

This graph illustrates the cumulative costs versus benefits with all figures brought back (discounted) to the value of investment as if made in 2007. When the value of the investment is taken into account in this manner, the cumulative benefits exceed the cumulative costs in 2013.

Figure 11.2  **Cumulative benefits exceed cumulative costs**

Check the discount rate being used in your organization. Identify the benefits over time and give these values discounted to the base year, as you did for costs. Calculate the net present value and benefit-to-cost ratio for each year of your analysis. The net present value (NPV) is calculated by subtracting the present value of costs (PVC) from the present value of benefits (PVB):

**NPV = PVB - PVC**

A positive NPV is the usual decision criteria applied for acceptable projects. The benefit-to-cost ratio (benefit: cost) is a fraction that represents the return (or benefit) on the investment (cost). Usually, the denominator (the cost) is reduced to 1:

**B:C = PVB/PVC**

For example, if a $100,000 investment yields a return of $260,000, the benefit-to-cost ratio would be 260,000:100,000 or 2.6:1. Investments that have a ratio greater than 1:1 will at least break even.

You can assess how changes in key parameters might affect the overall results. To do this, you need to rework the calculations for different implementation scenarios. These scenarios might incur different costs or lead to different benefits that must be accounted for in the analysis. This is called *sensitivity analysis.*

These basic steps have been adapted from those presented in Tomlinson and Smith (1991). You can find more detailed information on their published methods for conducting GIS benefit–cost analysis, by referring

| Cost per year | 2007 (base year) | 2008 | 2009 | 2010 |
|---|---|---|---|---|
| Actual cost of maintenance contract | $100 | $100 | $100 | $100 |
| Cost discounted to base year (using discounting rate of 4%) | 100 | 96 | 92 | 88 |

Figure 11.3    **True value of money used in the cost model**

to the *International Journal of Geographical Information Systems* 6(3): 247–256.

## Migration strategy

Crafting a good migration strategy is dependent on the scope of the effort. Obviously, the installation of a small system in one department requires a radically different strategy than a major "roll-out" of an enterprise-wide system in a large organization. In almost all cases, however, the new GIS will be implemented in the context of existing data handling systems that need to migrate from the old to the new. So regardless of the scope, you need to plan the sequence of events in this process and provide timelines for dealing with the old systems as well as the new.

### Legacy systems and models

The term legacy systems is an IT euphemism for an existing (sometimes quite old) technology platform that will be phased out by new technology. But legacy systems also represent the current way of doing things and these things, in the form of the business processes used to carry them out, must also be migrated. Complicating matters, because they support ongoing operations, these systems and processes must be migrated seamlessly into the new system with minimum disruption to business. This is quite a tightrope to walk.

Just as you have allowed time in your planning for new system acquisition, training, and break-in, so must you allow time for phase-out of legacy systems and reallocation of resources. This usually means a planned period of overlap between legacy systems and the new system. The annals of IT professionals are littered with stories of organizations that terminated critical legacy systems prematurely—on day one of new system implementation—with disastrous results. The key to not joining their ranks is to resist pulling the plug on any legacy system until you have proof that all of the needed data and functionality has been reliably migrated to the new platform.

The migration of existing business models can be a real challenge. Many have taken years to develop and refine, and they support business processes that must carry on within the organization. Since the need for the business model or process continues, there are three options for migration:

1. Rebuild the model so that it can be implemented in its present form into the new GIS-centric technology.
2. Improve the model, perhaps by replacing some of the assumptions with actual measurements using the GIS.
3. Abandon the model to design and build an entirely new model that takes advantage of GIS capability and makes new workflows possible.

These are some of the questions you will ask yourself:

- How difficult is it to map the process or model into the GIS data structures?
- How long will it take to do this?
- Who will do it? Are the people who designed the original model still available?

- What are the new GIS capabilities that you would like to access—can they be integrated into the old model or is a model redesign and rebuild necessary?

In considering these issues, you will identify many of the impediments to and possibilities for an appropriate migration strategy.

The migration from legacy systems to new GIS architectures is extremely dependent on the vendor offerings, both those already in place and the new ones to be acquired. For example, an Internet map service was developed four or five years ago from an older geographic (coverage) file system. A significant amount of software was written to create a publication database from the older file system.

Let's say that today your organization is considering replacing this old application with newer, server-based technologies. In addition to the cost of acquiring new software, it is also time to upgrade hardware and migrate the entire database to the new database platform. The most significant benefit of moving to the new technology is that publishing is accomplished "out of the box" and there is virtually no new application software to write. You fully expect that the new service will be more reliable than the old application, and that the cost of maintaining the old application code base will be largely eliminated, because with the hardware getting old and reliability expected to decline, keeping the old application would not be worth the associated costs.

## New considerations

Moving from old to new systems or applications brings up new matters to consider. Present management with those that require attention:

- **Age:** Is the system or application slowing the forward progress of the organization?
- **Costs:** Consider the costs of a new system, developing a new application, and transition. Will capable staff be available? Will training or hiring be required?
- **Benefits:** Is it necessary to do this transition now? Weigh the benefits to be gained by the transition.
- **Future transitions:** Will the proposed transition meet future business needs? Will legacy applications work alongside new applications developed on the new GIS in the future?

There are also technical considerations. Again, it is easy to find oneself extremely dependent on vendor offerings—those in place and new ones acquired. The movement to enterprise operations also involves dealing with data standards and data integration issues related to mapping from one schema to another. With gap analysis, you need to identify any functions not yet available in the new GIS but possibly required by one of your information products. If custom applications need to be built for them, prepare for the wait time by managing expectations.

## Pilot projects

Some organizations are more comfortable taking the GIS plan and implementing it incrementally via pilot projects. A pilot project is essentially a test run for part of—or for a small-scale version of—your planned GIS. For example, an organization with offices in multiple regions may want to establish the pilot GIS first at headquarters and in one of the regions.

This way, before wider implementation, users can build experience and gain an understanding of the kind of administrative and communications problems that might be encountered. Similarly, within one department it may be wise to focus on a selected subset of information products or even subsets of the database as first steps in implementation.

Pilot projects are useful in demonstrating the planned GIS to management and potential users. They also serve in evaluating the performance of the proposed system, solving data problems before the final cost model is developed, and verifying costs and benefits.

State your intentions clearly, though, and be aware that pilot projects are often conducted with ulterior motives. Vendors tend to encourage pilot projects on the assumption that once an organization brings in their system, it is more likely to buy it. Indeed, pilot projects can bias the procurement process. Be wary of the ploy of some senior managers who use a pilot project as a way to get GIS proponents off their backs without spending very much money. People in lower management lean toward pilot projects sometimes simply because they can get the GIS moving without the "hassle" of a thorough planning process. Clearly stating the objectives will help you avoid these pitfalls of the piloting process.

Avoid pilot projects if any of these are the motivating factors. An appropriate pilot project should always be launched in the context of your planning and should, in fact, be part of the plan from the beginning. If you have planned adequately and now want to start implementing incrementally, a pilot project may be a useful approach.

# Risk analysis

To ensure a successful GIS implementation, you must thoroughly evaluate the risks associated with your implementation strategy and the potential for project failure. The basic approach to risk analysis is to consider the questions that emerge within each of the five steps that follow:

1. Identify the types of risk involved in your project.
2. Discuss the nature of the risks in the context of the planned implementation.
3. Describe the mitigating factors that will minimize the risks.
4. Assess the likelihood and seriousness of each risk to the project and give it a score.

5. Summarize the level of risk. (Summarize the scores from step 4 into one final score with which upper management can evaluate the project in terms of overall acceptability of the risks involved.)

## Step 1: Identify the risks

To identify they types the risks involved with your project, evaluate the following factors:

## Technology

- Is the technology being adopted new?
- Is this the first release of the software or hardware? If so, does it have bugs or flaws?
- Are there gaps in the technology that prevent it from fully supporting your needs? If so, do you need to enter into a contract with the vendor before acquiring the system to ensure that the gaps are filled?

If the proven technology cannot create more than 80 percent of your information products, you are in a very high-risk category.

## Organizational functions

- Can you foresee any functional changes in the mission of the departments or changes in departmental functions?

These changes can take a long time and add complexity to your project, which increases risk.

## Organizational interactions

- Organizationally, are multiple agencies involved?
- Are they geographically dispersed?

Working with multiple agencies or multiple locations adds complexity—and its incumbent risk—to your implementation.

- Are changes in management required?

These changes may take a long time; you need to determine if you can succeed without change or during a protracted change process.

## Constraints

- Are there budget constraints?
- What is the timing of the project?

Adequate funding and a realistic time frame are essential for success.

## Stakeholders

- Are the stakeholders at multiple levels—federal, state, local, and private sector?
- Is involvement from the public, the media, and lobby groups required?

It is important to involve all stakeholders in the process so they buy in to your solution; yet the greater the number of stakeholders, the higher the risk. Negotiating and coming to agreement during the planning process can mitigate these risks.

## Overall complexity

- What is the overall complexity of the project?
- Are there federal regulations you must meet?
- Are multiple vendors involved?

Complexity in your implementation increases the amount of time you will need to deal thoroughly with each issue.

## Project planning

- Is your project planning well defined?
- Is your implementation strategy consistent with the existing business strategy?

Realistic planning minimizes risk. If the objectives of the project are not well defined, you may spend large amounts of time and money on the wrong things.

## Project management

- Are you using proven methods?
- Is there built-in accountability?
- Is there built-in quality control?

## Project scheduling

- Are scheduling deadlines reasonable?
- Do you have project-management tools to identify project milestones?

Project management and project scheduling are necessary to keep your project on time and within budget.

## Project resources

- Do you have adequately trained staff?
- Is there a knowledge gap in your organization?

If you do not have adequately trained staff, you will need to develop a plan to acquire or train them.

## Step 2: Discuss the risks in context

After identifying the risks, take each one and talk it over in the context of the planned implementation. For example, can your staff handle the new technology, or do you risk creating (or widening) a knowledge gap with this implementation? Discuss the new technology in relation to your staff's existing skill level until you come to a better understanding of the level of risk faced and how the risk can be mitigated.

## Step 3: Describe ways to mitigate the risks

Once each risk has been identified and discussed, consider mitigating factors and methods that could minimize the risks. Regarding the knowledge gap, two provisions could be made to reduce the risk of implementing new technologies with an untrained staff:

- Assess the current staff's skill level with an eye toward developing a training program.
- Decide to purchase software only from companies that have an established training program and budget for the necessary training.

## Step 4: Assess and score each risk

Assess the likelihood and seriousness of each risk to your project and give it a score. To quantify the risk associated with a knowledge gap, you could ask the following questions:

- How likely is it that your staff's skills will be insufficient to work with the new system?
- How seriously will this affect both project implementation and the agency/department itself?

If you have addressed your staff's skill level, you can assess the likelihood of the risk. You can determine the seriousness by relating the risk to the effect it will have on your system implementation and organizational functionality. Assign each risk factor a numerical weight that reflects its high, medium, or low level.

## Step 5: Summarize the level of risk

The final step is to summarize the risk factors. From the sum total of the scores produced in step 4, compute the average. Use this average score to determine if the project's risk level is acceptable to the organization. It is the organization taking the risk, so don't be surprised if it has its own approach to risk analysis. Major organizations often do. If yours does, follow its methodology for assessing risk. If the planned project meets its standards for level of risk, it's time to plan your GIS implementation strategy.

# Plan the implementation

*The implementation plan should illuminate the road to GIS success.*

You know what your organization needs; it's time to ask how to get it. What is the timeline going to be? Are there obstacles looming to stop us from implementing GIS? Do we need to add staff? The planning methodology's last stage begins with considering issues that affect GIS implementation and ends with presenting your implementation plan to management.

After a few last tasks and addressing all the issues left to consider, you will spell out your recommendations in the executive summary section of your final report and in a professional presentation to the executive board. Your report should do several things very effectively:

- Recommend an actual strategy that outlines the specific actions required to implement your GIS
- Highlight the latest (if any) extra implementation actions or special concerns that have been identified
- Include a list of actions and concerns for senior management to consider
- Reflect all of the previous planning work and include all of the relevant documents to justify your recommendations

Those documents covering the whole project can be in a cardboard box, as appendixes inside ring binders, to back up your final report. The report itself begins with the executive summary section, followed by six sections (described on pages 178–79):

1. Strategic business plan considerations
2. Resultant information requirements
3. Conceptual system design
4. Recommendations
5. Timing
6. Funding alternatives

After submitting it to the steering committee for review, then making the necessary adjustments, you can make your presentation to the executive board.

This presentation is important on several levels, but don't expect it to be the silver bullet. The executives should agree with your implementation plan already because you have informed them by keeping them in the loop all along. If you haven't and they don't, no presentation is going to convince them. On the other hand, these people have backed you up for a year or more, paying for your every move, so they deserve a presentation of the highest quality to tell them what you've been doing. If you have done your job, they probably will have read every word of your report beforehand and are expecting this presentation to be the opportunity to nod their approval. So lay before them what there is to approve, specifics that spell out such things as whether their GIS should be a server-based system or not; what budget year the costs will fall into; how many extra staff positions are needed, to be paid from which budget; and so forth.

## Implementation planning

Implementation planning is a critical juncture in your efforts because this is when the impact of the underlying change (which can be profound) will be felt. Implementation is when the messiness of the real world intrudes on your so-far orderly planning process. Only through a clear-cut path toward final implementation can we expect our efforts to result in positive change.

Since developing an implementation strategy involves many simultaneous tasks, teamwork comes into play. You will form a GIS steering committee, if you haven't already, along with a system development team. You will contact all the organizations and departments involved, if you haven't done so already, in order to synchronize your efforts and troubleshoot any problems. To facilitate technology procurement later, early on you will invite vendors to submit proposals as to how they would deploy hardware and software for GIS most cost-effectively.

Meanwhile, you will consider all the various strategic components that enter into your GIS implementation, including the all-important staffing and training requirements, the timeline, allocation of tasks, costs, and your recommendations for alternative strategies and for mitigating risk. You will draw on information about data and conceptual design you've already gathered and referenced in your preliminary design document to make specific recommendations.

This chapter addresses the tasks and issues involved in planning for implementation. Your plan's goal is to win funding for GIS implementation. Yet, this measured, step-by-step approach serves another purpose: by facing—before actual implementation—the issues you must consider in order to compile the plan, you further buffer your project against failure. Insuring a successful implementation first time out can be vital because you won't always get another chance.

You need support from users almost as much as that from funding. Keep in mind, with the introduction of any new information system into an existing operation, there are bound to be bumps in the road. Even if you adopt industry-standard hardware platforms and use only well-tested GIS software, your application programs may still have bugs during their first releases. Long-term GIS managers consider that they manage three interconnected items: budget, schedule, and functionality. Any two will affect the third. You should prepare users for this, to manage expectations, while at the same time letting them know that their clearly communicated feedback will help you fine-tune the system into well-oiled machinery.

In one sense, this period before moving into actual implementation is the last step in the planning process. Obviously, the planning for GIS continues as long as there is a system to operate, but that original window of planning before a project launches will soon be shut. From then on, everything will happen in real-time in a production environment. For your implementation plan to become a successful guide, you must devise it by thoroughly considering all the factors that apply to your situation. Addressing the issues detailed in this chapter should prepare you well for making your GIS implementation strategy recommendations.

## Organizing your project

Before starting a GIS implementation, it is important to consider how the most productive relationship between management and GIS staff could be organized. Clarification of roles and responsibilities and establishing good lines of communication will greatly aid the implementation of any GIS. The GIS steering committee and the system development team are the key players in fostering this.

A *GIS steering committee* helps you make decisions regarding project management, changes in project scope, and what to do if your project gets behind schedule. As the fundamental link to senior management in your organization, the GIS steering committee should take an active role in the GIS decision-making process, helping you decide, among other things, when you need to reprioritize or scale-down a new application or project extension (see figure 12.1).

The makeup of a steering committee will vary according to an organization's nature and size. At large sites, the steering committee could include the project initiator (known as the project sponsor), the GIS manager, at least two customer representatives, a management representative, and a technical expert to reinforce the technical perspective of the GIS manager. At medium or small sites, the steering committee could include the project sponsor, the GIS manager, one customer representative, and a management representative (see figure 12.2).

The *system development team* oversees design implementation, reviews progress, and identifies problems as they arise. The team reports to the project steering committee. The team can be as small as one or two people at a small site or an initial four or five people at a medium site (it will tend to grow). Whatever its size, its tasks are consistent. The team's primary functions are shown in figure 12.3.

The makeup of the system development team will differ depending on the size and nature of the organization, yet in all cases, the system development team should include a GIS manager. At large sites, the team might include the GIS manager, an expert from the business side of the organization (who thoroughly understands how the application helps), a GIS technology expert, and a GIS database analyst (who understands the logical data model and linkages between the different data elements).

At small or medium sites, the system development team might include just a GIS manager, an expert from the business side, and a database analyst. If one person must do many of the jobs required, as the system is being developed, he or she should bring together the types of expertise of the specialists just mentioned.

| Responsibility | Description |
|---|---|
| Review the system development team reports | GIS steering committees should meet monthly to review reports from the system development team. It is important that the steering committee be actively involved in the decision-making process. |
| Review GIS project status | During the steering committee meetings, the current status of the GIS project relative to the implementation milestones should be reviewed. |
| Identify and give early warning of problems | Reviewing the progress of the project compared to its schedule will help to identify problems as early as possible and allow adjustments to be made. |
| Make necessary adjustments | Every time a GIS project requirement changes or something needs to be added or deleted, the change should be documented. If you can manage a project within the scope that was already identified, the likelihood of finishing it on time is good. One way to manage the scope is to put the steering committee in the position of determining when you will expand a project and when you will not. |

Figure 12.1  **GIS steering committee responsibilities**

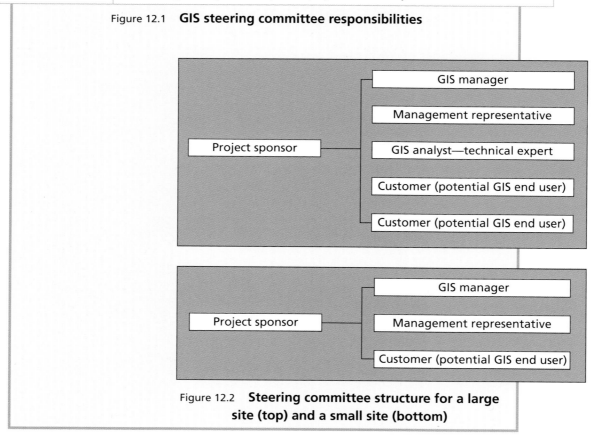

Figure 12.2  **Steering committee structure for a large site (top) and a small site (bottom)**

| Responsibility | Description |
|---|---|
| Solve design problems | The system development team discusses and resolves design problems as they arise. |
| Focus activities on the critical path | The critical-path method is one of a number of project-management tools that can be used. It identifies the tasks and the sequence of tasks most critical to complete the project on schedule. Noncritical tasks are also identified. These are tasks that can be delayed without affecting the overall project schedule. The critical-path method is often useful for focusing the system development team on the most important activities in the development of the project. |
| Balance workload assignments | The system development team is responsible for balancing the workload and assignments given to staff. |
| Meet regularly and report progress | The system development team prepares periodic progress reports (usually monthly) for the steering committee. The system development team should have regular development meetings. Initially, these might be daily meetings, then weekly. You should set up a formal schedule and reporting process where every week the team meets to at least touch base. Too often, a programmer will make some assumptions about requirements and then spend one or two weeks creating something that does not work. Frequent meetings are a way of trapping problems such as this and getting back on track quickly. |

Figure 12.3   **System development team responsibilities**

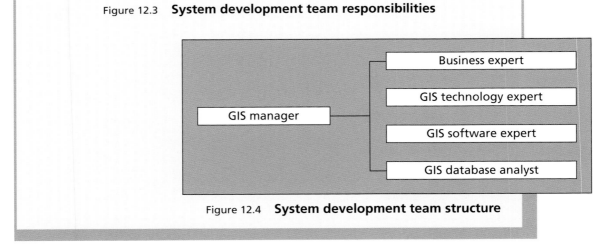

Figure 12.4   **System development team structure**

## Staffing and training

No part of GIS planning is more important than staffing and training. It would be almost impossible to overstate the degree to which a successful GIS is dependent on the staff that builds it, manages its evolution, and maintains it over time. The best GIS plan in the world will not launch a successful GIS—that takes people.

Discuss staffing issues with each department affected by GIS implementation. Staffing a GIS is a long-term operational cost and a major expense for all systems.

The number of staff associated with a GIS depends on the nature and size of an organization. Large organizations, with widespread user groups and complicated applications, could require a wide range of staff—from network and database administrators to GIS specialists and programmers, and of course managers to oversee the work of these individuals. In small organizations, staff members may have to wear many or all of the hats, but that can also work. For example, as the sole GIS manager you may have to take charge of the GIS planning, system design, and administration. A lone GIS analyst may have responsibilities spanning different software packages and applications.

The first line of division breaks between the core GIS staff, which is the cornerstone of your GIS, and the GIS end users; the two groups that require special attention as you set up a working team. Crucial staff, but not really part of either of these, is the management group and system administration team. The basic staff positions required for a GIS implementation all have associated skill requirements. (These are described fully in appendix A, along with much more on staff requirements and training options for bringing both GIS staff and end users up to speed.)

Whenever GIS remains underused, a primary cause is lack of staff training. It should go without saying that if people cannot make the system do what they need, they'll quickly abandon it and stick with the old, safe way of doing things. And who could blame them. They have a job to do, and the mere existence of a high-tech GIS system is not going to help them. It's not going to run itself either. It takes a live, thinking human being to frame a spatial problem in the context of a GIS. In order to get meaningful answers to their questions, people need to know how to apply the tools to the work as they understand it. Train, train, and then train some more will become your rallying cry.

### Key issues to address in implementation planning

Department staffing
Training regime
Institutional interaction requirements
System requirements and data sharing
Legal review
Security issues
Existing computing environment
Migration strategy
Risk analysis
Alternative implementation strategies
System procurement

## The knowledge gap

Often organizations must revisit the areas of staffing and training in response to changes in technology. If their current staff lacks the skill sets to make the best of technologic advancements, some combination of new hires and training of current staff can fill the gap. The term *knowledge gap* describes a phenomenon that results from the new capabilities of technology growing faster than an organization's ability to use them. In the case of GIS technologies, there was no knowledge gap before 1990: people were still more capable than their GIS systems (figure 12.5).

By 2000, the rate of GIS development had risen above the normal growth trend of institutional management skills. This means that systems are now more capable than people, and the ordinary incremental growth rate in skills within an organization does not keep up with developments in technology. Recently, the relative curve of GIS

development has leveled off somewhat, but management still has a lot of institutional learning to do before truly making use of the full capabilities of GIS. The projected knowledge gap has clear implications within an organization's training strategy and budget commitments, but it also bears on the ability of higher learning institutions to provide some of the needed skills training.

The degree to which an organization can improve its collective skills base will have a direct bearing on how well and how far the technology will be adopted within the organization. These skills are the tools that an organization uses to actually leverage technology in order to increase productivity. Only by recognizing that a knowledge gap exists and implementing efforts to fill it in can one realize that the knowledge gap is also an opportunity gap.

Some organizations attempt to circumvent the knowledge gap by hiring consultants to operate the GIS,

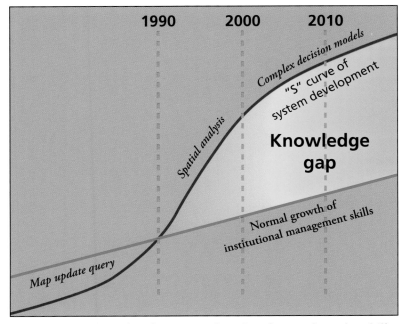

Figure 12.5 **GIS technology: Accelerating faster than the skills to use it**

under the assumption that these "hired guns" will bring the needed knowledge into the company. While this is certainly a possibility, there are few instances where it can be fully recommended. Hiring a consultant is just another way of buying the skills that you really need in your organization. It is a short-term solution to what may be a long-term requirement.

Consider the tale of a Canadian oil company that spent $200,000 implementing a complex environmental GIS application. When the application was finished, the two key staff members left, and there was no one remaining at the company who could use the system. Everyone involved in the planning and implementation must have felt like they'd been wasting their time. The moral of this story is that the host organization needs smart people in place who can really use the system.

### Training program

After determining the staffing needs for your GIS implementation, assess the GIS capabilities of your existing staff and determine an appropriate training program by personnel category. Emphasize that continuous employee training will be necessary for all GIS staff and spell out how it should be included in the budget. The all-important core GIS staff will require ongoing training to keep them current on new methods and technology. Recommend an employee training program that provides for the necessary levels of GIS staff.

Building a strong internal staff is a process, not an event, in most cases; the process itself can foster a dynamic atmosphere of opportunity. Highly selective hiring practices and ongoing training are a must, of course. But you must also create conditions that are favorable to learning and foster independent thought. This is also part of the forward-thinking approach to managing change. Provide interesting and challenging tasks, a supportive management environment, and continuing opportunities for knowledge development

(including training and formal interaction with other GIS professionals).

Use appendix A on staffing and training as a guide for the required training and its delivery.

## Organizational issues

Management and organizational issues come into play at all stages of the planning process; at the time of GIS implementation they take precedence. Implementation becomes more complicated when working with other organizations, but it's probably worth it. The richer database and more utilitarian system that ensues will actually get used, allowing for further GIS applications to be created.

To succeed in your GIS efforts you must involve all the stakeholders in the planning and implementation process. A stakeholder is any person, group, or organization with a vested interest in your project now or in the future. These stakeholders could include organizations with which you have interactions, as well as the end users of your planned GIS-related services (the public citizen or the business customer), the media, and lobby or special-interest groups.

You may have already made contact with other organizations and partners; now you must revisit and clarify these relationships and where necessary firm them up.

These relationships will all be different. Some may be more formal and even include legal dimensions. For example, a city planning department might be legally required to immediately report the opening of new streets to the keepers of an emergency route mapping application. Less formal relationships might evolve with other organizations sharing common causes or purposes, such as a network of conservation groups agreeing to share environmental data for their mutual benefit.

You must consider how the relationships that your organization has with these disparate external partners will affect your GIS project. Ask yourself the following questions:

- Who among these partners might hinder or prevent your system implementation (i.e., are there any showstoppers)?
- Who needs to be kept informed about your project to ensure that you have continued support?
- What will happen if another organization fails to maintain its commitments to your GIS project?
- Who is responsible for managing the relationship?
- What would happen if the relationship ended?

## Institutional interaction requirements

If there is a need to interact or cooperate with other organizations, agencies, or departments in the course of your GIS project, consider whether agreements relating to the responsibilities of those involved are necessary. Such agreements should, at a minimum, be documented in a memorandum of understanding (MOU). If the system depends on these interactions, formal contracts are required.

Enterprise-wide GIS systems are starting to proliferate, so the mandate to include the data requirements of every organization and department involved is worth repeating: all should be included in the planning process.

## Data sharing arrangements

Increasingly, your GIS will require data from several sources, which leads to the need for a systematic data sharing relationship with one or more other departments or organizations. Your implementation strategy must acknowledge the nature of any data sharing arrangements that will be part of the GIS. Armed with your clear understanding of the information products to be created and the data requirements of your GIS, contact each of the agencies, organizations, or departments that will be involved. For example, in the case of state or municipal organizations, these contacts might include local government organizations, state

organizations, federal organizations, partnerships, and multiagency bodies.

If your plan calls for data fundamental to your GIS to come from outside your own organization, you should enter into some kind of a formal agreement (such as a memorandum of cooperation or a legal contract) with the other organization or agency. This agreement should address the following:

- What will happen if the other organization fails to supply its portion of the data?
- Who is responsible for correcting and updating data in a timely manner?
- What backup and security is in place to ensure continued access to the data?
- Who will decide what further data is collected and shared?
- Who will fund the data gathering (including maintenance and updates)?
- Who will be responsible for coordinating the regular data administrative tasks?

Since data exchange can reduce the costs of data acquisition (typically a significant cost of a GIS implementation), there is a strong spirit of data sharing, particularly among U.S. federal and state agencies. Although that has been tempered somewhat in this era of intensified security concerns, sharing can be beneficial.

Oftentimes before or during implementation, organizations discover that other organizations have data previously unknown to them or information that they consider of value. For example, in Australia, six or seven state government agencies were found to have data potentially useful to one another. While there had been little or no sharing of data before, during the GIS planning process they recognized that simply by sharing the data they had already developed, they could produce new and better information products with significant benefits to each agency. In other words, sometimes creating interagency relationships can yield substantial financial benefits for all parties.

## System requirements and data

Your preliminary design document lists the work to be done by the system, including the information products that have to be created, the system functions required, and the data needed in the database. Before recommending the actions required to put the system in place, be sure you've taken into account data requirements of all the departments and other organizations sharing data within your GIS.

## Data exchange concerns

Important technical issues related to data exchange can trip you up if ignored, including the data format and accuracy, the metadata standards, and the data's physical location. Two key questions should be answered to identify how multiagency or multiorganizational data exchange affects your project:

1. Which information products require multiagency data?
2. Is the benefit that will accrue to the agencies from the new information products the reason for multiagency planning?

If the answer to the second question is yes, you have a strong reason to cooperate on data exchange, and you might also have the leverage to request joint funding of the planning process.

Once data is developed, it is important that each organization and department use it properly, so another task on your list may be creating clear user guides and metadata.

## Departmental resistance

Since data can be a large cost of your GIS, sharing data may make sense for all concerned; that doesn't mean it's always easy. You may encounter resistance to data sharing between departments in your organization for several reasons:

- The data may be poor and reflect badly on the department.

- To some, data means power; possessiveness may rear its head ("it's mine").
- When data represents responsibility for a function, it can be a department's ticket to budget appropriations.
- The source department may not regard other departments as capable of properly using and maintaining the data.
- Personality conflicts; institutional conflicts.

It must be in the self-interest of the departments to share. Either they will benefit from information products they are now able to make, or they need to demonstrate their compliance with instructions from on high (treasury board directive, cabinet agreement, government policy directive).

## Legal review

Your final report should recommend a legal review if legal issues are associated with the use of data in the GIS. For example, even though you won't be using the original paper documents again after automation, you may be required to preserve them if they contain legal descriptions for land parcels in the United States.

In the field of surveying, original paper maps may have to be retained as a legal requirement. To date, digital data does not have the same legal status as the written record, and in the event of a legal dispute, it is the paper map that will be used. This may change as surveyors adopt new technologies.

During preparation of your implementation strategy you should check with the acknowledged legal experts closest to your situation. The rapid acceleration in the use of GIS data by government and other institutions is raising many new and interesting legal questions related to the transition of maps from paper to digital forms. Realize these legal issues are out there and make sure any that pertain to your GIS are thoroughly investigated before deciding how they might factor into implementation planning.

You should also recommend measures to reduce the risk and liability associated with possible errors in your organization's GIS data and information products. There are various types of error in data, and it is important to understand your organization's liability and recommend actions to limit that liability. Erroneous data may result from faulty data input methods, human error, or programs or measuring devices that are used incorrectly. Some errors are more serious than others, and the resulting liability can affect other applications. GIS managers need to know the extent of their liability.

## Security issues

You must conduct a security review to determine the type and amount of security necessary to protect your GIS from damage. Through an appraisal of the security review, for your final report you can make recommendations on how to reduce the chance of system damage and data corruption.

Traditionally when referring to *security*, the primary thought in mind has been protection of your investment in data. Sadly, terrorism concerns are with us these days, too, bringing a more layered meaning to the word. In such an atmosphere, off-site data duplication and functioning system capabilities become more important. Some agencies need zero or minimal down-time arrangements in order to provide "business continuance."

The concept of security in depth is helpful. Although no security solution is perfect, a layered defense is most likely to approach the degree of protection necessary. Every level of the architecture should be protected by the appropriate access control, beginning with controlled access to the desktop environment. Consult the acknowledged experts first to see what approach to reviewing security issues is advisable in your organization.

## Protecting your GIS investment

System backups and data security are designed to protect your GIS investment. One of the major GIS benefits that come to organizations is the increasing value of their databases as they grow over time. Whatever the current value of your database, if it is properly maintained, its value in five years will increase dramatically. The value of information derived from the GIS database increases due to the improved business processes the GIS functionality delivers. The successful GIS will often quickly become an integral part of an organization's daily operations. This is why a sound security plan is required.

The risk of your system or data being destroyed or somehow compromised is real and deserves serious attention. Any information system is vulnerable to both deliberate and accidental damages. A disgruntled employee might purposely corrupt data, hackers may steal information, a computer virus could find its way into the server through e-mail, or terrorists could destroy the buildings involved. Natural disasters also pose a threat. Earthquakes, fires, hurricanes, and lightning are all examples of natural hazards that could disrupt a GIS.

While deviant behavior and natural disasters are intriguing subjects, threats more common to many organizations are found in day-to-day operations. Consider the potential effects of coffee spilled in the wrong place; a well-intentioned employee who accidentally deletes or corrupts a database; or a power disruption with no automatic battery backup.

## Conducting a security review

When conducting a security review, examine the physical, logical, and archival security of your databases (figure 12.6). Physical security measures protect and control access to the computer equipment containing the databases. Physical security guards against human intrusion and theft (security doors, locking cables) and environmental factors such as fire, flood, or earthquake (fire alarms, waterproofing, power generators). Here are some recommendations for physical security:

- Restricting access to the room in which main data storage terminals are located
- Reviewing construction plans for new stations as available
- Installing fire and intruder protection alarms
- Implementing document sign-out and follow-up procedures

Logical security measures protect and control access to the data itself, either through password protection or network access restrictions. A common security measure is to specify that only database management staff have editing and update rights to particular datasets. Here are some additional ideas on logical security:

- Develop a policy for terminal access
- Protect and control all storage media
- Develop a schedule for virus scanning
- Create a matrix showing access by document type

Archival security means ensuring that systems are backed up and that these backups are stored correctly in remote off-site locations. Legally many organizations are required to archive their data. This means that the system must include functionality that creates these archives. Raw data transfers are not enough: metadata, information about past coding and updating practices, and the location of data must all be stored to allow for

quick recovery in the event of a system failure. Consider the following ways to ensure archival security:

- Establish an off-site facility to store archived data
- Establish an audit trail to track copies of datasets
- Capture every transaction

After your initial security review, consider how current and future security risks might affect what you recommend in the final report. These recommendations should take into account physical, logical, and archival issues related to security.

## Existing computing environment

You have already outlined in conceptual form the infrastructure needed to support the new GIS. Review your conceptual system design for technology (chapter 10) before finalizing it as part of the implementation strategy. Your organization may have significant time and money invested in the existing technology base (see "Migration Strategy," chapter 11). Your implementation strategy recommendations should take your organization's hardware and software preferences into account.

The GIS that you propose to implement almost undoubtedly represents new technology and processes in your organization. Very rarely will your planning process lead to a system that is completely new from the

| Physical security | Logical security | Archival security |
|---|---|---|
| Prevent access to main data storage from the back stairs. | Develop a policy for terminal access. | Establish an audit trail for copies of data. |
| Review the construction plans for the new building to ensure appropriate climate control. | Create an access matrix by document types. | Establish an off-site backup facility. |
| Build a public workroom so staff don't have to go into the vault room to do their work. | Review protection of storage media. | Create and organize metadata. |
| Initiate document sign-out and follow-up procedures. | Purchase antivirus software. | Purchase storage media. |

Figure 12.6    **A typical security review**

ground up. Instead, the typical GIS plan must consider how the GIS will integrate with the existing computing environment, the so-called legacy systems.

As their name implies, legacy systems bring along a history of usage, and people will continue to rely on them. Clean connections to legacy systems are crucial to overall project success. Written organizational standards and policies on system-integration issues related to the GIS will help smooth the implementation process, reduce resistance to a new computing system, and build support among end users.

## System integration issues

By now, you've already considered the following aspects of the existing computing environment in which your GIS must coexist; now revisit them and optimize any needed upgrades or changes to hardware and software already in place.

Current equipment: List the current vendor platforms in use across your organization (including remote sites).

Layout of facilities: Gather or create diagrams of facility locations and their associated network facilities (by department and site).

Communications networks: List all the types and suppliers of networks intended for use by the GIS link (dedicated, in-house, commercial). Understand what's happening on both the local and wide area networks. What are the protocols: TCP/IP, IPX, NFS? What are the bandwidths for each link that will be used by the GIS (e.g., T3, T1, ISDN)?

Potential performance bottlenecks: Identify missing or inadequate communication links, fault tolerance, system security, and response-demand issues.

Organizational policies and preferences: Consider the IT culture of your organization. Is all hardware from a single preferred supplier? Is there a standard operating system in use? If policies for procurement and standards for use have been adopted or maintenance relationships established, consider these carefully. Adopting different

systems may lead to problems with support and acceptance and to a need for additional staff training.

Future growth plans and budget: The GIS must work within the fiscal framework of the organization. Budgets set must be adhered to, so the GIS manager must always keep an eye on costs and ensure the work is efficient and affordable. If money runs short, things like breadth of user applications, system performance, or reliability will take a hit. Initial budget projections should be considered in later benefit–cost analyses.

## Migration strategy

You have examined the existing computing environment of your organization. Now you must recommend a migration strategy for moving from the existing system to the new GIS. Include with this strategy detailed plans for merging the new system with legacy systems. Recommendations should address whether or not to replace, rebuild, or merge the new system with modeling techniques used by any legacy systems.

## Risk analysis

Implementation can be affected by four major groups of risks: technology, budget constraints, project management and scheduling, and human resources. Recommend steps to mitigate the risks identified. Include the results of the risk analysis in the final report to help ensure that senior management is aware of any implementation difficulties identified beforehand. (Review the risk analysis section of chapter 11.)

## Alternative implementation strategies

Include alternative strategies for implementation in the final report. Recommending more than one strategy (even if you have a strong personal favorite) shows that you're looking for the best approach for your organization. Consider using pilot projects with a subset of the geographic extent, particularly if you're concerned about the ease of integration of any particular datasets. Beware, however, of using a pilot project as a replacement for planning. That approach inevitably leads to an incomplete system design and a certain measure of frustration and wasted time.

## System procurement

How you will procure your system is part of implementation planning. You must consider two key factors: the procedural requirements of your organization and the characteristics of the planned system.

Many organizations have purchasing requirements that become more rigorous as the expected expenditure increases. Low-cost, generic products can often be purchased with minimal fuss. Acquisition of more expensive products and services may require most, if not all, of the following steps leading up to decisions about procurement..

This list represents about the most elaborate procurement process you could encounter—the average organization might include only half of these steps. Whatever your organization requires, by listing all of these steps in the final report you show that you have accounted for those required

during your acquisition planning. Follow the steps that apply when it comes time to procure your hardware and software technology and services.

**Step 1: Request for qualifications (RFQ)**

The RFQ is a request for qualifications from each potential technology vendor. The RFQ is optional but done early in the procurement process. In response, the vendor should identify the types of systems it has provided along with a track record of experience. This will help you determine which vendors qualify as able to provide systems similar to the one that you plan.

**Step 2: Request for information (RFI)**

The RFI is particularly important if you have a large procurement that could be so coveted by vendors as to result in potential protests from vendors.

**Step 3: Request for proposals (RFP)**

The RFP invites vendors to propose the most cost-effective combination of hardware, software, and services to meet the requirements of your organization. (Detailed guidelines for how to prepare an RFP appear in appendix D.) In your RFP, ask the vendors to put their proposals into a format that you specify. This will allow you to develop a rating system for proposal comparisons.

### Selection criteria

The final choice of your GIS is based primarily on its ability to perform the functions specified to create the information products. This is the first litmus test of whether the system is acceptable. Other factors that play into the selection criteria include cost, training availability, system capacity and scalability, system speed, system support, and, last but not least, vendor reliability (i.e., their financial stability, position in the marketplace, and verified references).

Having already prioritized and classified the functions based on their frequency of use and relative importance to total system functionality, you can use this information as selection criteria. Also use the rating system you've developed for proposal comparisons.

In your recommendation for technology acquisition, be sure that the equipment to be procured will be sufficiently used from the outset. At least 50 percent of the equipment's capacity should be used in the first year of acquisition. It follows that it is cost-effective to have a continuous technology acquisition budget to maintain your system. You should recommend the allocation of resources to keep your system cost-effective (see "Acquire technology" on page 182).

If you are procuring a major enterprise-wide system and benchmark testing is planned, let the vendors know that their proposals will face these tests.

**Step 4: Receipt and evaluation of proposals**

Identify who in your organization will serve as evaluators and spell out the criteria that they'll be using to make that evaluation. These criteria are often a key part of the RFP.

**Step 5: Benchmark test**

Benchmark testing involves verification of the proposals from the top-rated vendors to ensure they can perform the tasks and functions necessary for the planned system and communication network (see appendix B). Vendors may not wish to participate in a benchmark effort if you request extensive testing but are not planning to make a relatively large acquisition. In the event that thorough benchmark tests are not carried out, the purchaser should request a demonstration of system capabilities that includes the full functionality required for the organization. Always, caveat emptor—let the buyer beware.

**Step 6: Negotiation and contract**

Negotiation and contract often involves cooperation with your purchasing and legal staff. Personnel from these two departments can really help during contract negotiations, but as the manager, just make sure you review the contract to ensure that the technical requirements are properly addressed.

**Step 7: Physical site preparation**

Make sure that the site is properly prepared before the system is installed. This seems like an obvious point, but it can mess you up if overlooked. Are the necessary servers and appropriate network connections available for system installation? Is the computer room properly ventilated? Does each GIS team member have a chair and a desk?

**Step 8: Hardware and software installation**

Specifying who will install the system's hardware and software depends on the complexity of the system. In some cases, the vendor will provide this service. If your organization has the technical staff available, you could install the system in-house. Basic PCs have evolved a long way. It's possible to take delivery of a boxed computer and have it set up and running in less than an hour. Often, the vendor and the client are both involved in system installation.

**Step 9: Acceptance testing**

Within the RFP you would have specified the methods chosen for acceptance testing after system installation. These tests often require the hardware components to operate without error for a given period of time. With many of the widely used components available today (e.g., personal computers and their operating systems) these tests are of limited added value. When planning acceptance tests, consider testing the system's ability to integrate with existing databases and software and test all these connections. Network connectivity problems are always a major source of bugs and should be tested hard for possible problems.

## Recommendations

While addressing all the aforementioned issues that apply to your situation, you are developing the GIS implementation strategy you will present to executive management. These are the choices you have made, the actions you are recommending, the timetable for your implementation plan. These recommendations will be a key component of the final report and presentation you will give to the board, after approval from the steering committee. After the steering committee reviews the final report, you will note any extra implementation actions now required or any new concerns identified during the review process, then add them to your final recommendations.

### GIS steering committee review and approval

The information prepared during the planning process is the basis for your recommendations, and the steering committee should already be fully conversant in it. After thoroughly reviewing your implementation strategy (and the planning materials backing it up), the committee will approve, revise, or reject the recommendations. If you've done your homework, the approval should come quickly and with renewed enthusiasm for the mission. Never rely on a consultant to do this review. It must be undertaken by staff inside the organization, and preferably by a group and not an individual, to reap the strength of combined views.

The GIS steering committee can, of course, adjust the implementation plan. They should also provide ongoing support during and after implementation. This committee is an integral and permanent part of the GIS team effort. The members might change, but the committee will always be needed.

## The final report

In constructing the final report, lay out your recommendations for GIS implementation and what you've done and discovered that has led you to these conclusions. This is why you've done the work—to win approval to get the system in place—so make it good. The report itself will probably be anywhere from fifty to a hundred pages in length, with the executive summary section at the front (though you will write it last). It will be supported by a set of appendixes, placed in ring binders suitably labeled in a cardboard box, full of all the technical information you've generated.

The subsequent presentation of your recommendations in front of the executive board should also be of the highest quality. Go over the entire project and tell them what you've been doing. The beginning was all about finding out the strategic goals of the organization, its way of doing business, and the information products necessary to help move the organization toward these goals. You found out what data would be needed to produce that information, the software required to get it,

and the hardware and communications infrastructure to support it. You projected the costs in your benefit–cost analysis, then asked yourself how do we get that in place? What's going to stop us from implementing this? One by one, you came up with ways to overcome obstacles like the knowledge gap. Realizing that a trained staff is paramount to success, you thought about staffing and training, and now you're recommending exactly what the organization needs. Don't drag out the work that's been done to back up these recommendations. It stays in the ring binders in the cardboard box. It's enough to say what it contains.

Do tell the board enough in your presentation and in the pages of the final report so that they can approve the implementation plan. They need the specifics in front of them, such as the timeline—"you need two extra staff positions in budget A by a particular date"—and so forth.

The final report is composed of these six components, which follow the executive summary:

1. **Strategic business plan considerations:** A synopsis of the mandate and responsibilities of the organization—a summary of what they do and their business model for success. This leads to understanding what they need to know and how GIS and the information products will be effective helpmates in the strategic effort toward realizing these goals. Remember that GIS means change. In an enterprise, because its implementation may alter the way they do business, it becomes particularly important to keep the focus on how GIS serves their business. In executive terms, this is a mind shift. They need to know why you're recommending they go to a server-based system or not, for example. You will have kept them informed every step of the way, of course, so the executives will already have a feeling for what you're proposing because they will have contributed to establishing these terms. You simply need to be sure to clearly link your recommendations to the organization's goals, so that in approving your plan the executives are confirming their shared mission.

2. **Resultant information requirements:** A brief introduction to the information products that will be created and the datasets that must be acquired to generate them. List the information products by their titles and groupings, along with the datasets they require, also listed by name. You won't include the MIDL here, but you will say that all its data, as well as the full IPDs, are in the appendixes of your report.

3. **Conceptual system design:** The synopsis of the work on technology. You have identified the most suitable data design and software/hardware system design and the communications infrastructure necessary to support it. Show how you came to these conclusions. Why did you choose this particular data model? How does this specific client-server architecture best meet the needs of the organization?

4. **Recommendations:** Points out the most direct path forward for putting GIS in place. This is the implementation plan you are proposing that has been approved by the steering committee. Your understanding of the organization's needs and what's required from GIS to meet them has led you to formulate these specific, practical recommendations. Be sure to include the benefit–cost analysis here. Don't neglect to recommend a migration strategy for moving from the existing system to the new GIS. When you are recommending alternative implementation strategies, you may want to include a pilot project as one of the options, but be careful how it is used.

5. **Timing:** Set forth the dates that show the timeline for your recommendations. Use a Gantt chart to show the milestones.

6. **Funding alternatives:** Detail the budget for all this. Here you are saying, the funds for one thing will come from budget A and the funds for something else from budget B. There may be external sources that will allay these costs such as grants or data-sharing arrangements. Recognizing that managers worry about the financial effects of technological change, you should emphasize that technology is getting cheaper and faster. Maintaining out-of-date equipment is a waste of funds, and so is buying beyond capacity. It's better to spend a little every year to keep up with technology—about 20 percent of your total acquisition budget is a guideline that works. Technological change is going to happen, so you manage it with incremental budgeting and an understanding of system life cycles.

After completing these sections, write the executive summary section and place it at the front of the final report. After one more review by the steering committee, give the report to executive management and prepare to put on a dynamic presentation to the board. This presentation may be a formality, but it is an important one. Remember this is affirmation time, a chance for the board members to give the formal approval that makes the implementation happen.

## Implementation change

The business model of the modern organization is characterized as dynamic. Implementing a GIS to fit this model is a continuing process of adjusting to change, since it occurs in an ever-changing environment. There are changes in technology, both in hardware and software. But there are also sometimes subtle, sometimes profound, changes in the business needs of your organization and perhaps in the institution itself. As institutions shift gears to keep up with advancements in technology, the knowledge gap widens, which in turn signals even more challenge in the areas of staffing and training. So much change needs to be managed. Managing change starts with understanding the types of change.

### Technology change

If you don't think technology is changing GIS, consider that over just the past fifteen to twenty years, the hardware used for GIS has evolved from mainframes to minicomputers, from minicomputers to workstations, from workstations to personal computers, and now to handheld devices. The use of servers as mainframes linked on a network is increasing significantly. Operating systems have changed from being proprietary and hardware dependent to hardware independent. To accommodate these changes, GIS software has constantly evolved.

Change is generally a good thing when it comes to technology, as we began to explore in chapter 10 with the latest figures on the rate of technology change and the life cycle of technology. New versions of software and hardware do actually make the work easier and more cost-effective. Newer hardware brings significantly faster performance and cheaper storage, making work easier. New versions of GIS software offer easier use, simplified procedures, and reduced repetitive work. New user-friendly versions tend to fix bugs, becoming less error-prone and more stable and reliable.

The swift rate of change in technical capability also brings its share of challenges. Advancements in technology move faster than the changes in institutional requirements, and to meet this challenge you must employ the criteria of cost-effectiveness. Rapid advancements in technology mean that maintaining older software and hardware can become prohibitively expensive in less than five years. Vendors must offer maintenance for new hardware and software. Over time, they increase the price for maintaining older technologies to focus more of their resources on the latest technology, encouraging the migration to newer versions.

## Institutional change

The business needs of most organizations change incrementally over time. The staff gains more experience, new ideas and approaches are brought in, and new information products to support the new business needs are requested. This is the natural growth cycle of a successful business operation. Incorporating the new

information products into the GIS workload will present no significant problem, if you have planned for growth in advance.

Occasionally, major institutional changes occur, such as the merging of companies or departments of government, major changes in mission for all or significant parts of the organization, or changes due to recession or other budget constraints. In such cases, it may be that one organization has done no GIS planning, while the other is quite advanced. Regardless, a new overall suite of information products will probably be required, involving new datasets and database designs. In this event, you should review the entire GIS plan and put in place new enterprise-wide planning, considering all the new ramifications for benefit–cost, technology acquisition, and communications that come with it.

The rates of change in technical capability and change in institutional business needs are illustrated in figure 12.7. The differences in the rate of change are dramatic, but they can be managed. The challenge for the GIS manager is to provide the maximum business support while minimizing expenditures. He or she manages the changes in technical capability on the basis of cost-effectiveness. When new information products are introduced in response to changing business needs, this is managed by maximizing support for the business of the organization.

In the early days of GIS, plans were typically updated on a five-year cycle. These days five years is too long; things change too fast. To determine when your implementation plan will become outdated, you must carefully assess the technology changes that have occurred since preparation of the last plan. When updating the implementation plan, the most important factors for you to consider are the following:

- The need for the continued availability of existing information products in the most cost-effective manner

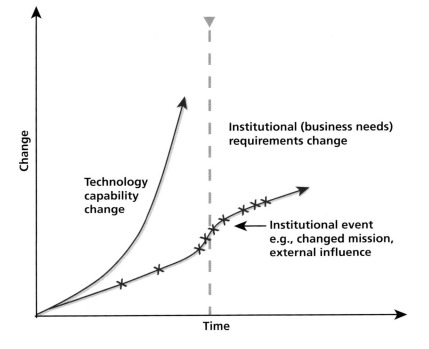

**Figure 12.7   Adding information products (x) to manage major change**

- The expansion of the information "product line" to meet the changing business needs of the organization

## Managing change

The best advice for managing change is exactly the same that informed your planning for a GIS from the first step forward: Start with the goals and objectives of the entire organization in clear focus. Keep in mind that you will be talking about change whenever you approach management for approval to add information products or acquire new technology; so it is best to update management regularly, just as you keep your plan itself up to date.

## Start with an enterprise-wide plan

Enterprise-wide planning allows for maximizing the benefit that can be gained from GIS. Note that enterprise-wide planning does not mean enterprise-wide implementation. (In the end, it may be prudent to implement only a small part of the plan at first and build on the success of that part for further implementation.) The point is that, while it's usually satisfactory to implement incrementally, it's always best practice to plan comprehensively. When you do, you can identify the most important system functionality on an enterprise-wide basis. You can intelligently consider GIS communication requirements throughout the organization. Time spent in enterprise-wide GIS planning is the best investment related to GIS that you can make because it sets you up for success.

The wise advice is to plan early and as broadly as possible. But you also need to plan within the normal life of an organization. The one exception to that relates to special circumstances that can be imagined but are out of the ordinary. For example, planning can and should be adopted for one or a small set of very high-priority information products created in response to crises or natural disasters.

Be a bit wary of out-of-the-box software with available data to produce so-called standard or all-purpose useful information products (followed by another and another). With such generic information products, after a while, demands and problems start to arise, and you are forced to actually think about what you are doing. Again, your planning, like each information product, needs to fit the specific mission of your organization.

## Add information products

Adding new information products after the GIS is up and running is not a problem, but it does require careful management because now you must weigh priority of need for the new against the old. First, you will revisit the steps you took in activity planning (chapter 7) to determine the priority level of the new information products just as you did for the original products when you were creating the MIDL. But this time, recognizing the demand new products will place on the data-entry schedule, you will consider whether displacement or delay might affect generating the other information products and their benefits.

In essence, you must formally manage the process of scheduling new information product design and generation in the context of the existing information product priorities, data availability and readiness, activity timing, and revised onset of benefit from other information products.

Information product design, particularly for more complex products, can be a time-consuming process and must be judged in the context of the life cycles of the technology being used. For example, if the technology currently in use is late in its life cycle and has only one year until obsolescence, a major information product design should probably wait and take advantage of the new technology.

If waiting allows for significantly reducing the amount of time needed to develop the product, it could measurably reduce its costs. Alternatively, you could always go forward with the original design, but only with the full understanding that its benefit cycle will be limited; it may face abandonment, or adapting it to the new technologies when they finally arrive may require significant effort.

## Acquire technology

These days, you can—and should—use much more of the capacity of the procured technology right from the outset. You should plan to use at least 50 percent of the capacity of the equipment you choose in the first year of its acquisition; otherwise, buy less. The old paradigm of buying the largest equipment possible from the current budget and planning to use 10 percent of its capacity in the first year, 20 percent the second year, 50 percent the third year, and so on over a five-year cycle is no longer cost-effective. Given the increases in equipment capacity and the cost reduction over each twelve-month period, you can do better.

In other words, to transform this type of change into the opportunity it really is, you need to set up a continuous technology acquisition budget to maintain your system cost-effectively, and senior management needs to allocate the resources for this. Hardware, software, training, and data all need to be procured bearing in mind the life cycle of both the technology and the information products.

To do this, describe your GIS as part of the organization's infrastructure. As with other elements of this infrastructure, two types of funding are necessary:

- Funding for ongoing operation and maintenance
- Funding for capital investment

A common approach to ongoing capital investment is to estimate the life cycle of the asset and annually budget for an appropriate amount in a capital replacement (or sinking) fund. For example, three years may be the estimated life cycle for a desktop workstation. If your organization has sixty of these workstations, you should budget funds to replace twenty per year.

In common practice, hardware extends its useful life by cascading down through the organization; older workstations are assigned less-demanding tasks, while high-end workstations are replaced on the acquisition budget. Many organizations also regard data acquisition as a capital investment item rather than an operation and maintenance expenditure.

### Inform management about change

Continual change raises a number of questions for the GIS manager:

- How do you secure support for a technology that is constantly evolving?
- How do you convince management that system upgrades are necessary?
- How do you secure funding for training costs?

When facing such questions, keep in mind that GIS implementation will move forward because an organization expects to benefit from using a geographic information system. Never forget your role in educating yourself and senior management about change. Keep up with change—anticipate it, prepare for it, and even make it happen—and your route can lead you straight to the benefits and opportunities change carries with it. Both technology and business needs change with time, and you need to stay on top of it all.

As you will have seen for yourself by now, GIS itself means change—the kind of change that brings benefits—so you are keeping senior management apprised of change when you keep them informed about the benefits received from the GIS as they become known. Your proposals for support required for upgrades and training must be presented in the context of these benefits. Provide management the opportunity to see how the GIS minimizes cost while maximizing support for business solutions. Revisit the benefit categories in your benefit–cost model to remind yourself what specifically to look out for. Identify policy changes that were substantially influenced by information received from the GIS. As demonstrable benefits occur, provide these in a continuing series of reports to senior management. To maintain the cost-effectiveness of your system, you'll do regular budget planning for which you can use these reports as reference.

### Keep your plan current

Based on what you know now, it makes sense that the GIS implementation plan will require continual review. It must be periodically updated in response to changes in your organization and to keep pace with technology trends. Determining when to update the GIS implementation plan requires a careful assessment of the changes that have occurred since preparation of your final report or the last plan. View the components of your GIS as assets that depreciate and require a certain level of investment to stay cost-effective. Minimize the total cost of the GIS implementation while maximizing support for business.

Again, as at so many moments during the planning process, when updating the implementation plan, the most important considerations revolve around your information products and how you really need them to be. Ask yourself and your team what needs to be done to ensure both the continuing availability of existing information products for your organization and the needed expansion of the information product line as scheduled. Then make your plan for doing what needs to be done.

As at every stage of the planning methodology, if you ask the right questions, the answers will lead you to the next step in planning a solution. In that way, no matter how much change happens or will occur, in planning you have the means to adjust to it. Fortunately, planning is like thinking: the ability to do it is always there when you need it.

# GIS staff, job descriptions, and training

A good GIS staff is an invaluable tool for a manager. Money can buy more hardware and software, but even money cannot create the motivation and enthusiasm essential to a successful staff and a successful GIS implementation. It takes people to build, manage, and maintain a GIS, so part of planning for a GIS is making sure you will have enough staff with the appropriate skills and training.

## GIS staff

Consider everyone directly concerned with the design, operation, and administration of the GIS as the GIS staff, including the end users, the management group, and the systems administration team. The core GIS staff, however, is where you expect to find the more specialized GIS skills, and it includes the GIS manager and GIS analysts.

### GIS manager

The GIS manager requires skills in GIS planning, system design, and system administration. Ideally, the manager would also possess hands-on, technical GIS skills—most effective GIS managers come from the ranks of GIS doers. The responsibilities of this position vary depending on the type of organization. In smaller organizations, the GIS manager may be the only person involved with the GIS; so the same person who negotiates data sharing agreements with the next county over is also pushing the buttons on the GIS when the data itself shows up. In very large organizations, often the GIS manager is in charge of coordinating the GIS staff, working with multiple departments, and overseeing the development of an enterprise-wide database. An emerging trend is toward the creation of geographic information officers (GIOs), who become the true champions and executors of GIS innovation within an organization.

## GIS analysts

GIS analysts are persons with GIS expertise working in support of the GIS manager. In smaller GIS organizations or in a single-department GIS, the GIS analyst may be one person with a broad range of GIS skills; large organizations may need several GIS analysts, among whom you might find titles such as these:

- GIS technology expert—responsible for the hardware and network operations of the GIS
- GIS software expert—responsible for application programming
- GIS database analyst—responsible for administration of the GIS database
- GIS primary users
- Professional GIS users—support GIS project studies, data maintenance, and commercial map production
- Desktop GIS specialists—support general query and analysis studies

## GIS end users

It is helpful to think of the end users of your GIS as an important staff component because they affect the design and use of the GIS. They may include the following:

- Business experts—key employees with intimate knowledge of the processes your GIS is attempting to improve; they provide the GIS manager with major input regarding design and management of the GIS.

- Customers—clients of the GIS who are served by it, including business users requiring customized GIS information products to support their specific business needs, as well as the more casual Internet and intranet map server users, people accessing basic map products invoked by wizards or Web browsers.

Once the GIS is implemented, the management group merits special attention as part of the end-user category. The fundamental purpose of a GIS is to provide to management new or improved information for decision-making purposes. At this level then, the managers actually become customers, whereas up until now they have been involved in helping you pass through the hurdles of the organizational bureaucracy. The managers could be the project sponsor, a member of executive management who will be using the application (or its output), or a management representative who can serve as the conduit delivering management's requirements. While not the core GIS staff, they are nonethelss vital to GIS success.

## System administration staff

A large organization needs a system administration staff to play an important role in the day-to-day operation of the computer systems supporting the GIS. Staff members may include the following:

- The network administrator—responsible for maintaining the enterprise network
- The enterprise database administrator—responsible for the administration of all databases that interact within the organization
- The hardware technicians—handle the day-to-day operation of computer hardware within the organization, including maintenance and repair

## Staff placement

Once you've identified the GIS staff required, you must decide where the positions fit into your organizational structure, a decision that will affect the role and visibility of the GIS department. There are four main levels in which GIS staffs are typically placed:

1. Within an existing operational department: In this scenario, staff is tied to a specific need and budget. It is difficult for staff at this level to serve multiple departments.

2. In a GIS services group: This group serves multiple projects but still has the autonomy and visibility of a stand-alone group.

3. At an executive level: This placement signals a high commitment from management. Staff have high visibility and the authority to help coordinate the GIS project. The downside is when GIS staff at the executive level become isolated, fostering the perception among the rank-and-file of being out of touch with critical stakeholders.

4. In a separate support department: The more old-fashioned notion of IT would place any new information system staff in a centralized computing services department. This is the "systems" group in many organizations.

# GIS job descriptions

Clear job descriptions are essential before hiring begins. Outlining GIS roles provides you and your prospective employees with a common understanding about the position and its requirements. Job titles and descriptions will also come into play during job evaluation and performance reviews. Most GIS job descriptions of the same titles are similar; however, they do vary depending on the software used within an organization, size of the system, specific job responsibilities required, and type of agency or company seeking to fill the position.

If your organization is new to GIS, the human resources department will not have suitable job descriptions for the type of GIS personnel you need, so you'll have to write them yourself. Refer to the sample GIS job descriptions here, and be sure to design your own just as realistically. Obviously, you want the best person for the job, but if you require that your digitizing technicians have master's degrees, you will probably never find a digitizing technician.

## GIS manager

Provides on-site management and direction of services to develop, install, integrate, and maintain an agency-wide standard GIS platform. This position will be responsible for developing, implementing, and maintaining special-purpose applications consistent with the agency's mission and business objectives. Requirements: must have proven experience in project-design and work-plan development; database system and application design; maintenance and administration of a large Oracle SDE database. Successful candidates must have a B.S./M.S. in geography, planning, or related field and three to five years professional experience implementing in-depth, complex, GIS solutions involving RDBMS and front-end application development. Applicants must also have knowledge of and ability to apply emerging information and GIS technologies (particularly Internet technologies); experience in project management; experience working with Oracle databases; and excellent interpersonal, organizational, and leadership skills. Experience with object-oriented methods and techniques is a plus.

## Enterprise systems administrator

This position will provide user support, resolve UNIX- and NT-related problems, perform systems administrative functions on networked servers, and configure new

UNIX and NT workstations. Requirements include a B.S. degree in computer science or other related college degree with experience in computer systems area or three or more years working in systems administration functions in a client-server environment. Must be familiar with multiple UNIX platforms and have high skills with both UNIX and NT commands and utilities. Good problem-solving skills and the ability to work in a team environment are mandatory.

## GIS application programmer

The GIS programmer will design, code, and maintain in-house GIS software for custom applications. Position requires the ability to interpret user needs into useful applications. Candidates should have a B.S./B.A. degree or higher in computer science, geography, or related earth sciences. All candidates must have two years or more of programming experience with one of the following: VB, C++, or GIS vendor-specific programming languages. Previous experience with programming GIS applications and knowledge of GIS search engines is a plus.

## GIS database analyst

Responsible for the creation of spatially enabled database models for an enterprise GIS. Typical tasks include setup, maintenance, and tuning of RDBMS and spatial data, as well as development of an enterprise-wide GIS database. Position is also responsible for building application frameworks based on Microsoft COM approaches. Position requires at least a B.S./B.A. in computer science or geography. Candidates should have a strong theoretical GIS and database design background and experience with Microsoft COM objects approach. Preference will be given to candidates with experience in modeling techniques used by the enterprise.

## GIS analyst

Responsible for the development and delivery of GIS information products, data, and services. Responsibilities include database construction and maintenance using current enterprise GIS software, data collection and reformatting, assisting in designing and monitoring programs and procedures for users, programming system enhancements, customizing software, performing spatial analysis for special projects, and performing QA/QC activities. Requires a B.A. degree in geography, computer science and planning, engineering, or related field or an equivalent combination of education and experience. Candidates should have one to two years experience with GIS products and technologies, especially those currently used by the enterprise. Applicants should have experience with various spatial-analysis technologies, and knowledge of current enterprise spatial server engines is a plus.

## GIS technician/Cartographer

Responsibilities include all aspects of topographic and map production using custom software applications, including compilation from various source materials, generation of grids and graticules, relief portrayal, creating map surround elements, digital cartographic editing, text placement, color separation, quality assurance, symbol creation, and cartographic software testing. Successful candidates will have strong verbal and written communication skills and have a B.A./B.S. or M.S. degree (depending on position level) in geography, cartography, GIS, or related field; experience or coursework in GIS software and macrolanguages, Visual Basic, or graphic drawing packages; and familiarity with remote-sensing and satellite imagery interpretation. Candidates should provide a digital or hard-copy cartographic portfolio for evaluation.

# Training

Consider how the people within your organization will use the GIS before developing a training program. GIS staff and GIS end users will require different types of training.

## Core staff training

The core GIS staff members comprise the cornerstone of your efforts. They are responsible for creating, maintaining, and operating both the data and the system infrastructure. They will require up-front and ongoing training to keep them current on new techniques and methods. (You may need to consider training for system administration staff as well.)

The training program developed for the GIS staff could involve courses in database management, application programming, hardware functionality, or even geostatistical analysis, depending on their relative and collective skill sets. The training your staff receives should complement their job responsibilities. These are the people responsible for maintaining a product for your users. A well-trained staff is crucial for the continual success of a GIS.

## End-user training

The training required for GIS end users is understandably much less involved than that for core GIS staff members. Often a single interface or Web application is all that an end user will ever see, meaning the application can be taught in as little as minutes.

Many vendors provide training courses related to their own software, and some even cover basic GIS theory and applications as necessary. Self-study workbooks that include software to practice with provide another flexible learning alternative. GIS is inherently a multidisciplinary endeavor, so training in other areas beyond the actual software continues to play a major role.

## Manager training

Even if, ideally, the person hired as GIS manager has technical competency in GIS, these skills must be continually updated if the manager hopes to give meaningful direction to his or her staff. Also, of course, GIS managers must demonstrate effective management skills—or work to acquire them. Courses designed to help in specific areas such as general management skills, project management, strategic management, and total quality management can all be helpful.

## Training delivery

Training can be delivered in many flexible forms these days, thanks to wonders like the Web and cheap air travel. Face-to-face classroom courses are available from vendors or educational establishments, either at their premises or on-site with you. Web-based training, distance learning, and self-study workbooks are all options for training in GIS and related areas. Whatever method is used, sufficient time and resources for training and related activities (travel, preparation of assessment, follow-up reading) must be provided.

# Benchmark testing

*Appendix*
*B*

A benchmark test is a comparative evaluation of different systems in a controlled environment. The test is used to determine which system can handle the anticipated workload in the most cost-effective manner.

Benchmark testing is appropriate if you are planning to procure a large-scale system. It may cost a vendor about $40,000 to put on a benchmark test. If the system you're going to buy will cost $10,000, no vendor is going to conduct a benchmark test for you. The system is too small to make benchmarking cost-effective. That is why such tests are generally conducted only for large system acquisitions, and they are getting harder to recommend to vendors as system prices fall.

A benchmark test is not simply a demonstration of what a system can do. The objectives are to find out whether each system under test can perform the required tasks and to determine each system's relative performance with respect to these tasks. A benchmark test should be designed to verify that the system can perform the functions necessary to create the information products in a timely manner. It should evaluate whether each system can handle the data required, produce the information products needed, and carry out the core functionality. The focus of the tests should be functions that you will use most often.

The test is also used for assessing the price of the proposed system compared to its performance.

## What you provide vendors

You should provide vendors with information on functional requirements and throughput capacity. Vendors who want to participate in the benchmark testing will then respond with details of a proposed system configuration and the cost of system acquisition and maintenance. The system configuration details would include the type and capacity of the equipment, storage devices, network capacities, and the number of input and product generation workstations. Such details might also be accompanied by descriptions of system capabilities, support services, company characteristics, and contractual commitments in any prebenchmark proposals.

You already gathered information for the functional requirements you need to pass along—you did so during the planning process, when you considered the following aspects of the anticipated workload:

- The information products created by the system in each of the first five years
- The relative importance of each information product to the daily work of the organization (the assigned priority) and the wait tolerance of each information product
- The system functions required to create each information product
- The data required to create the information products
- The yearly volume of each data type required to create the information products

During the conceptual system design for technology, you summarized and classified the functions required by the GIS in a functional utilization table and graph. This provides you with the following details:

- The total set of system functions required
- The frequency of anticipated use of those functions
- The relative importance of those functions

Having determined the functionality required, and thereby the anticipated workload, you can now establish the throughput capacity of the system. Throughput capacity is the amount of work that the GIS must be able to carry out over a period of time, which is a function of the combined capabilities of the system software, hardware, and network bandwidth.

## Testing guidelines

A benchmark test is a compromise between exhaustive and inadequate testing. You should aim to keep the test as compact as possible while still producing reliable results. To minimize the testing effort placed on the vendors, while still allowing yourself to gather the information required, you can adopt the following guidelines:

- Send approximately 85 percent of the test data and all of the test questions to the vendors two months in advance of the test. This gives the vendors ample time to create the required databases and set up their systems to perform at optimum levels during the test.
- Make sure that each vendor receives the same data and test questions. This uniformity permits the testing of all vendors on an equal basis. It also permits you to create testing scenarios with known answers.
- Provide approximately 15 percent of the test data on the first day of the benchmark test to permit real-time observation of data entry and data updating.
- Choose a set of information products that is representative of your organization's needs, including some that require rapid response, some that are mission critical, and some that are high-capacity business support applications.
- Carefully choose which information products to test to ensure that the proposed system has the capacity to create the other information products required by your organization.

- Test most thoroughly those frequently used functions required for the highest-priority information products. Less-used functions or lower-priority functions should be tested the least, but all functions should be tested at least once. Any insufficiently tested functions can be tested in a separate section of the test specifically designed for that purpose.

## Logistics of testing

You need to address other questions, concerning the logistics of testing. These include the following sections.

### Where should the test be conducted?

It is usually preferable to hold the benchmark test at a site chosen by the vendor. They may choose their own company headquarters. However, if the new system will be embedded within an existing enterprise network, it is better for the client to provide an isolated network that emulates the multiple data transmission speeds encountered in their network with wide area connections. If the client provides the testing site, the vendor should supply the proposed hardware at the client's site using the vendor-recommended protocols. If it is not possible to establish the network test at the client's site, the network may be simulated at the vendor's site with provision made to closely monitor network traffic volumes.

### When should the test be carried out?

The vendors should select the test dates. Once the testing dates are chosen by all the vendors, send the questions and materials to the vendors by courier at appropriate intervals to ensure that each vendor has the same amount of time between when they receive the materials and their scheduled testing date.

### Who should manage the testing?

A benchmark test team should manage the process and evaluate the results. This team should be composed of key client personnel, such as users, technical-support staff, consultants, and managers. It is important for the users to have a sense of ownership in the decision. It is also wise to include technical support and management staff. They will be crucial allies during implementation and in providing ongoing support. These different perspectives will help make the selection decision a better one.

### Who should monitor the tests?

A subset of the management team should monitor the actual tests. Ideally, this monitoring team should consist of a minimum of two and a maximum of four persons, including technical staff with previous benchmark test experience or one or two experienced GIS consultants, plus one or two staff from your organization who have firsthand knowledge of the GIS analysis required. The same monitoring team should preside over each benchmark test in the procurement.

### Who pays for the testing?

Current practice is to share benchmark test costs between the client and the vendors. The client typically underwrites the cost of test preparation, materials, provision of an isolated network for testing, test monitoring, result analysis, and reporting. The vendors accept costs of database creation, installation of hardware on the isolated network (if required), and performing system tests.

## Evaluation and scoring

Benchmark testing is conducted to ensure that the proposed system can perform the functions you need to generate your information products. Without testing a

193

proposed system adequately, you risk making a purchase with little value to your organization. Proper evaluation is part of adequate testing.

Your evaluation of the functional requirements should answer the following questions:

- Can the systems being tested perform the functions specified in the RFP?
- What is the relative performance of different systems on a function-by-function basis?
- What is the effect of the proposed system configuration and network utilization design on the ability of the system to generate the required information products in a timely manner?

The functions you wish to evaluate should be identified in each section of any benchmark test guidelines provided to the vendors. Each information product has performance requirements (e.g., wait tolerance) specified.

A benchmark test team, together with anyone involved in preparation of data and answers for the benchmark test, should evaluate the functionality. (The monitoring team is an important part of the benchmark test team.) To evaluate functionality, the benchmark test team needs the following:

- All observations made by the monitoring team during the benchmark tests
- The indicators of system performance by function measured during the benchmark tests
- The results of the verification performed after the benchmark tests

Each function should be allocated a score using the scoring system from the table bellow. This scoring system should be provided to vendors in the RFP. When the test is complete, the benchmark test team should discuss each function to arrive at a unanimous decision for the final scores.

Now you should assess how the production of information products will be affected by the functional capability. To do this, use your list of information products ranked by

| Score | Function appraisal | Criteria |
|---|---|---|
| 0 | Outstanding | All of the qualities in appraisal totally integrated into an operational system—the best in the industry. |
| 1 | Excellent | Elegant, well-thought-out solution for individual functions—very fast and user friendly. |
| 2 | Very good | Fast and user friendly. |
| 3 | Good | Adequate and fast or user friendly. |
| 4 | Satisfactory | Adequate. |
| 5 | Functional | Function can be performed. Needs minor improvement for speed or ease of use. |
| 6 | Functional with limitations | Function can be performed. Needs substantial improvements for speed or ease of use. |
| 7 | Partial only | New software development required for part for function. |
| 8 | Absent or not demonstrated | New software development required. |
| 9 | Absent and constrained | Impossible or very difficult to implement without major system modification. |

Figure B.1   **Criteria for system evaluation**

priority. Assign a 0-9 function score to each function invoked to make each product, determine the total and average score for each product, and determine the worst score for any of the functions required to make each product.

These results will be sufficient where there is a substantial difference in functional capabilities between the systems under evaluation in the benchmark test. It should be clear if one or more of the systems includes restricted functionality that prohibits the making of high-priority, frequently used products.

Where differences between systems are less pronounced, you'll need to produce a graph like the one below to help in your decision making. Plot the highest function score obtained for each information product on the vertical axis against the priority ranking for each information product (on the horizontal axis). Plot a separate curve for each system you have tested.

If there are no overlaps of the separate curves for each system on your graph, then the preferred system on functional grounds will be the one appearing highest on the graph (as on the left). If the curves on your graph

overlap (as on the right), you must make a judgment depending on the relative importance of high-priority versus low-priority products.

## Throughput capacity

Again, throughput capacity is the amount of work that your system must be able to carry out over a period of time. To evaluate throughput capacity you should determine system performance for data input, information product generation, and network capacity utilization.

### Data input

Calculate personnel time required for data input. When setting up your benchmark tests make sure you can extrapolate personnel time for each dataset planned for input in each year of the five-year planning horizon. Determine data storage requirements; estimate these in terabytes, gigabytes, megabytes, or kilobytes for each dataset as appropriate.

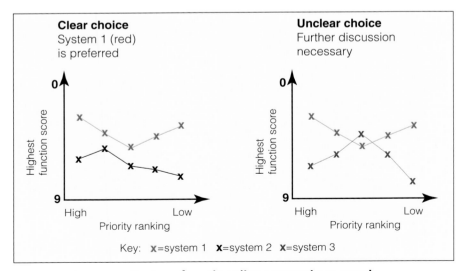

Figure B.2   **System functionality comparison graph**

## Information product generation

Estimate the data volume by data function for each information product. Use the master input data list and the information product descriptions to generate this estimate. Use the measures of system performance by function and data volume collected during the benchmark test to calculate personnel time, CPU time, network capacity utilization, and plotting time to generate each information product (if plotting is needed).

Compare these results with the results for the same variables generated during the benchmark test. After the benchmark test, you should be able to estimate the following, by year:

- The total personnel time required to input data
- The core performance metrics required to input data and create information products
- Storage requirements of the system
- The network capacity utilization to create the required information products at the specified wait tolerances
- The plotter hours required for information product generation

Compare the results of personnel time used for daily input and information product generation with personnel availability. Convert the results to operational costs by year using hourly rates, so you can assess the overall use costs for each system.

The core utilization figures will require adjustment if the core type used by the vendor during the benchmark test is different than the core metrics proposed for acquisition by your organization. When necessary, you can use the relative performance ratios provided by computer manufacturers. In general, advise the vendor to use the proposed core type for the benchmark test. Compare the results of the system resource use calculations with the system configuration proposed by the vendor. This will allow you to determine if the proposed configuration can handle the workload.

## Network capacity utilization

When enterprise networks are needed for information product generation and tests have been conducted on an isolated controlled network, a quantitative evaluation of network capacity utilization is possible.

The benchmark test results allow you to calculate the effect on the network caused by use of the GIS. The benchmark test gives the percentage of network capacity utilization by information product for single and multiuser conditions. These numbers can be extrapolated to estimate, by year, the network capacity utilization associated with the generation of the proposed information products. Estimates will reflect the hardware and protocol options and data search engine optimization design recommended by the vendor. You should compare these estimates with the client network administration numbers on network percent capacity availability in the same time period.

The measures to be tested should be specified in the benchmark test guidelines and sent to vendors.

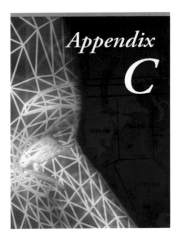

*Appendix*

*C*

# Network design planning factors

| Network design planning factors | | | | | |
|---|---|---|---|---|---|
| | Data per display | | Traffic per display | | Kbps traffic per user | |
| Client platform | Kbpd | Adj Kbpd | Kbpd | Mbpd | 6 dpm | 10 dpm |
| File server client | 1,000 | 5,000 | 50,000 | 50.000 | 5,000 | 8,333 |
| Geodatabase client | 1,000 | 500 | 5,000 | 5.000 | 500 | 833 |
| Terminal client | 100 | 28 | 280 | 0.280 | 28 | 47 |
| Web browser client | 100 | 100 | 1,000 | 1.000 | 100 | 167 |
| Web GIS desktop client | 200 | 200 | 2,000 | 2.000 | 200 | 333 |

Figure C.1 **New network load factors**

A system design performance factor is derived for six primary ArcGIS architectures, starting with average data requirements per query. Each of these analyses follows:

## 1. File server client

This represents a standard GIS desktop client accessing data from a file server data source. Data required to support display is 1,000 KB per query. Traffic between the client and server connection is 5,000 KB per query (file must be transferred to client to support query of data extent required for display). Converting data to traffic yields 50,000 Kb or 50 Mb per display (8 Kb per KB with 2 Kb overhead per traffic packet). Traffic per user depends on productivity, 5,000 Kb with 6 displays per minute and 8,333 Kb with 10 displays per minute. Typical GIS power users generate an average of 10 displays per minute.

## 2. Geodatabase client

This represents a standard GIS desktop client accessing data from a geodatabase data source. Data required to support display is 1,000 KB per query. Data is compressed in the geodatabase, reducing data transfer requirements to 500 KB per query. Converting data to traffic yields 5,000 Kb traffic per query (8 Kb per KB with 2 Kb overhead per traffic packet). Traffic per user depends on productivity, 5,000 Kb with 6 displays per minute and 8,333 Kb with 10 displays per minute. Typical GIS power users generate an average of 10 displays per minute.

**Caution:** The two client/server architectures above are normally supported over an Ethernet LAN environment. Only one transmission can be supported over a shared LAN segment at a time; when multiple transmissions occur at the same time with current switch technology, transmissions are cached on the switch and fed sequentially across the network. Too many users on a shared segment can result in performance delays. For this reason, maximum traffic on shared Ethernet segments is typically reached by about 50 percent of the total available bandwidth (due to probability of transmission delays at higher utilization rates).

## 3. Terminal client

This represents terminal client access to standard GIS desktop software executed on a Windows terminal server. Data required to support display is 100 KB per query (display pixels only). Traffic between the client and server connection is 28 KB per query (average 75 percent compression with Citrix ICA protocol). Converting data to traffic yields 280 Kb traffic per query (8 Kb per KB with 2 Kb overhead per traffic packet). Traffic per user depends on productivity, 5,000 Kb with 6 displays per minute and 8,333 Kb with 10 displays per minute. Typical GIS power users generate an average of 10 displays per minute.

## 4. Web browser client

This represents browser client access to a standard Web map service. Data required to support display is typically 100 KB per query (typical size of image data transfer generated by Web mapping service). Traffic between the client and server connection is 100 KB per query (no additional compression).

Converting data to traffic yields 1,000 Kb traffic per query (8 Kb per KB with 2 Kb overhead per traffic packet). Traffic per user depends on productivity, 100 Kb with 6 displays per minute and 167 Kb with 10 displays per minute. Typical GIS Web clients generate an average of 6 displays per minute. Note: If peak map request rates are given, 1,000 Kbpq would be the more accurate network design factor for assessment purposes.

## 5. Web GIS client

This represents GIS desktop client access to a standard Web mapping service. Data required to support display is 200 KB per query (based on typical user-selected display resolution—pixels per display determines traffic requirements). Traffic between the client and server connection is 200 KB per query (no additional compression). Converting data to traffic yields 2,000 Kb traffic per query (8 Kb per KB with 2 Kb overhead per traffic packet). Traffic per user depends on productivity, 100 Kb with 6 displays per minute and 167 Kb with 10 displays per minute. Typical GIS Web clients generate an average of 6 displays per minute. Note: If peak map request rates are given, 2,000 Kbpq would be the more accurate network design factor for design purposes.

**Caution:** The three architectures above (3, 4, and 5) are normally supported over WAN environments. Only one transmission can be supported over a shared WAN segment at a time; when two transmissions occur at the same time, transmissions are cached at the router and fed sequentially onto the WAN link. Transmission delays will occur as a result of the cache time (time waiting to get on the WAN). For this reason, optimum performance on shared WAN segments is typically reached with less than 50 percent of the total available bandwidth (due to probability of delays at higher utilization rates).

## Acknowledgment

The author would like to express appreciation to Dave Peters of ESRI for providing these network planning factors and the network traffic transport time and performance per CPU tables in chapter 10. For more detailed information, please refer to his *System Design Strategies* white paper referenced in the "Further reading" section of this book.

# Appendix D

# Request for proposal (RFP) outline

Early in your implementation planning process, you may want to write a request for proposals (RFP) and send copies to hardware and software vendors in contention for your business. An RFP invites vendors to propose the most cost-effective GIS solution to a specified business need. Well-crafted RFPs are not shopping lists of hardware and software to be procured, but rather descriptions of the work that has to be done by the system. An RFP also specifies how the selection and actual procurement will be carried out, so that vendors can propose realistic options based on the most complete information.

Sometimes the actual RFP may be preceded by a request for information (RFI), which many organizations use to solicit assistance in the development of their final RFP. Savvy technology managers realize that early input from tech suppliers can be very instructional—vendors spend a lot of time thinking about how to implement their particular technology. Sometimes an RFI is nothing more than an early draft RFP. RFIs are particularly useful when the scope of your system is likely to be large. You can include the draft RFP when you send the RFI to vendors, asking them to respond with a letter of intent to bid and any comments. This step helps you to design an RFP that is not inadvertently biased toward one vendor or another.

The RFP for a major procurement is typically a single document supported by substantial appendixes. (For a smaller project, the single document may be all that is needed.) The primary document lays out the requirements, while the appendixes provide details, such as the master input data list, the information product descriptions, copies of government contract regulations, worksheets for product cost and data conversion estimates (to standardize replies from vendors), and overall data processing plans pertinent to the GIS.

This primary document of the RFP should include the following:

**General information/procedural instructions:** Here, you cover the acquisition process and schedule, the vendor intent to respond, instructions on the handling of proprietary information, proposed visits to vendor sites and debriefing conferences (if deemed necessary), clear rules for the receipt of proposals (date, time, place), and finally, arrangements for communications between the organization's contact person and the vendors.

**Work requirements:** This section is the most substantial part of the RFP. It should list the work to be done by the system, expressed specifically in the context of the information products that have to be created, the system functions required to produce the information products, and the data needed in the database. Limit the main text of the RFP to a listing of what is required, and leave supporting definitions and any necessary descriptions to the appendixes.

Here's a checklist of work requirements that every good RFP should include:

- The full set of information product descriptions (IPDs)
- The master input data list (MIDL)
- Data handling load estimates over time by location
- Functional utilization estimates over time by location
- Notes on existing computer facilities and network capabilities
- Lists of any special symbols required (for maps, etc.)

**Services to be performed by the vendor:** Typically, vendors are contracted to supply and install the hardware and software systems and to train the new users. But sometimes in-house staff takes on part of that work. In any case, clear, complete written documentation in the form of user guides must be created. After installation and start-up training, also plan for ongoing maintenance and upgrades to the system. Spell out what you want the vendor to do.

**References:** Good vendors are more than happy to provide reference sites of existing customers running similar systems. After you receive the references, call the other customers yourself to hear their experiences.

**Financial requirements:** You will be making some significant financial decisions, including whether the hardware equipment will be leased, lease-purchased, installment-purchased, or purchased outright, and depreciation and tax considerations may come into play. The RFP should solicit the cost of the recommended approach along with several alternatives and their respective costs. It should include the instructions on use of financial worksheets, if any, and the licensing terms and conditions on purchased data and software. If you require estimates of operating costs from the vendors, be sure they account for staff hourly rates. Maintenance on software should be a guarantee of prompt upgrades to new versions and technical support from the vendor, so you want to ask for that in writing, too.

**Proposal submission guidelines:** Describe the required format, the number of copies needed, and the proposal content, including appendixes. (Choose a format that will facilitate your comparing and rating proposals from the various vendors.) Specify any mandatory contractual terms and conditions, or any specific financial requirements.

**Proposal evaluation plan:** This part of the RFP details the structure of whatever committees you will use to evaluate the proposal. With the RFP, step through the evaluation process and lay out the criteria that will be applied in the final decision making. These are the rules of engagement, as it were. Take care to explain the procedure with clarity—you want all minds in agreement, within the organization and among the vendors, on the process to be followed. If the system will be subjected to benchmark and acceptance testing, spell out the testing processes. This is particularly important in major procurements; most organizations contemplating major procurements have firm procedures for these steps. Both the organization and the vendors have a stake in your producing a clear, explicit RFP.

# Writing the preliminary design document

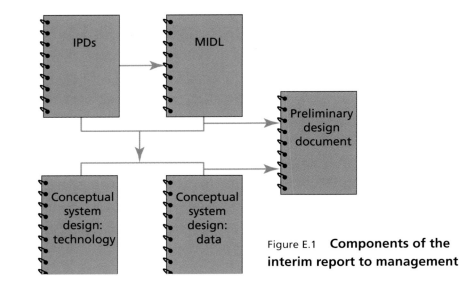

Figure E.1 **Components of the interim report to management**

The preliminary design document (introduced in chapter 10) is the culmination of all your planning work before the end stage planning for GIS procurement and implementation. Just as you sought commitment from upper management with your planning proposal at the beginning, now you must seek executive approval to move forward into planning the strategy for actual implementation. With this preliminary report, you will describe what your organization needs from a GIS and all the specific requirements GIS needs fulfilled in order to produce what is needed. This organized, straightforward report functions as the basis for the system you're recommending: the design for data and for the computer technology that will best support your organization through GIS. To win approval from upper management, it should be thorough, presented in an objective, reportorial style, and include the following sections.

# Executive summary

The preliminary design document begins with a summary of your findings and recommendations, so you're going to write this first section of the report last. Senior officials, who are short on time and low on GIS knowledge, probably will read this part only, so you want it to be convincing. After you've completed the report, review it in its entirety, paying close attention to the recommendations section. Gather this information into summary form and create the section that management will see first, the "Executive summary."

# Introduction

Include a brief introduction describing the report's purpose and structure. Include a table of contents in this section.

# Data section

The data section details the design and development of the database and its effect on system design. Structure it to include the following subsections.

## Dataset names

There is little to build on without first identifying the datasets. You'll find the name of each in the MIDL.

## Data characteristics

Gathering this information also from the MIDL, identify the physical and spatial characteristics of each dataset. Report the medium of the source data (e.g., paper maps, Mylar sheets, CDs, tape disks, or floppy disks). If the data is already in digital form, identify its format (e.g., TIGER, .E00, .DXF, or .txt files). Report the size of each dataset, map projection, scale, and datum. Carefully note any dataset that will require conversion to the chosen projection or scale. Finally, be sure to include the type and amount of error tolerance for each dataset.

## Logical data model

The conceptual database design is a high-level view of how the database will work. You've already used the logical design as a preliminary layout to fill in the conceptual design in accordance with a specific data model. Now for the conceptual database design, report the database contents, including all of your data elements and their logical linkages. Begin organizing the data thematically here, clustering such topics as landownership, transportation, and environmental areas together. Include diagrams of the relationships between data elements. This step will lend some perspective on the overall database and the complexity of its data relationships.

# Conceptual system design for technology

The technology section of the document defines the remaining components of the conceptual design for your organization. Clearly identify your planned use of the technology within the following subsections.

## Function utilization

Report the function utilization in the main document or as an appendix. It should contain an overview of the software functions required to create the information products. Gather this information from the steps you did earlier in summarizing and classifying your function requirements, and include your table or graph.

## System interface requirements

Describe the system interface requirements you have identified. For example, your GIS applications may require a link to scanned images and documents that are already managed by an existing software program. If this is the case, specify the need to access these databases and where they live. Include detailed information about the specific software, as an appendix if needed.

## Communication requirements

In this subsection, review the existing communication infrastructure and identify the network communications required to support the GIS. Also report all locations within the organization requiring access to GIS and the number of GIS users at each location. You first established this information in chapter 7 ("Define the system scope") and clarified it further early in this chapter. Refer back to it and report your findings.

## Hardware and software requirements

Describe the existing hardware and software standards and policies of your organization, as well as the proposed hardware and software configuration for the new GIS. If necessary, discuss any system configuration alternatives based on your organization's policies and standards.

Document any issues of compatibility between the existing computing standards and the proposed system configuration. Suggest how this proposed configuration might integrate with other systems, already used or planned for use, within the organization.

## Policies and standards

Report the policies or standards regarding the implementation of technology that exists within your organization. If there are no specific policies or standards that might affect the conceptual design, note this here.

## Recommendations

The last section of the preliminary design document is the clear-cut recommendation for a system design. All the previous sections have been strict reportage—facts and findings from your earlier work. This section is where you and your supporting team can actually declare your advocacy for the system's final configuration.

Base your recommendations on logical decisions. Draw from the data and technology sections of this report and use your staff to help with the decisions, then make the design recommendations for both software and hardware technology. You are recommending the overall design required to meet the needs of your organization, not a specific choice among the offerings of vendors. In fact, avoid brand endorsement as much as possible at this stage.

Make the recommendations clear and concise. You have reached a critical point in the planning process. The assessment of needs, data, and technology is complete. The recommendations take all of this into account and provide a basis for asking for approval to proceed with planning for procurement and implementation.

## Appendixes

Consider anything supplemental but not vital to understanding the core of the design as a candidate for an appendix. For example, it's essential to provide all the IPDs and the MIDL as appendixes (this way, too, they will be at hand for reference when you write your final report, the plan for implementation in chapter 12).

Finally, write the "Executive summary" and place it at the front of the document.

# Lexicon

This lexicon is a reference to the most important functions that your GIS software should provide. Many of the GIS function entries include examples of their use. This is not a comprehensive list of GIS functions, but rather an accessible, convenient subset of the most commonly used functions, which will help you prepare information product descriptions (IPDs) and functional specifications.

You will discuss GIS functions during several stages in the GIS planning process:

- During the technology seminar (chapter 5), to ensure that the planning team shares a common vision of what a GIS is and to encourage the use of a common vocabulary to assist communication.
- During the development of IPDs (chapter 6), to identify the GIS functions necessary to create an information product.
- During conceptual system design (chapter 7), to assess function use to help evaluate system requirements in preparation for making procurement recommendations (chapter 10) and planning implementation (chapter 12).

The lexicon is designed to boost your planning efforts in at least three ways:

1. Broaden your knowledge of the full range of GIS functions that should be available in a comprehensive system. (Most GIS users access only about 10 percent of the functions available to them on a daily basis.)
2. Enable you to write a description of your needs in a way that will be understood by any user or vendor. Users and vendors of GIS software tend to become well-versed in the terminology of their particular software. Different software, however, may have different terms for the same function or concept. Therefore, a software-independent description—not tied to any brand name—should facilitate communication even when terminology varies.
3. Allow non-GIS users to appreciate the full capabilities of a GIS. Many of those involved in GIS planning, as well as senior managers, clients, and members of an organization's information technology department, may be new to GIS software. The lexicon will help you help them understand its potential to serve their interests.

*The name of each function is followed by a brief description of the process or ability you should expect from it, via the software you choose. Functions that are considered high-complexity are flagged by an asterisk (\*).*

The lexicon is divided into the following sections or task categories; you'll find each function under the overall task it most often supports:

Data input

Data storage, data maintenance, and data output

Query

Generating features

Manipulating features

Address locations

Measurement

Calculation

Spatial analysis

Surface interpolation

Visibility analysis

Modeling

Network analysis

# Data input

### Digitizing

The process of converting point and line data from source documents into a machine-readable format. Manual methods employing a digitizing table or tablet are widely used, but, increasingly, these methods are being replaced by scanning, automatic line following methods, and transferring data files already in digital format. Many users, however, still use a manual digitizing technique for small amounts of data or when other methods are too expensive. Digitized data often needs editing or reformatting.

### Scanning

The process of creating an electronic photocopy of a paper map or document. You can use a flatbed or drum scanner, depending on the size of your map or document and the resolution you require. Scanning results in data that is in raster format (see raster-to-vector and vector-to-raster conversion, below). The data layer produced will contain all of the detail on the input map or image—including features you may not want to collect. For this reason, post-processing of scanned data is common. Scanned raster images are useful as a background for vector data, as they provide good spatial context and assist interpretation.

### Keyboard input

The process of manually typing alphanumeric data into machine-readable form; used infrequently because the dangers of human error are high and inputting multiple entries and checking are labor-intensive. Occasionally, keyboard entry is used to label data taken from hard-copy maps or, less frequently, to input coordinates for map corrections or very simple maps.

## File input

The process of inputting data, which uses tabular data or text from ASCII or word-processor-generated files that have already been manually typed and checked.

## File transfer

Allows you to input data that has been created with some other software or system. The data file being transferred may come from external, commercial data providers or from other systems within your own organization (for example, GPS or CAD). Data can be transferred from disk, CD-ROM, the Internet, or downloaded directly from field-data collection devices. This data might need to be reformatted to make it compatible with your GIS.

## Raster-to-vector and vector-to-raster conversion

Processes that change the format of data to allow additional analysis and manipulation. During vector-to-raster conversion, you should be able to convert both the graphical and topological characteristics of the data. You should also be able to select cell size, grid position, and grid orientation. During raster-to-vector conversion, creation of topology is necessary. Editing and smoothing of data may be necessary to create an effective vector representation.

## Data editing and data display

These functions should be possible at any time during digitizing and may apply to points, lines, and labels. On-screen displays or paper plots of errors assist editing. A range of functions for displaying different portions or different features of a dataset is essential. Functions that should be available for edit and display include the following:

- Selecting one or more datasets for display and editing
- Selecting a specific area within a dataset for editing
- Selecting features (points, lines, labels, etc.) to be displayed
- Selecting a feature or set of features to be edited
- Querying the attributes of selected features
- Indicating line ends (nodes) on request
- Rotating, scaling, and shifting one dataset with respect to another
- Deleting all user-selected features, codes, or data types in specified areas
- Deleting a user-selected feature using attributes or the mouse
- Adding a feature using the cursor, keyboard, or mouse
- Moving all or part of a feature
- Creating and modifying areas interactively
- Changing label text or location

## Create topology*

The ability to create digitized lines that are intelligently connected to form polygons or networks in two or three dimensions. Ideally, the process is automatic and includes error correction procedures (e.g., "join line endpoints within specified tolerance distances" or "remove small overshoots"). Alternatively, errors could be highlighted on-screen for you to edit and correct using standard graphical editing functions. The ability to perform topological operations on a selected part of the database is desirable, rather than involving the whole database each time.

## Edgematching*

An editing procedure used to join lines and areas across map sheet boundaries to produce a single, seamless digital database. The join created by edgematching needs to be topological as well as graphical. An area joined by edgematching should become a single area in the final database, and a line joined by edgematching should become a single line. Edgematching functions should be able to handle small gaps in data, slight discrepancies, overshoots, and missed and double lines. If these gaps and errors cannot be handled automatically, you should be alerted to their presence so that other methods of correction can be applied. Edgematching functions should allow you to set a tolerance limit for automatic editing.

## Adding attributes

The process of adding descriptive alphanumeric data to a digital map or to an existing attribute table. Attributes are characteristics of geographic features (points, lines, and areas). They are typically stored in tabular format and linked to the features. When there are a significant number of attributes associated with features (or sometimes for database design reasons), attributes may be stored in separate databases within your GIS or within another database management system (DBMS).

## Reformatting digital data

The process of making digitized data or data transferred from another system compatible with your system. Reformatting ensures accessibility or assists conversion to the system software format. Reformatted data should be topologically and graphically compatible with other data in your GIS. You may need to reformat data so that it complies with organizational standards. Reformatting may involve additional digitizing, adding extra labels, automatic editing, and the editing of attribute data.

Automated reformatting is increasingly important as users wish to integrate multiple data formats (from open or proprietary sources) into their GIS directly or make their own data available to others over the Web. Interoperability programs are available that allow direct reading and export from multiple sources.

## Schema arrange

The process of automatically combining two classification systems into one acceptable classification according to a set of rules. Usually carried out during the process of automated reformatting.

# Data storage, data maintenance, and data output

## Create and manage database

The process of organizing datasets using good cartographic data structures and data compaction techniques. Database creation and management permits easy access to data when a GIS contains several datasets, particularly if some of these are large.

In most cases, data will be input into a system from map sheets, images, or documents that cover large, contiguous areas of land. The data from these sheets must be edgematched into a combined database with a consistent data structure. This will allow analysis and query functions to be applied to part or the whole database.

## Edit and display (on output)

The ability to edit and display output map products on-screen is necessary to create effective information products. This process requires a wide variety of functions for editing, layout, symbolization, and plotting. Editing on output includes all of the editing capabilities used on input.

Appropriate symbolization assists presentation of results and simplifies interpretation of data. To facilitate symbolization, your GIS should include a wide variety of symbols that can be used to display points, lines, and areas; the ability to locate and display text and other alphanumeric labels; and the ability to create your own symbols

## Symbolize

The process of selecting and using a variety of symbols to represent the features in your database on-screen and on printed output. To create high-quality output from a GIS, you should use a wide variety of symbols to represent the features stored in the database on-screen and on printed output. Functions for symbolizing should permit the following:

- Use of standard cartographic symbols
- Filling areas with patterns of symbols or cross-hatching of different densities
- The representation of point features at different sizes and orientations
- The use of multiple discipline-oriented sets of symbols (for example, geological, electrical, oil, gas, water, and weather).

## Plot

The process of creating hard-copy output from your GIS. Printing and plotting functions in your GIS should allow the production of "quick-look" plots on-screen and on paper, spooling or stacking of large print jobs, plotting onto paper or Mylar sheets in a range of sizes, and registration facilities to permit overprinting on an existing printed sheet.

## Update

The process of adding new points, lines, and areas to an existing database to correct mistakes or add new information. After the initial creation of a digital database, periodic updates may be necessary to reflect changes in the landscape or area of interest. New buildings and roads may be constructed and old buildings and roads may be demolished. Quarries or forests may change in their extent or ownership, requiring updating of both the spatial extent and attributes of the data. You may need to update data to correct errors in the data.

Many of the functions for editing and display will be useful for updating, as will functions for heads-up digitizing on-screen. The ability to undo work is important, and there should be transaction logs, backup, and access protection for files during updating.

## Browse

Browsing is used to identify and define an area or window of interest that can be used for other functions. During browsing, no modifications to the database should be possible, but you should be able to select areas by specifying a window or central point, and pan and zoom. After identifying an area of interest, you should be able to edit, measure, query, reclassify, or overlay data.

## Suppress

Suppression is used to remove features from your working environment so that they are omitted from subsequent manipulation and analysis. As opposed to querying, which is normally used to select features you're interested in, suppression is used to omit features you're not interested in. For example, you might have a data source that contains all the roads in your study area, but you want to work only with the major highways. You can suppress all features other than the major highways so they are excluded from subsequent overlay, display, and plotting operations.

## Create list (report)

The creation of lists and reports can be part of the process of generating final or interim information product output. Also, information products themselves may be in the form of tables, lists, and reports. Functions in your GIS should allow you to do the following:

- Create user-specified lists of the results of any function generating alphanumeric output
- Produce subtotals, summary totals, and totals from lists of numbers
- Perform arithmetic and algebraic calculations based on given formulas
- Perform simple statistical operations, such as percentages, means, and modes
- Create list titles and headings in a range of standard formats and easily prescribed custom formats
- Sort data
- Create reports of system errors to permit corrections to be made easily

### Serve on Internet

Serving GIS or map data over the Internet usually involves displaying interactive maps that allow users to browse geographic data. In addition, many map servers allow users to view attributes, query the database, and create customized maps on demand.

## Query

### Spatial query

The process of selecting a subset of a study area based on spatial characteristics. The subset can be used for reporting, further study, or analysis.

Spatial queries are usually implemented by selecting a specific feature or by drawing a graphic shape around a set of features. For example, an irregular study area boundary may be plotted on-screen and all features within this boundary selected, or an administrative area might be selected with a single mouse click and used as a subset of the area for further study.

Querying a database can become complex and involve questions of both spatial and attribute data. For example, "Which properties are on the east side of town?" might be followed by "Which properties have four bedrooms and are available for sale?"

Queries are one of the most commonly used GIS functions. A good system will offer several alternative methods for querying to meet the needs of a range of users.

### Attribute query

The process of identifying a subset of features for further study based on questions about their attributes.

Attribute queries are usually implemented using a dialog that helps build the question or by using a special query language, such as structured query language (SQL). The questions "Which roads have two lanes?" and "Which properties are zoned residential?" would both result in the selection of a subset of features for further study.

## Generating features

### Generate features

The ability to create new features and add them to the database. Generating functions should allow features to be defined easily, with no limit on the number of new features that can be added to the database or on the number of points in any position. Names or codes can be attached to new features.

The types of features that you should be able to generate with your GIS include points, lines, polygons, circles, grid cell nets, and latitude-longitude nets.

## Generate buffer

The ability to generate zones of specified width around point, line, or area features. Around point and area features, these zones are generally called *buffers*, while zones of interest around line features may be called buffers or *corridors*.

A user-specified buffer distance is used to generate these buffers and corridors, and the system should automatically resolve overlaps and inclusions in cases where features are complex or highly convoluted. Buffers may be necessary both outside and inside area features such as lakes. For point, line, and area features, buffers at different distances (multiple buffers) should be possible. Constant- and variable-width buffers should also be possible, including buffers that intersect each other. Buffer width should be able to be set from the attributes of the features concerned, without operator intervention.

## Generate viewshed*

Involves manipulating a digital elevation model (DEM) to identify areas of the terrain that are visible from one or more viewpoints. The viewpoints may be any point along a line (such as a road) or in a user-defined polygon. Viewshed maps help find well-exposed places for communication towers or more amenable locations for parking lots, for example.

## Generate perspective view*

The ability to generate a three-dimensional block diagram showing the nature of the surface relative to three axes from a digital elevation model. Hidden line removal, hill relief shading, and the ability to plot symbols and cross-hatched areas on the surface plane are desirable to achieve a good quality output.

With scene generation, an advanced form of generating a perspective view, you can generate three-dimensional objects (for example, buildings, trees) and add them to the view. The realistic visualization this provides allows you to dynamically view the scene (perform fly-bys over and under the scene) and dynamically label the features on the passing scene.

## Generate elevation cross section*

The ability to generate a graph showing a cross section through a digital elevation model, along a user-defined line of any length or orientation. It is useful if the locations of features that cross the line of section (for example, roads) can be annotated.

## Generate graph

The ability to create a graph of attribute data. Graphs are used to display two attributes: one measured along the x-axis and the other along the y-axis. You should be able to illustrate data distribution with symbols, bars, lines, or fitted trend lines. Graphs can be drawn in place of maps or used to supplement them.

# Manipulating features

## Classify attributes

Classification is the process of grouping features with similar values or attributes into classes. Many datasets contain a wide range of values. Classifying the data into a number of groups, or classes, for presentation or analysis helps illustration and interpretation. For example, population totals for one-kilometer grid cells may range from zero to several hundred in a study area. Displaying all possible values on a single map, using a different color for each one, could result in a map so multicolored as to render it impossible for a user to interpret. For presentation purposes, up to eight classes are normally used, but for analysis more classes may be appropriate.

## Dissolve and merge

Allows the removal of boundaries between two adjacent areas that have the same attributes. A common attribute is assigned to the new larger area. Using these functions, the boundaries between adjacent areas with the same attributes are dissolved to form larger areas; tables containing attribute values from the joined areas are then merged to give one value for the resulting larger area.

This function may be necessary after an edgematching or reclassification operation (although in some cases it may be important to retain the boundaries between areas—for example, administrative or political boundaries).

## Line thin*

The ability to reduce data file sizes where appropriate, following input, by reducing line detail. This function reduces the number of points used to define a line or set of lines, in accordance with user-defined tolerances. Some of the points along the line are weeded out to reduce the total number used to represent features. It is important that the general trend and information content of lines be preserved during the process.

## Line smooth*

As opposed to line thinning, line smoothing involves adding detail to lines to represent a feature more effectively. Line smoothing functions use tolerances to smooth lines by adding extra points and reducing the length of individual line segments. A smoother appearance results. A number of different functions for line smoothing may be available in a GIS.

## Generalize*

A process to reduce the amount of detail when displaying features. Generalization techniques are used to permit effective scale changes and to aid the integration of data from different source scales. A large-scale map (1:50,000) redisplayed on-screen at a smaller scale (1:250,000) would appear cluttered and difficult to interpret without the aid of generalization techniques.

### Clip

Allows you to extract features in the database from a defined area. This function is also commonly referred to as *cookie-cutting*. Whether you define the area on-screen with the mouse or by using another feature in the database (such as an administrative area), the result is a new data layer containing only the features of interest within your study area. The original data layer remains unchanged.

### Scale change

Involves changing the size at which data is displayed. A scale change is usually performed in the computer rather than at the plotting table. Zoom-in and zoom-out functions should be available, as well as the ability to specify the exact scale at which you want to redisplay data. Line thinning and weeding operations or line smoothing may be incorporated in scale reduction. Line dissolving and attribute merging functions usually need to be invoked prior to broad-range scale reduction. Particular attention should be paid to the legibility of the final product, including labels.

Changing the scale of a dataset before integrating it with other data should be undertaken with caution, as data is best manipulated and analyzed at the scale of collection. As a general rule, if the data is to be used in analysis, you should avoid changing a dataset's scale to more than 2.5 times larger or smaller than the scale of the original source.

### Projection change

Allows you to alter the map projection being used to display a dataset. You may need to change the projection of a dataset to enable integration with data from another source. For example, you would do so with data digitized from a map that uses the universal transverse Mercator projection if you wanted it to be overlaid by a data layer using an equal-area cylindrical projection. Your software should provide functions for changing data between a range of common projections or map datums.

### Transformation*

The process of converting coordinates from one coordinate system to another through translation (shift), rotation, and scaling. Transformation involves the systematic mathematical manipulation of data: the function is applied uniformly to all coordinates—scaling, rotating, and shifting all features in the output. It is often used to convert data in digitizer units (most often inches) into the real-world units represented on the original map manuscript. Data from CAD drawing files may require transformation to convert from page units to real-world coordinates and permit integration with other data.

### Rubber sheet stretch*

Used to adjust one dataset—in a nonuniform manner—to match up with another dataset. If you have two data layers in your GIS that you need to overlay, or one map on a digitizing table that needs to be registered to another map of the same area already in the system, rubber sheet stretching may be necessary. The function allows maps to be fit together or compared. Using common points or known locations as control points, the rest of the data is "stretched" to fit one data layer on the other. Rubber sheet stretching is frequently used to align maps with image data.

### Conflate*

Conflation aligns the lines in one dataset with those in another and then transfers the attributes of one dataset to the other. Conflation allows the contents of two or more datasets to be merged to overcome differences between them. It replaces two or more versions of the dataset with a single version that reflects the weighted average of the input datasets. The alignment operation is commonly achieved by rubber sheet stretching.

One of the most common uses of conflation is in transferring addresses and other geocoded information from street network files (for example, TIGER/Line files from the U.S. Census Bureau) to files with more precise coordinates. Many files contain valuable census data but may be deficient in coordinate accuracy. Because attributes are valuable, conflation procedures were developed to transfer the attribute data to a more desirable set of coordinates.

### Subdivide area*

The ability to split an area according to a set of rules. As a simple example, given the corner points of a rectangular area, it should be possible to subdivide the area into ten equal-sized rectangles. The boundary of the area may be irregular, however, and the rules applied may be complex. The rules will allow factors such as maximum lot size and road allowances to be taken into account during subdivision planning.

### Sliver polygon removal

A sliver polygon is a small area feature that may be found along the borders of areas following the topological overlay of two or more datasets with common features (for example, lakes). Topological overlay results in small sliver polygons if the two input data layers contain similar boundaries from two different sources. Consider two data layers containing land parcels that will be used in a topological overlay. One data layer may have come from an external source—perhaps provided in digital format by a data supplier. The other data layer may have been digitized within the organization. After they are overlaid, it is likely that small errors in the location of parcel boundaries will appear as sliver polygons—small thin polygons along the boundaries.

Automatic functions to remove sliver polygons are available and are commonly incorporated within both topological overlay and editing functions. You should have control of the algorithms used for sliver removal. In particular, you should be able to control the assignment algorithm that will determine to which neighboring polygon a sliver is assigned or how it is corrected.

## Address locations

### Address match

The ability to match addresses that identify the same place but may be recorded in different ways. This function can eliminate redundancy in a single list (for example, a list of retail store customers), but is more frequently employed to match addresses on one list to those on one or more other lists. Address matching is often used as a precursor to address geocoding. The user can specify various levels of matching probability.

### Address geocode

Address geocoding is the ability to add point locations defined by street addresses (or other address information) to a map. Address geocoding requires the comparison of each address in one dataset to address ranges in the map dataset. When an address matches the address range of a street segment, an interpolation is performed to locate and assign coordinates to the address. For example, a text-based data file containing customer addresses can be matched to a street dataset. The result would be a point dataset showing where customers live. The resulting points must be topologically integrated with the database and usable as new features in the database. The new features should be usable by other system functions in combination with the rest of the database.

## Measurement

### Measure length

The ability to measure the length of a line. Measurements in a vector database may be calculated automatically and stored as part of the database. In this case, length can be retrieved from the database with simple query operations. In other cases, measurements may be calculated after you click on a source feature of interest. For example, you might select two locations from your on-screen map, then ask that the distance between them be calculated.

### Measure perimeter

The ability to measure the perimeter of an area. Measurements in a vector database may be calculated automatically and stored as part of the database. In this case, perimeter can be retrieved from the database with simple query operations. In other cases, measurements may be calculated after you click on a source feature of interest. For example, you might select a field from your on-screen map, then ask that the perimeter be calculated.

### Measure area

The ability to measure the area of a polygon. Measurements in a vector database may be calculated automatically and stored as part of the database. In this case, area can be retrieved from the database with simple query operations. In other cases, measurements may be calculated after you click on a source feature of interest. For example, you might select a land parcel from your on-screen map, then ask that the area of the parcel be calculated.

This function of your software should also have the capability of calculating the area of a user-defined polygon. User-defined polygons may subdivide existing area features in the database. In this case, only that part of the area feature within the user-defined polygon should be measured. The function should measure interior areas contained within polygons (for example, islands within lakes) and subtract them from the overall area of the feature. In other words, it should be possible to implement three levels of "stacking" in area calculations without operator intervention. For example, you should be able to measure the area of land mass in a polygon that includes a lake that, in turn, contains an island, on which there is a pond.

### Measure volume*

The ability to measure the amount of three-dimensional space occupied by a feature. Volume measurements can be calculated when surface digital elevation models of features have been incorporated into the database (for example, you could measure the volume of a mountain, the volume of a lake, or the volume of an aquifer).

## Calculation

### Calculate centroid*

This function calculates the centroid of an area (or set of areas or grid cells) within a user-defined region. It generates a new point at the centroid and automatically allocates a sequential number to each centroid in the region. A useful technique for labeling polygons created during digitizing, centroid calculation is often performed automatically on new areas created by dissolve and merge or by overlay operations.

### Calculate bearing

The ability to calculate the bearing (with respect to true north) between two or more points in a database. This is a geometric calculation based on the relationships between features. You should be able to perform this calculation independently or in combination with other arithmetic, algebraic, or geometric calculations in macroprograms and iterative procedures.

### Calculate vertical distance or height

The ability to calculate the vertical distance (height) between two points in a digital elevation model. The calculation of vertical distance between two points should be possible wherever the points are located in the region covered by the digital elevation model.

### Calculate slope

Calculation of slope (change in surface value) is the ability to calculate the slope along lines, or the average slope of an area.

### Calculate aspect*

The ability to calculate the compass direction toward which a slope faces. This function requires a digital elevation model and a user-specified area. The average aspect of the region should be calculated, weighted by the amount of land in each aspect category.

### Calculate angle and distance*

The function that can generalize the shape of a linear feature into a set of angles and distances from a starting point. The user should be able to set angular increments and constrain the calculation to any known point along the linear feature.

### Calculate location from a traverse*

The ability to calculate the route and endpoint of a traverse, given a starting point and directions and distances of travel. It should be possible to enter the resulting route and endpoint (a point or grid cell) into the database.

### Arithmetic calculation

The ability to perform operations such as addition, subtraction, multiplication, and division. You should be able to perform arithmetic calculations independently, perform arithmetic calculations in combination with algebraic and geometric functions, incorporate arithmetic calculations into macroprograms, change variables and components of algorithms, and establish iterative procedures.

### Algebraic calculation

The ability to perform operations based on logical expressions. You should be able to perform algebraic calculations independently, perform algebraic calculations in combination with arithmetic and geometric functions, incorporate algebraic calculations into macroprograms, change variables and components of algorithms, and establish iterative procedures.

### Statistical calculation

Statistical functions perform simple statistical analyses and tests on the database.

Increasingly, statistical functions are common in GIS software programs; however, for more sophisticated analysis, data may have to be transferred to other statistical packages. Statistical functions should allow you to calculate mean, median, standard deviation, variance, percentiles, cross-tabulations, and regression.


## Spatial analysis

### Graphic overplot

The ability to superimpose one map on another and display the result on-screen or as a plot to see the intersection of the datasets. When you use graphic overplot, the datasets are not integrated in the database and no new datasets are created. This function merely produces a visual impression of the interrelationships between two (or more) datasets.

Graphic overplotting is commonly used to combine thematic data layers to give a context for interpretation. For example, you might display the boundary of your study area, the roads within the areas, land-use polygons, and rivers and lakes before performing queries or other analysis. Graphic overplotting can also be used to display the results of analysis in a way that aids interpretation. A land-use dataset might be overplotted on a landscape surface to provide a three-dimensional visualization of the changes in land use across a study area.

## Topological overlay*

Topological overlay of one map on another will produce new data as a result of the combination of two input data layers. The attributes of the two input layers will be combined into a new set of attributes for the accompanying output layer.

Three types of topological overlay are frequently used:

### Point in polygon

Point in polygon overlay allows you to superimpose a set of points on a set of polygons, determine which polygon (if any) contains each point, and add the results to the database as attributes of the points. If a point is contained within a polygon, the attributes of that polygon are added to the point.

### Line on polygon

Line on polygon overlay allows you to superimpose a set of lines on a set of polygons. Lines are broken at intersections with polygon boundaries, and the attributes of the polygon that each segment of the line crosses are added to the attributes of that segment.

### Polygon on polygon

Polygon on polygon overlay allows you to superimpose two polygon datasets. The result is a topologically integrated version of the two input datasets that can be used to create a new output map or for further analysis. Polygons in the output map will have attributes from both of the input maps.

## Adjacency analysis*

The ability to identify areas that are next to (adjacent to) each other, particularly those that share a common boundary.

## Connectivity analysis*

The ability to identify areas or points that are (or are not) connected to other areas or points by tracing routes along linear features.

## Nearest neighbor search*

The ability to identify individual or sets of points, lines, or areas that are nearest to other points, lines, or areas specified by location or attributes.

## Correlation analysis*

The ability to compare maps that show the same area, but that represent conditions in different time periods. Correlation can be a very useful management tool. Quantifying and explaining the differences between two maps requires determining and comparing the differences between them. Correlation is one method for doing this. It may involve using overlay techniques and statistical functions.

### Linear referencing*
The ability to associate multiple sets of attributes with any portion of a linear feature. These attributes can be stored, displayed, queried, and analyzed without affecting the underlying linear data's coordinates. Linear referencing models linear features using routes and events.

A route represents a linear feature such as a city street, highway, or river. Routes contain measures that describe distance along them. These measures provide an explicit location for data that describes parts of the route. The attributes associated with any occurrence along the linear features are known as events. Events are stored in a tabular database rather than with the data's geometry; therefore, they do not affect the underlying spatial data. These events are accessed as needed from the tabular database.

Linear referencing allows the computation of locations of events on linear features based on an event table for which distance measures are available.

## Surface interpolation

### Interpolate spot height*
The ability to predict the height of any point in an area from a digital elevation model. A new point is generated with height as an attribute.

### Interpolate spot heights along a line*
The function that can predict heights along lines using a digital elevation model. For example, if you have a digital elevation model and a hydrology network, interpolation can be used to generate points along streams at fixed increments of height (for example, ten feet) above a given point on the stream. The same technique could be used with other networks, such as roads or pipelines.

### Interpolate isoline (contour)*
The ability to generate lines showing equal elevation from a set of regularly or irregularly spaced point values. If the values are height values from a digital elevation model, contours will be created. If the point values represent pressure readings, isolines are created.

### Interpolate watershed boundaries*
The ability to generate areas of drainage using a digital elevation model and a hydrology network. Many terms are used to refer to the areas of drainage, including drainage basin, watershed, basin, catchment area, and contributing area.

# Visibility analysis

### Line of sight*

These functions compute the points, parts of lines, and sections of polygons that are visible along a line between a given target and a point of observation. Line-of-sight calculation requires a surface. Commonly, surface data comes from a digital elevation model (DEM). If you were physically located at one point in your dataset (say on top of a mountain), a line-of-sight calculation will establish whether you would be able to see from that point to a target point (such as a lookout tower on another mountain peak some distance away).

### Generate viewshed*

Generating a viewshed involves manipulating a digital elevation model (DEM) to identify areas of the terrain that are visible from one or more viewpoints. (Also in "Generating features" category.)

# Modeling

### Arithmetic modeling*

Used to add, subtract, multiply, or divide the values of one or more input datasets to calculate the values for a resulting dataset.

### Weighted modeling*

Allows you to assign weighting factors to individual datasets according to a set of rules, and to overlay those datasets and perform reclassify, dissolve, and merge functions on the resulting concatenated dataset. This may be done to identify regions with specific characteristics (for example, zones suitable for development). In this instance, proximity to market may be given a higher weight in the modeling process than slope or aspect characteristics of the land.

# Network analysis

### Shortest route*

Functions to determine the shortest or minimum value path between two points or sets of points on a network. The minimum value may be expressed in terms of, for example, cost or time. When complex network analysis is not required, shortest route functions may be sufficient for many users. Shortest route can be used on any type of network data, including transportation, river, pipeline, or cable networks.

### Network analysis*

Functions that allow you to perform a range of operations on network data. Shortest route and connectivity functions are simple forms of network analysis. More complex analyses are often necessary on network data for electrical, gas, and communications applications. The analyses that may be required include simulation of flows in complex networks, load balancing in electrical distribution networks, traffic flow analysis, calculation of pressure loss in gas pipes, and optimization of complex delivery routes with tight constraints of time and load.

# Further reading

## Books

Boyles, David. 2002. *GIS Means Business: Volume 2.* Redlands, Calif.: ESRI Press.

Brewer, Cynthia. 2005. *Designing Better Maps: A Guide for GIS Users.* Redlands, Calif.: ESRI Press.

DeMers, Michael N. 2004. *Fundamentals of Geographic Information Systems.* 3rd ed. New York: John Wiley & Sons, Inc.

Fleming, Cory, ed. 2005. *The GIS Guide for Local Government Officials.* Redlands, Calif.: ESRI Press.

Eason, Kenneth. 1989. *Information Technology and Organizational Change.* London: Taylor & Francis.

Foresman, Timothy, ed. 1998. *The History of Geographic Information Systems.* New York: Prentice Hall.

Harmon, John E., and Steven J. Anderson. 2003. *The Design and Implementation of Geographic Information Systems.* New York: John Wiley & Sons, Inc.

Huxhold, William E., Eric M. Fowler, and Brian Parr. 2004. *ArcGIS and the Digital City: A Hands-on Approach for Local Government.* Redlands, Calif.: ESRI Press.

Longley, Paul A., Michael F. Goodchild, David J. Maguire, and David W. Rhind. 2002. *Geographic Information Systems and Science.* New York: John Wiley & Sons, Inc.

Mitchell, Andy. 1999. *The ESRI Guide to GIS Analysis, Volume 1: Geographic Patterns and Relationships.* Redlands, Calif.: ESRI Press.

Maguire, David, Michael Batty, and Michael Goodchild. 2005. *GIS, Spatial Analysis, and Modeling.* Redlands, Calif.: ESRI Press.

Muehrcke, Phillip, and Juliana Muehrcke. 1998. *Map Use: Reading, Analysis, Interpretation.* Madison, Wis.: JP Publications.

Ormsby, Tim, Eileen Napoleon, Robert Burke. 2004. *Getting to Know ArcGIS Desktop: Second Edition.* Redlands, Calif.: ESRI Press.

O'Sullivan, David, and David Unwin. 2002. *Geographic Information Analysis.* New York: John Wiley & Sons, Inc.

Sommers, Rebecca. 2001. *Quick Guide to GIS Implementation and Management.* Park Ridge, Ill.: Urban and Regional Information Systems Association.

Tang, Winnie, and Jan Selwood. 2005. *Spatial Portals: Gateways to Geographic Information.* Redlands, Calif.: ESRI Press.

Thomas, Christopher, and Milton Ospina. 2004. *Measuring Up: The Business Case for GIS.* Redlands, Calif.: ESRI Press.

Tomlinson, R. F., and M. A. G. Toomey. 1999. GIS and LIS in Canada. In *Mapping a Northern Land: The Survey of Canada 1947–1994,* ed. Gerald McGrath and Louis Sebert. McGill Queen's University Press.

Wade, Tasha, and Shelly Sommer, ed. 2006. *A to Z GIS: An Illustrated Dictionary of Geographic Information Systems.* Redlands, Calif.: ESRI Press.

Zeiler, Michael. 1999. *Modeling Our World: The ESRI Guide to Geodatabase Design.* Redlands, Calif.: ESRI Press.

Zeiler, Michael, and David Arctur. 2004. *Designing Geodatabases: Case Studies in GIS Data Modeling.* Redlands, Calif.: ESRI Press.

## Web sites

The following Web sites include extensive reading on topics of relevance to GIS managers:

Home of the leading GIS software.
www.esri.com

The official GIS home of the U.S. Geological Survey.
www.usgs.gov

The U.S. Census Bureau's FAQ section.
https://ask.census.gov

University of Edinburgh's GIS information clearinghouse.
www.geo.ed.ac.uk/home/giswww.html

## Journal articles

Buliung, R. N., and P. S. Kanaroglou. 2004. On Design and Implementation of an Object-relational Spatial Database for Activity/Travel Behaviour Research. *Journal of Geographical Systems* 6(3): 237–62.

Calkins, Hugh W., and Duane F. Marble. 1987. The Transition to Automated Production Cartography: Design of the Master Cartographic Database. *The American Cartographer* 14(2): 105–19.

Haklay, M., and C. Tobón. 2003. Usability evaluation and PPGIS: Towards a User-centred Design Approach. *International Journal of Geographical Information Science* 17(6): 577–92.

Poch, M., J. Comas, et al. 2004. Designing and Building Real Environmental Decision Support Systems. *Environmental Modelling and Software* 19(9): 857–73.

Tomlinson, R. F., and Douglas A. Smith. 1991. Assessing GIS Costs and Benefits: Methodological and Implementation Issues. *International Journal Geographical Information Systems* 6:3.247–56.

Wilcox, Darlene L. 2000. Now What Do wWe Do? Using Cost-benefit Analysis for Strategic Planning. *GEOWorld* 13(2): 42–4.

Wilcox, Darlene L. 1990. Concerning "The Economic Evaluation of Implementing a GIS." *International Journal of Geographical Information Systems* (April–June).

**White papers**
The following papers can be found in PDF format on the companion Web site to this book located at www.esri.com/esripress/tgis

*A Descriptive Study of the Usability of Geospatial Metadata.* A reference to a usability study on the FGDC metadata standard done in Florida.

*Building GIS Catalogs and Implementing a Metadata Catalog Portal.* ArcNews article and white paper on metadata and its role in GIS.

*Building Robust Topologies.* A paper on how and why ESRI implemented its particular topology format.

*Migrating from ArcInfo Workstation.* Ideas and concepts in ArcGIS for ArcInfo users.

*System Design Strategies.* An overview of system design philosophy from the ESRI perspective, updated quarterly by Dave Peters.

# Index